TEACHERS' EXPECTATIONS AND TEACHING REALITY

TEACHERS' EXPECTATIONS AND TEACHING REALITY

EDITED BY WITOLD TULASIEWICZ AND
ANTHONY ADAMS

ROUTLEDGE
London and New York

First published 1989
by Routledge
11 New Fetter Lane, London EC4P 4EE
29 West 35th Street, New York, NY 10001

Printed and bound in Great Britain by
Biddles Ltd, Guildford and King's Lynn

British Library Cataloguing in Publication Data

Teachers' expectations and teaching reality
   1. Western World. Education
   I. Adams, Anthony, *1933–*
   II. Tulasiewicz, Witold
   370'.9182'1

ISBN 0-415-00552-3

Library of Congress Cataloging in Publication Data

Teachers' expectations and teaching reality / edited by Anthony Adams
   and Witold Tulasiewicz.
      p. cm.
   Bibliography: p.
   ISBN 0-415-00552-3
   1. Comparative education. 2. Education — Europe. 3. Teachers —
Training of — Europe. I. Adams, Anthony, II. Tulasiewicz, Witold,
1928- .
LB43.T43 1989
370'.94–dc19   88-37480
                                          CIP

CONTENTS

FIGURES

CONTRIBUTORS

Anthony Adams University of Cambridge, UK
Ulrich Aselmeier University of Mainz, FRG
Miriam Ben-Peretz University of Haifa, Israel
Raymond Bourdoncle National Institute for Educational Research, INRP, Paris, France
Françoise Cros National Institute for Educational Research, INRP, Paris, France
Patrick Dias McGill University, Montreal, Canada
Karl-Wilhelm Eigenbrodt Rabanus Maurus Gymnasium, Mainz, FRG
Hans-Werner Eroms University of Passau, FRG
Doug Holly University of Leicester, UK
Devorah Kalekin-Fishman University of Haifa, Israel
Friedrich W. Kron University of Mainz, FRG
Denis Lawton University of London Institute of Education, UK
Hermann Maier University of Regensburg, FRG
Wolfgang Mitter German Institute of International Educational Research, DIIPF, Frankfurt/Main, FRG
Brent Robinson University of Cambridge, UK
Witold Tulasiewicz University of Cambridge, UK
Günther Vogel University of Mainz, FRG

EDITORS' INTRODUCTION

This volume is the product of an ongoing discussion arising out of a research seminar based on the departments and schools of education in the Universities of Mainz, Haifa, and Cambridge to which colleagues from other universities, notably Leicester, Passau, Regensburg, McGill, and the National Institute for Educational Research in Paris were subsequently invited to add their contributions. The research group has been concerned with defining the learning needs of school students and with the delivery systems for a child-centred curriculum.

Part I provides a survey of the current educational situation in each of the major countries represented, highlighting such themes as the source of responsibility for the curriculum, the new patterns of educational structu: ? (including its government), the extended age of schooling and its relationship to vocationalism and employment opportunities, and teacher preparation.

Part II provides papers which highlight the current situation in school of a number of major subject areas which are considered from a European perspective and look especially at the interplay of teacher expectations and the teaching reality in classroom terms. Although these chapters are written by specialists in the different countries they provide a perspective applicable on a wider basis, largely as a result of the extensive programme of school visits undertaken by the contributors. These chapters range from those on the teaching of the mother tongue, to the teaching of modern languages, literature, humanities, mathematics, biological science, and the new technologies .

Part III draws together the cross-disciplinary

developments on a school-wide basis addressing itself to such topics as the politics of teacher education, teachers' interpretation of the curriculum, their professional independence, and their role relationship in respect of their students.

We feel that this publication is especially timely in view of the 1988 Education Act in England and Wales, the changes occurring in the Federal Republic of Germany, France, and Israel, and the need, in view of the 1992 Single European Act, to take a wider perspective on European education as a whole. This is the more urgent as there is a dearth of studies dealing with the cultural and educational implications of a united Europe compared with the recent (though belated) spate of discussion of the economic and business implications of the new 'Europeanism'.

This was highlighted for the editors, and some of their contributors, who participated in the series of seminars in the FRG in January 1988 which led to the following report in the Times Educational Supplement of 26 February 1988:

> German educationists, who have admired the British teachers' power to innovate without the constraints of external control, have strongly criticized the move towards centralism embodied in the Education Bill ... West Germany is planning to increase the amount of time available for teachers to innovate by 30 per cent. Testing of students is seen only as part of a teaching process and not as a device for public scrutiny of schools or for 'policing' the state curriculum ... It seems ironic that at a time when major innovations in Western European education are seeking to build upon patterns well-established in England and Wales, this country should now be turning to a system from which West Germany is striving to escape.

A word must be said about the various chapters. Those in Part I represent the current situation in the countries concerned as a result of change. The chapters in Part II, on the other hand, consider not just present developments but a number of proposals, still awaiting implementation and arising out of the situation; Part III consists of more general analyses of the situation and its implications for a school-student-based curriculum and the preparation of teachers.

Our thanks are due to Denis Lawton, Director of the London Institute of Education, for his interest and willingness to contribute a chapter on the implications of our work for the politics of teacher education, and to Wolfgang Mitter, Director of the Comparative Education Research Unit of the German Institute of International Educational Research for his contribution on the 'revision of reform' in his country.

We also wish to thank the British Council for its generous support for the work of the seminar in its early stages, which has led to an earlier publication by the group. We should add that education will require more funding of this kind if European and international co-operation in the field of education is to be given the status it merits for the well-being of the generation of students in the 1990s.

Finally, we owe a particular debt of gratitude to John Cairns at the University of Cambridge Department of Education for his help in the typing of the text and for many valued comments on the contents of the various chapters.

Witold Tulasiewicz and Anthony Adams
Cambridge

Part I

NATIONAL EXPECTATIONS AND THE CHANGING SCHOOL SYSTEMS

Chapter One

UK EDUCATION IN THE LATE 1980s: PRESSURES AND CONTEXTS FOR CHANGE

Anthony Adams and Witold Tulasiewicz

This chapter has been rewritten several times. This has been necessary because of a highly volatile context for discussion of British education. At the time of writing, the Education Reform Bill (derisively named GERBIL, after the miniscule rodent) introduced by the Secretary of State for Education and Science, Kenneth Baker, has just become an Act of Parliament. This legislation brings together into one single Act most of the developments of the previous ten years. We deal below with some of its more important implications as far as school education is concerned. Other important organizational matters such as the abolition of the Inner London Education Authority (ILEA) and the changes in the universities will concern us less in the context of this chapter. (1)

We must stress at the outset that the main thrust of this Act is to reverse the philosophy of British education which has been built on the belief that education should begin with the child and his, or her, needs: 'child-centred education'. The new Act, by contrast, highlights the obligation of the education system to society, the latter based upon the idea of economic value (seen essentially in trading terms) of the educational process, the education for 'market-place forces' in essence. The crucial concepts in this new educational context are, therefore, on the one hand 'accountability', and on the other 'consumerism', both of which are alien to British education as a whole which, spearheaded by the grammar schools, provided the basis for the expansion of the idea of <u>Secondary Education for All</u> as a right in the years immediately before and after the Second World War. (2)

3

The 1944 Education Act was intended as an extension to most of the population of an approach to education which had no commercial or narrowly utilitarian end but was seen as an education for living rather than for how to earn a living. Indeed, as late as 1975, an official inquiry on language and education saw fit to modify its formal terms of reference, drawn up by the then Secretary of State for Education and Science, one Margaret Thatcher, and widen these to justify its chosen title of A Language for Life. (3)

Hardly a year later the then Labour Prime Minister, James Callaghan, made a significant speech at Ruskin College, Oxford, which was to change the direction of British education for the next decade. Amongst the claims made that the education system was 'failing the nation', he argued that 'there is no virtue in having socially well adjusted members of society who are unemployed because they do not have the skills'. (4) This demonstrates that the reversal in educational policy we have described is not limited to one political party but represents a curious party consensus; although Callaghan's reference to 'skills' significantly did not link the inculcation of skills with a purely mercantile, 'cost-effective', view of what a 'skilled' nation might achieve. His emphasis was still upon the individual and his employability, as human fulfilment, rather than primarily the needs of the economy irrespective of individual well-being. This must be said since the speech was made against the backdrop of pressures being exerted by the International Monetary Fund in a worsening economic situation for Britain. All of this was to change with the monetarist policies adopted by the incoming Conservative administration which took over the Callaghan rhetoric but significantly changed its policy directions. The actual issues which were identified in the Ruskin College speech were:

1. the relevance of the school curriculum to the economic life of the nation;
2. the concern over adequate standards;
3. arising from the above, the accountability of the education service to the general public.

All three of these can be summed up in Callaghan's own words. After visiting schools he wondered:

Were they (the school students) also acquiring the skills they would need in later life? ... Was the curriculum sufficiently relevant for older children in comprehensive schools, especially in the teaching of science and mathematics? ... How did the examination system shape up as a test of achievement?

In developing his argument about these issues he claimed that the reason for the assumed malaise in education was that 'Many schools had developed experimental and expressive methods of learning more centred on the child and less on the subject.' The education service had to pay dearly for this misunderstanding of its functional role. In practice the evidence from Her Majesty's Inspectors of Schools (HMI) in their primary and secondary school surveys showed relatively few schools adopting what might be called experimental, child-centred curricula at that time. Rather, there were complaints by the Inspectorate of the lack of opportunity for talk within the classroom and too much stress on rote learning and approaches based on direct instruction by the teacher, providing evidence of an actual regression from the practice of the 1960s. (6)

In reflecting, therefore, in the late 1980s on the education system in England and Wales (significantly the Scottish educational system had been reformed as early as 1919 and 1937) (7), it becomes necessary not so much to concentrate on such issues as the availability of Secondary Education for All, as enshrined in the 1944 Education Act following Tawney's pre-war pamphlet, or upon comprehensive reorganization, as upon the educational agenda set successively by both Labour and Conservative governments.

In attempting a brief survey of the last twenty years of educational experience in Britain it is a temptation to single out the comprehensive reorganization of schools as a landmark. This is because the comprehensive school is now the basic pattern of schooling with well over 80 per cent of students attending such schools. On the other hand, within less than four years of reorganization of schooling on comprehensive principles under the Circular 10/65 legislation, (8) the new Conservative administration of 1970 attempted to slow down, indeed to reverse, the process by leaving the local education authorities (LEAs) free to decide whether or not they wished to reorganize instead of making this submission of plans mandatory. Less than ten years after Circular 10/65, in 1974, the new Labour government was back in power and made an attempt to reintroduce compulsory comprehensivization of the public sector but the original zest and zeal were somehow missing. (9) When again the Conservative party took over in 1979 one of its first education acts was to reverse the Labour party's legislation of 1976 without, however, attempting to dismantle the comprehensive system as a whole. Comprehensive schooling had, therefore, been something of a political football throughout this period of changing governments and comprehensive reorganization should not be regarded as one of the most important developments of education in the United Kingdom at the time.

Under the Labour governments of 1974-9 the education debate ultimately focused upon the three issues already mentioned:

1. the curriculum, with an increasing concern for subject centredness and the search for the basis on which to establish a core curriculum, leaving it none the less to the LEAs to deliver; (10)
2. the concern for monitoring and establishing standards in the schools, (11) and the discussions relating to new examinations at 18-plus and 16-plus, (12) though there was as yet no mention of national standards and criteria on which such examinations would be based.
3   the question of accountability with much greater concern for the relations between schools and industry, (13) and the role of parents and other 'users' of the system. (14)

The Taylor Report can be regarded as the first statement proposing to bring together the three parties of the educational service as partners: the financial provider of education (the LEA as the distributor of local and national funding), its professional executor (the teachers and other professionals), and its consumer (the employer and the child together with the child's parents).

These three issues were significantly linked in the unprecedented intervention by central government requiring LEAs to submit reports on Local Authority Arrangements for the Curriculum, the first time a national curriculum review of this kind had either been attempted or thought proper. (15) It had been a well-established view, to quote the words of an early post-1944 Minister of Education, George Tomlinson, that 'Minister knows nowt about curriculum'. The tradition that curriculum was no concern of central government was thus breached.

The curriculum debate and its associated issues had begun with Callaghan. However, when the Callaghan government left office the only substantive item that had been attempted in educational legislation was the new provision for school governing bodies, (16) which envisaged a partnership which included school students who were to have a place (albeit a small one) on governing bodies alongside teachers and parents as well as local authority represent-atives and community and economic interests.

The incoming Conservative administration at first took over many of the existing proposals and was groping its way towards implementing what had now been under discussion for some years, especially parental rights and the accountability of the service. (17) But it was not long before such moderate voices as those of its first Secretary of State, Mark Carlisle, were silenced by the voices of the new radical right, 'authoritarian populism' in Stuart Hall's phrase, (18) and education passed into the hands of one of the most intelligent and philosophically committed advocates of the then prevailing monetarist economic policies, Sir Keith Joseph. From 1982 the time for discussion was at an end. The Schools Council for Curriculum and Examinations, the forum where the voices of teachers and educationists were heard together in discussion, was abolished, literally at a moment's notice (with the chairman receiving a letter from the Department of Education and Science (DES) announcing this as Sir Keith was rising to speak in the House of Commons) and replaced by two separate bodies, the Schools Examinations Council (SEC) and the School Curriculum Development Committee (SCDC), both consisting of members nominated by the secretary of state rather than by teachers' organizations and other representative interests as the Schools Council had been. Instead of consultation, education policy was implemented through a series of Orders in Council backed up, when occasionally necessary, by legislation. This followed the general lines already established but in a much more direct way. The agenda remained much the same but the ordering of priorities was changed to make the consumer the main criterion by which all was to be judged. A significant breach of the non-selective principle in education was the legislation introduced to establish the Assisted Places scheme whereby the more able students were to be provided with free places in fee-paying independent (and therefore supposedly better) schools, at local authority expense. (19) Apart from rescinding the mandatory comprehensivization of the Labour administration this was the first educational act of the incoming Conservative government. This trend was further confirmed by the policy, since 1986, to establish City Technology Colleges (CTCs) catering for the technically gifted student with funding from industry. The 1980 Education Act, which established new powers for school governing bodies in abolishing student representation and failing to give teachers the large share of power that had previously been expected, ran contrary to the proposed Labour legislation in the same area. Here, too, it was the consumer rather than the provider of education whose interests appeared paramount. (The subsequent 1986 Education (No 2) Act, which can be seen as a fulfilment of the promises of the 1980 Act, fully confirmed this direction with a clear bias in favour of the populist notion of parent power in schools. (20) Significantly industry has been slow to respond to government initiatives on CTCs, no doubt sensing the inadequate justification for this policy and a reluctance on the part of many, including the influential Industrial Society grouping of employers, to damage their existing productive links with local comprehensive schools. In the summer of 1988 the policy changed yet again to extend the notion of selective schools, along the CTC lines, to include schools catering for the industrial arts as well. This whole approach bears a striking resemblance to the well-established North American concept of 'magnet schools', which have proved themselves to be very effective in major cities, such as Chicago, without, however, the divisive effect contingent upon a selective procedure.

Just as there proved to be less support than expected from industry for the CTCs, so too in the area of parental power, the National Confederation of Parent-Teacher Associations reacted critically to giving full curriculum control to parents not professionally prepared for this responsibility. An example of this was the provision in the 1986 (No 2) Act of the right of school governing bodies to veto the arrangements for sex education in schools, in spite of professional advice from the responsible LEA officers. (21) Other curriculum arrangements may be similarly affected.

One of the significant measures of the 1980 Education Act was the requirement that schools should publish prospectuses, outlining their philosophy of education and their curriculum, and also to publish examination pass-lists of their students to give parents more 'evidence' on which to base their choice of schools. (22) The intention was that the good schools would emerge as the ones to which parents wished to send their children; thus 'good' schools would become larger and better and 'bad' schools would be even less popular. The main result of this will be that the more articulate middle-class parents will exercise their powers of choice while many of the schools in the poorer areas will become 'sink' schools struggling to survive. In fact the annual surveys by HMI confirm this to have happened which led at least one Conservative MP to say that HMI should not be allowed to publish such reports.

The accountability to the consumer must in the eyes of the government be seen as the single most important criterion for the education service. (23) Such accountability to the consumer is also reflected in the desire of the government for more business and industrial interests to be represented on school governing bodies. The new Secretary of State for Education, Kenneth Baker, suggested in the phone-in referred to in the note above that governors of schools might regard themselves as 'shareholders', a blatant advocacy of mercantile practice in schools and a significant shift from the time when governors saw themselves as 'guardians' of the public service. This industrial enterprise analogy is reinforced by the further proposal that governing bodies be chosen by postal ballot, together with the growing practice of giving headteachers full financial control of their schools. The latter has become known in the rapidly developing jargon of the new education as 'Local Financial Management' (LFM).

Ironically alongside this concern with individual consumer involvement with education there has been a growing abrogation to itself of power by central government. The Labour government pointed the way towards this change and the Conservatives imposed it upon teachers and their schools. During the last two Conservative administrations, no area has been left without government intervention from the abolition of the statutory right to nursery schools and to school meals, (24) to the demands for greater accountability in Higher Education. The latter has led to a taking of money away from universities, especially in the area of research (research is seen as valueless unless it produces the goods in the market-place), the recognition of independent universities such as the University of

Buckingham and the suggestion that private funding should form the basis for much university finance. In the area of the school curriculum, the setting up of two separate bodies (one dealing with examinations and the other with curriculum) in place of the original Schools Council, with the emphasis placed firmly upon the work of the School Examinations Council (SEC), (25) reversed the well-established practice that examinations should follow, and not determine, the curriculum. In 1984-5, Sir Keith Joseph determined to rush through the introduction of the new 16-plus General Certificate of Secondary Education (GCSE) before he retired from office. The basic assumption underlying this was that there should be nationally agreed criteria to define what was meant by a particular school subject and national standards that would underpin the award of a particular grade in any subject. The long discussion that had been going on in the area of school examinations was circumvented when the new Examinations Council was charged with delivering the national criteria to the secretary of state in a remarkably short time. Many teachers complained about the indecent haste and expenditure at a time when their schools were badly starved of resources to such an extent that parents were being asked to provide funding for what might be regarded as 'extras' such as the provision of individual tuition in instrumental music.

The examination system proved relatively simple to reform and it was seen as a first step towards the reform of the curriculum as a whole. Sir Keith's successor, Kenneth Baker, from the moment of his appointment unleashed a veritable torrent of ideas on the schools in the area of curriculum and made clear his intention of introducing a national curriculum through legislation. Lip service is occasionally paid to the notion of consultation with HMI, advisers, and some subject associations, but it is clear that the national curriculum will be written by officials of the DES with a very strong input from the secretary of state himself. For example, when the working party on mathematics education was rejected by the secretary of state it led to the then chairman resigning. His replacement was a man much more in sympathy with the secretary of state's own views. (26)

The means to ensure the delivery of the new national curriculum by the schools is to be through the introduction of a nation-wide system of testing of school-children at ages

7, 11, and 14, in addition to the terminal GCSE examination. Significantly the Task Group on Assessment and Testing under Professor Black, established to advise on the new testing system, refused to take a simplistic view arguing against too rigid a system of tests divorced from teaching practice, especially in the early years. This remains a controversy to be resolved, with the Prime Minister in particular declaring herself in favour of a rigorous testing programme distinguishing between the performance of individual children and schools, with the results of such tests to be published.

The role of Her Majesty's Inspectors (though strongly denied and resisted by HMI themselves) (27) was also subtly changed by the introduction of mandatory publication and wider circulation of their Reports together with a tacit expectation that they would be more concerned with 'educational standards'. In this way HMI would become truly an inspectorial body rather than an advisory one concerned with teacher and curriculum development.

In the three areas in which successive administrations have engaged with the education process: curriculum, accountability, and standards, the weighting that has been given to these has changed from time to time. In the lifetime of the third Conservative government since 1987, however, the overarching factor for all three has been that of consumerism, education (like everything else) being a commodity which has to be paid for by its purchasers. The consumers' choice, whether as parents or governors (the children are not yet articulate enough to express their own views), often does not extend beyond seeing the advantage to their own children and their own children's schools ignoring wider matters of community concern. All this, in the light of the various proposals for increased parental power and individual schools' local accountability, that we have already discussed, linked with the much more direct intervention of the secretary of state in all aspects of education, is leading towards a combination of increasing power at the centre alongside a populist devolution of local power to those who can be trusted because they are 'people like us', men of power, that is the new managerial infrastructure that is to replace traditionally elected local government.

Similar policies in higher education are leading to more direct control and supervision by central government as evidenced in proposals to remove the control of polytechnics from the LEAs and to hand them over to a government-appointed funding council. No doubt the polytechnics, in this climate, will be competing for private sources of funding alongside the universities who are already being enjoined to do so. The universities' funding council's proposed method of allocating funds has been criticized by the Committee of Vice-Chancellors and Principals as well as by the Association of University Teachers.

We have argued that there has been a consistent policy underlying what has been done to education over the last ten years. We now propose to examine the outcomes of this policy of increased centralism in terms of what are its implications for schools on the one hand, and for teacher education on the other.

Naturally the initial speech by James Callaghan did not begin with his 'firm belief in the importance of education'. It must be seen in the context of a collapse in confidence in the economic base of society triggered off by the sharp increase in commodity prices. Along with other services, education had to justify its expenditure in market terms. In England and Wales this showed itself in a sequence of changes in the way of financing education. In the case of school and further education we had already seen the introduction of a 'block grant' system for expenditure, culminating in 'rate capping', legislation aimed to prevent LEAs from raising their own local revenue above certain limits, thus seeking to reduce their spending so as to strengthen central government control.

The need to justify expenditure on education led to an increased concern with the relationship between schooling, employment, and industry. This led to the assumption that the problems of structural unemployment, affecting especially the young in the inner city areas, could be alleviated if schools did more to prepare young people for working life, which gave rise to schemes spearheaded by the Manpower Services Commission on increasing 'training' as opposed to 'education'. Such training, which has meanwhile been extended to the 14-19 age range, regards schooling as a direct preparation for employment, often of a semi-skilled kind.

The Conservative government, therefore, institution-alized what had already been begun by the time they took office in terms of the Technical and Vocational Educational Initiative (TVEI) of 1982, which was administered significantly through the Manpower Services Commission, and therefore the Department of Trade and Industry (DTI) rather than through the DES. Like other Conservative schemes, tightening up on previous Labour proposals, TVEI was a call for a thorough reform of the curriculum in the wake of industrial upheaval and educational change. It covers the age range 14-18 and alters the mainstream curriculum by inserting new courses and skills, and encouraging a coherent approach to education-industry relations.

Although official statements suggest that the TVEI schemes will be open to everybody, in practice it is unlikely that the more academically able students will choose such options. In other words there is a reversion in all but name to the pattern of secondary modern and grammar school education. This could be further extended as a result of the 1988 Education Act's intention to allow some schools to 'opt out' of the LEA-based system and receive their funding directly from central government, widely recognized as a return in all but name to the old Direct Grant system.

Fortunately in spite of these general tendencies many schools took the opportunity of grabbing whatever money was forthcoming from the DTI (at a time when they were being increasingly starved of other funds) and used their TVEI grant genuinely to enhance their curriculum by setting up a series of option modules open to all students across the ability range. In this way it became possible for all to study a module in a practical area such as design and communication, or photography, or information technology, or to combine several such modules to lead to a qualification in the area.

The government in its emphasis upon vocationally oriented schemes was much influenced by the model of the 'dual system' in countries such as West Germany, ignoring the fact that the per capita expenditure on education in the Federal Republic of Germany is much higher than in the United Kingdom. Indeed the dual system in West Germany has become the subject of criticism precisely because the jobs for which the training is being provided are no longer available. In the United Kingdom certainly many of the young trainees on the schemes that began with the Youth Opportunities Programme (YOP) (the name has been changed regularly since then largely for cosmetic purposes) felt sadly let down when they found that there were no jobs for them to go to at the end of their training. Instead of providing money to invest in the public sector, it was made

13

available for employers to finance YOP schemes and, good though some were, in other cases they were seen by employers as a means of obtaining cheap and subsidized labour with no very adequate training programme linked with them. This skewed concern with vocational training has led to proposals in 1987, (effective in September 1988) that all young people leaving school should go either into the work-place or into some form of training, the option of being 'unemployed', and thus swelling the unemployment figures, no longer being open to them. (28)

In curriculum terms one of the most important symbols of the 1960s approach was the vogue for open-plan design in schools. This implied much more than simply a new architectural fashion. Behind open-plan design lay much more importantly the concept of open teaching, students and their teachers engaging together in a joint exploratory process of learning. Teaching styles such as those associated with 'politics in the classroom', teachers and pupils negotiating a curriculum together, were symptomatic of many new approaches. (29) This was linked with a belief in the value of the human individual ('growth' was a central metaphor for the discussion of education in this decade) and it was no accident that new cross-disciplinary subject areas such as humanities were developed at this time. Typically the term 'student' came increasingly to supplant that of 'pupil', the semantic shift encapsulating the changed relationship. The 'new' English, geography, science, mathematics, and religious education (to name but a few) took on this more 'open', inquiry-based approach; it was a period of dynamic curriculum renewal in traditional subject areas as well as one of curriculum development in the new areas of integrated humanities and science. (30) Indeed some imaginative programmes broke down the barriers between traditional arts and science curricula, such as Bruner's famous curriculum: 'Man - A Course of Study'. (31) Human beings are seen in their widest dimension: intellectual, emotional, social, spiritual, and physical. Although this involves a concern with the cognitive, affective, and psycho-motor domains, they are seen in a holistic way far removed from the more mechanistic approach of taxonomies of individual educational objectives.

In classroom practice this led to the development of the 'project' method of teaching with, very often, students concentrating upon joint assignments rather than individual work. One of the best examples of this approach is to be found in Sybil Marshall's An Experiment in Education which, in its account of a teacher working across age and ability levels, epitomizes much of the spirit of the times. (32) Mixed-ability classes and team teaching which emphasized the individual, albeit in a social context, were growing in popularity. By contrast, the present cult of selfish individualism is at considerable odds with the reality of the new possibilities for the wider extension of community that modern technology makes possible. It has happened at precisely the time when the ease of communications world-wide, through the new technology, has made more communal and co-operative structures of learning possible.

Instead of building upon these integrated models the proposed National Curriculum is likely to revert, even in the primary school, to an essentially subject-based model expressed in these terms in the consultation document and the 1988 Education Act supported by the national subject courses of study and the assessment system, criticized for failing to mention the skills students should be acquiring through cross-disciplinary work. (33)

Again, by contrast, the curriculum and organizational patterns of the 1960s led to new developments in assessment with opportunities for students to present their own selection of the work they felt represented them best (such as 'course work' or 'submitted work' in the Certificate of Secondary Education) rather than being subjected to an externally imposed examination of a traditional kind which tended to emphasize their failure in certain areas rather than their achievements. Indeed the concern came increasingly to be one for self-assessment with the primary accountability of the students being to themselves and to their own learning. Interest in profiling of students with their own contributions to their appraisal which date from this time continues and the acknowledged place of course work in the GCSE is a guarantee of its survival. (34)

The future will certainly be hallmarked by changing patterns of employment with few in permanent full-time work, and with a need for constant adaptation to changing work needs. (35) The new 'basics' are much more likely to be concerned with the importance of learning to live in harmony with others in a complex multicultural, less hierarchical society, than current developments seem to take for granted. It is significant that, in the proposed 'core curriculum' of the national curriculum, itself only binding on the LEA-maintained schools, English could be reduced to a

15

concern for grammatical minutiae with art, drama, and kindred subjects relegated to options (that is effectively marginalized) rather than forming part of the basic entitlement. This when, if we can solve the continuing economic problems, people ought to expect to have more time available for creative leisure.

What was seen in the 1960s as being at the heart of the teaching and learning relationship, the growth and personal development of the student, has become transformed in the 1980s into 'social and life skills' (often conceived of in a mechanistic manner, a socialization of the pupils into an acceptance of the status quo and their role within it). Whereas programmes such as the Humanities Curriculum Project in the 1960s sought to leave students asking questions with a healthy critical stance towards the world in which they lived, (36) social education programmes since the 1980s have often seemed to be aimed at producing a tame conformity.

This can be seen most easily in curriculum terms. The concept of the curriculum in the 1960s as a ground for negotiation between teacher and taught, with each student developing his or her own curriculum, is the antithesis of the pressure in the 1980s towards the core curriculum and towards national criteria, foreclosing any debate, and re-establishing the teacher as the mediator of a curriculum centrally controlled and defined by agencies which are not representative of the cultural, societal, and intellectual values of the population as a whole. Characteristic of the 1980s has been a move towards the crowding out of subjects such as political and social studies along with the introduction of criterion-based testing, (37) founded upon the assumptions held by those in power about what ought to be the attainments of pupils at specified ages largely leaving out of account any consideration of individual strengths or weaknesses.

Looking back over the last twenty years of public education we can turn on its head the question from the Ruskin College speech with which we began ('How are the schools failing the nation?') and ask rather how in the last decade the nation has failed its schools, not just in terms of the most obvious element (that is resource allocation) but in terms of the underlying philosophy and intention.

Given the implications of these changes for the teaching profession, there is now a need to write something about teacher education and teachers' preparation for the new reality. There can be no doubt that, with the disruption in schools and the collapse of teacher morale in the late 1970s and 1980s, there has been a decline in quality applications to enter the teaching profession both at Post-Graduate Certificate of Education (PGCE) and the Bachelor of Education degree (BEd) levels. This has been reflected in the serious shortage in such key subjects as the physical sciences, mathematics, craft, design and technology, modern languages, and, recently, English and (most seriously) in the number of excellent teachers leaving the profession disillusioned in their mid-30s. (38)

In an attempt to reverse this trend and to improve the quality of education in schools, Sir Keith Joseph addressed himself, notably in Circular 3/84, to the issue of <u>Teaching Quality</u>. (39) The status of teacher preparation has in the last twenty years undergone a significant change reflected in the terminology used, as in the case of 'pupils' and 'students'. In the mid-1960s it was impossible to refer narrowly to 'teacher training'; 'training' was seen as part of a process of 'teacher education'. The erstwhile Teacher-Training Colleges were renamed Colleges of Education. There was a new concern with academic rigour both in the relatively new area of education as an academic discipline in its own right as well as that of the established disciplines which, as school subjects, at least at secondary level, teachers would be teaching in their classrooms. This was associated with the growing enhanced status of teaching itself as an all graduate profession and the consequent growth of the BEd degree. Significant of this was the extension of initial teaching-preparation courses, all of which were now linked with degree-awarding bodies such as the universities or the Council for National Academic Awards, to a minimum period of three years from the previous two. This involved a large increase in the number of staff employed who wished to protect their own academic status and development as researchers and educators. Many young staff with high academic qualifications introduced from their university background a new intellectual emphasis into College of Education courses which in the 1960s and 1970s ceased to be narrowly instrumental.

The new input of intellectualism into teacher education in the mid-1960s also affected the professionalism of the young teacher. This was focused in 1975 by a national conference on teacher education in which there was an important debate between Brian Simon and Paul Hirst, when

17

the former argued for the enhanced role of educational theory as a means of equipping the new entrant to play a full professional role in serious educational debate. (40) Hirst, by contrast, saw educational theory as primarily enabling the students' performance in their first year of teaching, what has been called a 'narrow educational practicism'. (41) This debate foreshadowed the 1980s continuing controversy over teacher education: the term has now shifted back into 'teacher training'.

A positive contribution of the debate was the development of a much greater coherence between theory and practice in many courses both at the PGCE level and that of the BEd. For example in Cambridge, as elsewhere, there were successful programmes developed in teaching educational theory in the traditional areas of history, philosophy, psychology, and sociology of education through classroom-based incidents. (42)

A further positive element in the early 1970s was the impact of the James Report, (43) which envisaged a much extended period of initial preparation for teaching as well as establishing the function of the professional tutor, embodying a partnership between the training institution and the school in which the trainee teacher was to be initially employed. An important feature of this proposal was the equality of status in the partnership and the realization that each of the partners had their own particular skills to bring to the process. This burgeoning development, though never fully implemented, was weakened by subsequent proposals as presented in Circular 3/84, (44) and in the Green Paper of May 1988, (45) which tend to suggest that teacher education can be reduced to a mere practicism of learning classroom skills 'on the job', without undergoing a probationary year.

There had been no mention in James Callaghan's Ruskin College speech of the then ongoing serious debate about teacher education. By that time there appeared to be a surplus of teachers (a situation exacerbated by the drop in the birth-rate) and the government was anxious to close down 'unnecessary' colleges, especially those preparing teachers for the primary sector: a policy that, with hindsight, proved very short-sighted indeed. Both Labour and Conservative parties spoke from an instrumental view of the purpose of education which saw the preparation of young people for the working world as the sole purpose to be fulfilled. It followed that teachers had to be more

18

'accountable', to be seen to deliver what was required of them by 'society' for the money which they were paid as society's obedient servants. However, it was left to the incoming Conservative government to propose to change fundamentally the nature of teacher education.

The Secretary of State for Education and Science, Sir Keith Joseph, set to work with reforming zeal to transform ideas into instruments of policy. The first outcome of this in respect of teacher education was the White Paper, Teaching Quality, (46) which signalled the intention of a thorough overhaul of programmes of initial teacher preparation in the university as well as in the public sector of colleges of education and polytechnics and introduced the Inspectorate (HMI) into this (for them) new territory. There was now a two-pronged approach. First, to introduce a national curriculum to enable the maintained schools to meet the perceived needs of society, the independent schools being assumed to do this without legislation, a glaring example of the mixture of authoritarian, centralist, and liberal individual approaches to education. Second, to find ways of taming the schools and the teacher educators to implement such a curriculum at minimal cost to the Treasury.

What had been in the White Paper a matter for discussion became enshrined in the mandatory requirements of the subsequently issued Circular 3/84 which curtailed all further debate. (47) For all its seemingly innovatory approach, the Circular was a further example of what we have described as the consumerist approach: teacher education was to be 'improved' but at no extra cost to government or the consumer society. The one-year PGCE course was extended to a minimum of thirty-six teaching weeks with no adequate recognition of the extra demands that this placed upon staff and resources in both teacher-training institutions and schools. The James notion of partnership between equal, but different, institutions was replaced by the itself not unacceptable idea of locating as much teacher education as possible in the schools, but with the teachers expected to provide much of the input with no extra, indeed contracting, resources available to them. This ignored the specific intellectual skills and practical, as well as theoretical, expertise built up in the institutions of teacher education over the previous twenty years, while presupposing that the teachers themselves could find time to prepare themselves for their new duties without neglecting their existing pupils. The Circular as a whole, however important some of its detailed proposals, such as a concern with multi-culturalism and the world of work, was essentially a conserving document, designed to preserve the status quo in schools.

This status quo was itself to be narrowly defined, with an increasingly authoritarian government seeking to impose its will on schools, teacher-education institutions, and their staffs. The long-established (even if out-moded) machinery for settling school teachers' pay and conditions of service was replaced by the Teachers' Pay and Conditions Act, (48) which imposed a settlement of these issues on teachers, following a period of great industrial unrest in the schools, while the training institutions were brought into line by the establishment of the Council for the Accreditation of Teacher Education, (49) with no rank-and-file teacher-educators represented on it, which has laid down mandatory conditions without which teacher-education courses would not be approved. Both these steps created unrest and antagonism, (50) so that the mid-1980s were hall-marked by unprecedented unrest fuelled by the government's imposing solutions which proved to be divisive, setting teacher against teacher and exploiting the situation created by the multiplicity of teachers' unions in England and Wales. The new salary scales envisage a much more hierarchically organized profession, teachers being required under contract to work a laid-down minimum number of hours, with extra so-called 'Baker Days' when they have to be in school and with much bigger salary differentials for headteachers and deputies and (as we have already seen) much increased powers for heads. In effect, headteachers and deputies are to be seen as the equivalent to minor captains of industry (who are to be paid sufficiently to ensure their loyalty) while the classroom teachers are reduced to their nineteenth-century role of 'usher', symptomatic of the disdain and distrust with which the teaching profession as a whole has been treated. The notion of accountability has recently been extended by proposed legislation for the appraisal of teacher performance. (51) The schemes considered are potentially dangerous in shifting appraisal linked to professional development (which all teachers' organizations are united in supporting) to the device of linking evaluation with salaries, something that teachers, as a profession, had escaped from after the days of Robert Lowe's imposition of 'Payment by Results' in the nineteenth century. There is a further threat to the professional autonomy of teachers in that under the 1986 Education (No 2) Act politically controversial issues are excluded from discussion in the primary classroom, while morally controversial issues may also be banned by secondary school governors. (52) Both of these are notoriously difficult to define and there is the danger that teachers' views or opinions may be used against them.

Though we present a somewhat gloomy view of what is happening in education, this is no new thing. As long ago as 1911, Edmund Holmes, then a recently retired HMI, wrote his important book, What Is and What Might Be, which pointed the way to a new teaching reality. (53)

We are still far from translating this potential reality into practice. Yet some of the things that have happened in the last twenty years should give us cause for hope. We see these as comprising, at least, the following: the developments in alternative and community education; programmes bringing in productive links with the world of work; the redefining of the role of the teacher as a facilitator rather than simply as an instructor; and the development of support services and support teaching in schools to enable specialist subject teachers to draw upon their colleagues' skills to learn alongside their students, assisting them in their own learning as an interested fellow-learner, (54) especially so in the case of those students with 'special needs' no longer regarded as requiring teaching in separate schools. (55)

In many ways we see a continuing value in the educational programmes pioneered in the 1960s placed alongside the realities of the economic constraints and the technological revolution of the 1980s. In the area of teacher education for the realities of the 1990s, we would argue for a programme that will give young teachers a sense of their professionalism, a skilful blend of educational theory and effective classroom practice to make them aware upholders of the teacher's professional rights and responsibilities.

Chapter Two

RECENT TRENDS IN EDUCATIONAL POLICIES IN THE FEDERAL REPUBLIC OF GERMANY

Wolfgang Mitter

INTRODUCTORY REMARKS: TWO ESSENTIAL FEATURES OF CONTINUITY

Students of the history of formal education in Germany until 1945, examining the actual trends of educational policies in the Federal Republic of Germany, should include two features of continuity in their basic considerations. The first feature deals with the dominant role of the state which plays the leading role in the organization, administration, and control of schools and other educational institutions. This feature has origins in the period of early absolutism, when German princes began to regard policy affecting schools as an important task. The 'state' means, in this context, the centralized structure for legislation and government which can make use of a hierarchically constructed administration. The general nature of this fundamental stipulation was laid down in Article 144 of the 1919 Weimar Constitution and confirmed by Article 7 of the Basic Law (of the Federal Republic of Germany): 'The entire school system is subject to the supervision of the state'.

State control applies particularly to the horizontal stages of primary and secondary education. At university level the influence of the state is restricted to 'supervision' in the real sense of the word, for within this framework, the universities are allowed considerable autonomy in the discharge of their own concerns. State monopoly is also limited in the field of pre-school education. Supervision thus works in favour of the small local government units and the churches, as well as of private individuals and institutions. A further limitation occurs in those sectors of vocational

22

education which are provided outside the school system, that is by agencies of the labour market (industry, trade, services, agriculture). Here the state is content with outline legislation and allows the non-state chambers of industry, commerce, and agriculture extensive rights to regulate their forms of training.

The second essential feature concerns the tension between uniformity and variety. State monopoly in the education system and political and administrative federalism does not present us with a paradox because the Länder (states) of the Federal Republic each possess a centralized administrative structure. The important status of the Länder in matters of education, which has been reflected in their independent responsibility for all state institutions (including the legal supervision of universities) has a long historical basis. The Federal Republic has linked up with this traditional federative structure and even a change in the Basic Law in 1969 gave the Federal Authority outline legislative powers for the development of the university system and for collaboration in educational planning. Even in these areas, however, the Länder remain responsible for legislation affecting any changes in day-to-day standards and practices, such as the development of school syllabuses and determining the qualifications of teachers. The existence of these consultative bodies and the awareness of an educational public which disregards Länder boundaries certainly ensure that, even allowing for the important status of the Länder in matters of education. the traditional framework of an education system which is unified, at any rate in fundamental questions, continues to be effective. This endeavour finds expression also in the decisions of the Standing Conference of Ministers of Education and Cultural Affairs. So far as the most recent part of the history of education is concerned, mention must be made, in particular, of agreements on the reorganization of the final years in Gymnasien (grammar schools), enacted in 1972, 1977, and 1987, and on the reciprocal recognition of the end-of-course achievement standards in comprehensive schools in all Länder (1982). However, it must not be ignored that the pressure for unanimity in this body frequently slows down the implementation of decisions and may sometimes even defer them.

Whereas at the end of the 1960s and the beginning of the 1970s one could observe a certain trend towards convergence, recent years not only have reversed this trend,

but also on the contrary have favoured the revival of
policies signalizing divergence not only in special, but also
in fundamental matters, such as school selection and
admission procedures. The reasons for this are, on the one
hand, the fact that the legislative and executive bodies of
the individual Länder are made up of different political
power groupings: one-party rule by the Christian Democrats
(CDU) or the Social Democrats (SPD) or a coalition between
one or both with the Free Liberals. On the other hand, the
recent discrepancies in economic development, having in
particular opened a gap between the 'rich' South and the
'poor' North, affect the financing of educational measures.
Finally, there has been evidence indicating the existence of
feelings of Länder 'autonomy' in educational matters which
have had an impact on the arrangement of educational
structures and syllabuses. It is this autonomous component
which, besides the economic factor, explains that individual
Länder, even those governed by the same political parties,
may react differently to similar challenges. Therefore
students who want to get an insight into details of the
eleven Länder education systems may soon find themselves
in a labyrinth, as soon as they have left the basic level of
features found in the Federal Republic as a whole.

THE EDUCATION SYSTEM IN THE LIGHT OF 'CONTINUITY VERSUS REFORM'

Compared to the majority of European countries the
structure of the education system in the Länder of the
Federal Republic is characterized by a comparatively
distinct stability which is rooted in the tradition of the
nineteenth and twentieth centuries. Based upon a
comprehensive four-year primary school (which has been
extended to six years only in West Berlin and Bremen), lower
secondary (after the age of 10) education still mirrors the
former and traditional European scene, in so far as it is
generally organized in a tripartite system. It consists of two
selective types of school, the pre-academic Gymnasium and
the more practice-oriented Realschule, and the non-
selective Hauptschule, the West German variant of the
British secondary modern school. Even in the Länder (in
particular Hesse, North Rhine-Westphalia, and West Berlin)
which have built up systems of comprehensive and separate
(parallel) selective schools in competition during the past

two decades, the existence of the traditional system has not been seriously questioned.

There is still, however, a close link between each of the three types of lower secondary education and the network of upper secondary education, as far as the educational career of the majority of pupils is concerned:

1   from the lower and intermediate stage to the upper stage of the Gymnasium a pupil may proceed without formal admission procedures;
2   from the Realschule to the full-time vocational schools sector, as a rule, a pupil may proceed after formal admission based on the results of an examination;
3   from the Hauptschule to apprenticeship and part-time vocational schooling in the 'dual system' (part-time apprenticeship and compulsory schooling), as a rule the pupil proceeds without formal admission procedures, but dependent on the availability of training places in the specific branches or firms.

The 'stable' structure is reinforced by a network of school-type bound syllabuses which are focused on the ideal of Allgemeinbildung (general education) and organized round a broad core curriculum available in all 'general' types of schooling, and which has special regard to such foundation subjects as German (mother tongue), mathematics, and sciences; this is completed at the (lower and upper) secondary level by foreign languages, in most cases English. The core curriculum comprises the overwhelming part of the grade-bound syllabuses from the beginning of primary up to the end of lower (that is six years) secondary schooling. The outcome of the recent 'revision of the reform' at the upper stage of the Gymnasium will be dealt with later in detail. In this context, we must add that Allgemeinbildung, though in a reduced form, is also part of the syllabuses of full-time and part-time vocational schools.

The strength of the traditional stability, in terms of structures and syllabuses, has prepared the ground for the survival of the tripartite system (confined mostly to the lower secondary education level) and the failure of 'comprehensivization' on the one hand. On the other hand, it explains the maintenance of the comparatively well-balanced curricular proportions at the upper secondary level and, in particular, for the steadfastness of the 'dual system' (the most widespread form of vocational education) in overcoming the various assaults on it during the 1970s, and in reconfirming its present reputation, not least in the UK. Taking this strength into account, it is not surprising to discover the recent tendencies towards a 'revival of the past', as far as the political decision-making and its immediate impact on education are concerned. To illustrate this tendency, the following three sections of this chapter are given over to issues which may serve to provide an exemplary answer.

THE CONSOLIDATION OF THE TRIPARTITE SYSTEM AT THE LEVEL OF LOWER SECONDARY EDUCATION

It is true that, compared with the vast majority of West European education systems, the Federal Republic of Germany as a whole had been lagging behind on the march towards comprehensivization in the late 1960s and early 1970s. Even the Länder which were governed by Social Democrat-Liberal coalitions at that period, were not too keen on pushing their 'comprehensivization' reforms too far and held back from making lower secondary education in toto comprehensive. Therefore, it should not cause any surprise that in the traditionally conservative Länder of Southern Germany, namely Bavaria, Baden-Württemberg, and Rhineland-Palatinate, the few comprehensive schools which had been established never lost the status of 'experimental schools'.

On the other hand, the belief in the irreversible nature of the traditional tripartite system (with the aforementioned selective Gymnasien and Realschulen, and non-selective Hauptschulen), somehow, had lost ground in that period. This explains why even conservative politicians mostly represented in the Christian Democratic Union, as well as the more tradition-inspired educationalists had difficulty in formulating appropriate arguments against the need for structural reforms in favour of comprehensivization at the lower secondary education level. This was the period when the German Education Council (Deutscher Bildungsrat), an advisory body existing between 1965 and 1975, published its remarkable reports and recommendations which met with great acceptance, while resistance was articulated in rather a reticent manner, at least until 1973. The Structure Plan (Strukturplan), published in 1970 as the main document of the Council, was focused on the goal of equality of educational opportunity. The following aims were listed in the programme of educational reforms:

1 Modernization of the education system with reference to planning, school structure, and organization.
2 Democratization of education in which, it must be emphasized, the West German interpretation involves, not merely the opening of school and society to strata of the population hitherto underprivileged, but also the co-operation and joint decision-making by teachers, parents, members of the community, and finally even by pupils, in the way schools are set up and organized.
3 Introduction of curricula which aim to replace or, at any rate, reduce the function of traditional syllabuses. Underlying this desired change was the provision made in Saul Robinsohn's seminal book School Reform in the Light of Curriculum Revision, for the formulation of overall aims and detailed educational objectives, on the one hand, and, for instructions on teaching methods and guidelines on pupil and syllabus evaluation in order to complement the previously established lists of curriculum contents, on the other.

Comprehensive schools should greatly contribute to pursuing this programme. In order to smooth the transition from the four-year primary school to the comprehensive school and also to the still-existing majority of separate (parallel) schools of the tripartite system, a two-year orientation stage (Föderstufe or Orientierungsstufe) was established. Instead of holding entrance examinations as a prerequisite for admitting fourth-grade leavers to the Gymnasium, the orientation stage was to serve as a transitional arrangement of continuous assessment and pupil guidance. However, this innovation was modified, from the start, by conservative policy-makers, in that in the South German Länder, the orientation stage was set up in the traditional secondary schools themselves. The genuine variant, its establishment either at primary schools or as an independent institution, gained ground, though rather slowly, in the Länder governed by Social Democrats.

In the 1980s the pendulum has swung back towards consolidation and even restoration of the tripartite system. This trend had started in the mid-1970s already, that is long before the political change of the Federal government in 1982 which brought the Christian Democrats to power. In

Southern Germany (Bavaria, Baden-Württemberg, Rhineland-Palatinate) most of the few comprehensive schools
which, as has been mentioned, had only been admitted on an
experimental basis were 'dissolved', that is (re)transformed
into school types of the tripartite system. The most striking
case, however, has recently been presented by the Land
Hesse. In April 1987 the Christian Democrats (together with
the Liberals who, as in the Federal government, changed
their coalition partner preference from the Social
Democrats to the Christian Democrats) took office after
forty years' Social Democrat domination. Hesse had been
surpassed only by North Rhine-Westphalia and the city-state
of West Berlin as the Land where comprehensive schooling
had most markedly expanded. In the last year of rule by the
Social Democrats (together with the Green Party) the Hesse
Landtag (parliament) had enacted a law introducing the
comprehensive Föderstufe for all pupils of grades 5 and 6.
Only a few days after taking over government, the Christian
Democrats proposed a bill to the Hesse Landtag containing
the annulment of this law and its replacement by the new
Gesetz zur Wiederherstellung der Schulwahlfreiheit (law on
the restoration of free school choice) which was enacted on
27 May 1987. Christan Wagner, the new Minister of
Education, made it clear that his policy would include the
(re)transformation of all comprehensive schools into
traditional secondary schools. This policy has been actively
pursued during the early months of 1988. At the end of
August 1988 (the beginning of the school year 1988/89)
visitors to Hesse could discover that in some places the
existing comprehensive school had been turned back into one
of the three school types of the previous selective system.

The 'revisionist' policy aiming at reversing the trend
towards comprehensivization has been reinforced by the
following three initiatives which have resulted in laws or, at
least, have entered the stage of the parliamentary decision-
making process:

1   The open transfer from primary to all types of lower
     secondary education which had replaced the former
     selection procedures (entrance examinations to
     Gymnasien) in favour of parental choice, that is long
     before the orientation stage was introduced, was
     abolished in Bavaria and Baden Württemberg. The Hesse
     minister of education, following their policy, issued a
     decree on 5 February 1988 aimed at re-emphasizing the

selective character of the Gymnasium and the Realschule. From the school year 1988/89 onwards therefore, admission was to depend on the pupil's assessment report given by the grade 4 teacher of the primary school the pupil attended. Parents who did not agree with the report, were to have the right to insist on their children sitting an entrance examination (at a Gymnasium or Realschule). This measure could in fact be regarded as a return to the selective procedure practised up to the 1950s. This is noteworthy, the more so since it was the Christian Democrats who had so emphatically pleaded for parental choice of schooling for their children.

In the event, this harsh and apparently 'sloppily prepared' assault on the open transfer policy in Hesse was stopped, at least temporarily, by a judgement of the Hesse Court of Administrative Law (Hessischer Verwaltungsgerichtshof) on 20 June 1988, after some schools had already organized the prescribed entrance examinations.

2   As the 'moderate' alternative to comprehensivization the idea of permeability, an easy transfer between the three types of lower secondary school with access to near identical or similar syllabuses, though different teaching approaches, had been given much attention. This was because until the 1960s the grade-bound syllabuses in the tripartite system had been developed separately and were different. As an example, the Gymnasium syllabuses for the teaching of the German mother tongue emphasized grammar and German classical literature, while the Realschule syllabuses paid greater emphasis to the 'teaching of the commercial language'. Hauptschule syllabuses finally concentrated on the teaching of 'everyday language'. This differentiation of the syllabuses made it extremely difficult, if not impossible, for pupils to move to the 'higher' type of school, even when they were considered to fulfil the general ability and aptitude requirements. The reformed syllabuses were aimed at smoothing the differences by means of a process of approximation, a certain de-academization of the Gymnasium exemplar and, on the other hand, a measure of raising the academic levels of the syllabuses of the other two school types. Following the trend already manifested, for instance, in Christian Democrat governed Baden

Württemberg, the recent Hesse policy is directed towards returning to the situation existing before the reforms. This means breaking up the integration already achieved by the three existing school types.

3   In the course of the reform of the late 1960s and early 1970s, efforts had been made to build bridges between the hitherto strictly differentiated curricula derived from the academic syllabuses of the university disciplines, the derivation from the latter exemplified most closely in the case of the Gymnasium syllabuses. As a step towards this 'bridge-building' the Hessische Rahmenrichtlinien (Hesse Curricular Guidelines) contained, among other innovations, the reinforcement and extension of provision of 'social studies' consisting of history, geography and civics. In addition pilot schemes had been launched in the area of natural sciences to promote interdisciplinary links. Restoration, in this subject area means the return to the former departmentalized subject syllabuses which has already resulted in the abolition of the integrated subject of 'social studies'. These measures must be seen in the context of an overall policy of a retreat from general education objectives to curricular oriented content-bound syllabuses for individual subjects.

Hesse, therefore, following the South German trend has proved to be another hardliner in 'revisionist' policies. On the other hand, West Berlin and Lower Saxony, where the change of government from Social Democrat to Christian Democrat had already taken place at the end of the 1970s or the beginning of the 1980s, have pursued policies characterized by a remarkably delicate approach in revising the reforms that the Social Democrats had introduced. Thus West Berlin has retained the six-year primary school, while Lower Saxony, though allowing exceptions, has continued to acknowledge the legitimacy of the orientation stage as an independent institution as the 'rule'. Finally, it must not be forgotten that the continued existence of Social Democrat governments in North Rhine-Westphalia, Hamburg and Bremen has preserved the continuation of comprehensivization policies. Compared to the early 1970s it is not possible to speak, however, of clear strategies in this direction, the more so as the majority of parents (in all Länder) seem to favour the extension of the Gymnasium, as the most desired school type.

REVISION OF THE 'REFORMED' GYMNASIUM UPPER STAGE'

The recent development observed in the upper stage of the Gymnasium indicates another trend where 'revisions of reforms' have been going on. The three-year upper stage of the Gymnasium begins in the eleventh year of schooling, counting from the first grade of primary education. The tenth grade, though in most Länder already beyond full-time compulsory school education, counts as part of the intermediate stage of the Gymnasium, as does the final (tenth) grade of the Realschule. Since the school-year 1977/78 it has been reorganized in the 'reformed upper stage' on the basis of a Resolution of the Standing Conference of Ministers of Education and Cultural Affairs (KMK) passed in 1972. Departing from the traditional system of instruction in which individual subjects were taught in self-contained classes according to the age-group criterion (this system continues to prevail at the lower and intermediate stage) it substituted a system of course instruction across the upper stage. Entry requirements for individual subjects or groups of subjects remained, but pupils were given ample opportunity to choose the curriculum they wanted and to specialize within an extended range of available subjects. With regard to the traditional Gymnasium, the reform of 1977 has been of great significance in two respects:

1 Compared with the compactness of the traditional curricula which had obliged the pupils to take, though in three different curricular combinations (i.e. modern, classical, and scientific), four major and eleven minor subjects up to the Abitur, the 'reformed' syllabuses were characterized by a significant reduction to two major and approximately six minor subjects. Though the core curriculum has been kept rather broad, certainly compared with Britain, none the less, the reform of the upper stage has been seen as a break in the history of the Gymnasium and, consequently, been criticized by a great part of the public not given to supporting conservative policies.

2 The second component of the reform has proved to be even more 'revolutionary'. While in the previous system there had been a consensus that in each combination the group of major subjects had to consist of German,

mathematics, and one foreign language, the reform opened the door to the formal equality of all subjects which it is worthwhile to describe in detail.

Following the 1972 Resolutions the legal provisions of the Länder made a distinction between basic (Grund) and intensified/specialist courses (Leistungskurse) for the sake of structuring the whole syllabus with regard to achievement standards, where, needless to emphasize, there is considerable diversity among the syllabuses of different Länder.

The aim of Grundkurse (basic courses) is defined as being that of assuring basic education for all secondary school pupils. The Leistungkurse (intensified courses), on the other hand, are intended to provide in-depth pre-academic understanding and in some aspects extended knowledge of the subject in question. Despite the difference in view of specialization and intensity, there is, generally speaking, no fundamental distinction between the educational objectives of the two course types, but there is a difference of degree of quality and quantity. At the moment they differ primarily with regard to

1   the number of course hours per week (for basic courses usually three, for intensive courses five to six are required);
2   the complexity of the subject matter dealt with;
3   the degree of subtlety and abstraction in the material and concepts presented;
4   the degree to which pupils are expected to master the subject matter in question;
5   the requirement concerning pupils' ability to work independently.

As much as two-thirds of all instruction at the upper stage takes place in basic courses, while the pupils choose two (in Rhineland-Palatinate and the Saarland, three) specialist course subjects. One of the specialist courses must be a subject carried over from lower-secondary-level instruction, e.g. a foreign language (English, French, or Latin as a rule, in exceptional cases also a 'non-conventional' language, e.g. Russian or Japanese), mathematics or a science subject (physics, chemistry, or biology). Subjects offered from scratch in upper-level instruction at Gymnasien can be taken as a second specialist course, e.g. one of the non-conventional foreign languages (Spanish, Italian, Dutch, and others), economics or computer studies (information technology).

The aim of creating areas of specialization in specialist courses had been to ensure the high quality of pre-academic education and of the Gymnasium leaving certificate, the Abitur. However, pupils' choice of subjects in specialist courses does not predetermine their choice of subject when they enrol in higher education because the reform of the upper level has not in any way restricted the traditional right that the Abitur holder has acquired the Allgemeine Hochschulreife (general certificate) for entry to study any subject in higher education, though the numerus clausus has reduced this right somewhat by demanding high marks for studying certain subjects at university.

The subjects taught at school fall into three general categories of Studienbereiche (fields of study):

1   language, literature, and art
2   social sciences
3   mathematics, science, and technology.

Sports and religion, though not included in any of the fields of study, may be associated with any one of them. The Resolution of 1972 laid down the principle that each of the three fields of study must be represented among the subjects taken as a basic or specialist course by every secondary school pupil right through to the end of the upper-stage instruction and to the (reorganized) Gymnasium leaving examination, the Abitur. Pupils may not drop any of the fields of study nor replace one with the other two. As a result of this requirement the previous principle of the 'major subject' has been replaced by the fixed position of the Studienbereiche.

While the eleventh year of schooling serves as an introductory year, the four semesters of the course system comprising the twelfth and thirteenth years of schooling have been organized in rather a complicated way, as regards the principle of Studienbereiche and individual subjects, on the one hand, and the arrangement of basic and specialist courses, on the other. Taken as a whole, the curriculum of the 'reformed upper stage of the Gymnasium' (and, subsequently, the Abitur examination) mirrors the attempt to combine the traditional philosophy of a broad core curriculum, inherited from Wilhelm von Humboldt's neo-humanistic philosophy, with a maximum of individual choice for the pupils. The weakest and most crucial aspect of the reforms of the 1970s has been identified as the neglect of the growing second stage, that is the pre-vocational, as opposed to the preparation for university function of the upper stage. Critics have pointed to the need to enrich the curriculum by work-experience studies and other pre-vocational activities, at least in the form of basic courses or optional working groups.

As regards the implementation of the reform as such there have been continuous disputes among the public. From its beginning criticism has been directed towards the lack of staff and rooms necessary for a proper course system. Shortage of teachers has continued to restrict the number and nature of course choices possible, and it has often been the case that the staff available to take on subjects has not been trained to teach them. The disbanding of homogeneous age group classes has also been considered to be problematic, as impeding interpersonal communication. A further source of criticism by the public has been the diversity of regulations resulting from the aforementioned differences of implementation of reforms from <u>Land</u> to <u>Land</u> which increases the difficulty of changing schools.

Besides these ongoing points of criticism, the debate has widened into fundamental controversies about the extent of the mandatory core curriculum and the range of options to be conceded to the pupils. Some <u>Länder</u> have limited courses offered to specific subject combinations right from the beginning of the reform. Since the end of the 1970s the West German University Rectors' Conference has stressed the danger of premature specialization by pupils, advocating a restriction of options in favour of broadly based mandatory subjects. The Rectors believe that German, mathematics, two foreign languages, two science subjects, and history should be compulsory throughout the upper stage. These subjects are viewed as being an essential prerequisite of readiness for university study. However, sports, art, humanities subjects, and religion are also thought necessary components of the curriculum.

Beyond the issue of defining the concept of 'general education' to be implemented in a compact core curriculum there have been debates about the syllabus requirements in individual subjects. For example in German language studies associations the question has been raised whether, or to what extent, traditional literature studies should be replaced by analyses of actual texts written in everyday style, such as newspapers or magazines. Regarding literature studies as such, conflicts have arisen with regard to the proportion of compulsory to optional subject matter. Here freedom of choice (by the individual teacher, the whole team of subject specialists or, in participatory models, also the pupils) creates an additional item in the debate.

It is true that the division of the German literature syllabus into compulsory and optional units has existed for decades; it can be traced back to the reforms of the 1920s. Nevertheless until the reforms of the late 1960s and early 1970s there was undisputed consensus that certain German classical works, in particular Goethe's Faust, were considered part of the compulsory component of the German literature syllabus. It is precisely the abandonment of this consensus which has recently recaptured the attention of the policy-makers and the public; these conflicts have crystallized into the controversial reappraisal of the school's duty to teach the classics. The opponents of the 'conventional' view argue that the choice of texts and works must not be slanted towards traditional concepts in a one-sided way, but rather should be derived from those issues and problems now affecting pupils' minds and perspectives.

Another example may be given from the area of social studies. Here a battle has been fought over the position of history: should it maintain its autonomous position as a discrete subject or should it be integrated into a cross-disciplinary, sociologically oriented course? Since the beginning of the 1980s the trend towards 're-establishing' history as a subject in the core curriculum has gradually gained strength and momentum. A first landmark in this counter-movement was the decision of the Staatsgerichtshof (State Supreme Court) of Hesse in December 1981. It obliged education authorities to retain German and history as compulsory subjects up to the Abitur. This decision, though binding only on the Hesse Ministry of Education, exerted considerable influence on revision-bent policies throughout the Federal Republic.

In recent years the controversies have increasingly affected the educational policies of the three main political parties and, consequently, their representatives in the Länder governments, above all the ministers of education. While the governments formed by the Social Democrats advocate keeping the state of affairs achieved in the aftermath of the 1972 Resolution of the Standing Conference of Ministers of Education and Cultural Affairs (KMK), their counterparts in the governments formed (or dominated) by the Christian Democrats have clamoured for its modification. After several meetings the Standing Conference of Ministers of Education and Cultural Affairs came to an agreement at Karlsruhe on 4 December 1987. It has, after all, confirmed their willingness to reach a compromise in order to preserve the legal uniformity and general validity throughout the Federal Republic of the Allgemeine Hochschulreife (Abitur). This compromise consists of the following arrangements:

1   all pupils must take at least two subjects of the group consisting of German, foreign languages, and mathematics throughout the final two grades (four semesters) before the Abitur (whether they have chosen them as basic or specialist courses);
2   each pupil must take one course in one of the three natural science subjects (physics, chemistry, or biology) in each of the four semesters, or two semesters (courses) each in two science subjects provided they had been part of his or her curriculum in grade 11;
3   each pupil must take history (or another 'social studies' subject with an explicit historical component) throughout the last two grades.

THE DEVELOPMENT OF THE ABITUR

Some basic remarks should be devoted to the Abitur examination as it has been developed since the 1970s. It is administered in four subjects including two subjects taken as specialist courses and one additional subject, in all of which there are both written and oral examinations. In the fourth subject, however, there is only an oral examination. All three areas of study must be represented in the examination. Within the context created by the federal structure of the Federal Republic of Germany, and taking the assessment of scholastic achievement into special account, the Standing Conference of Ministers of Education and Cultural Affairs (KMK) has made efforts to bring about a joint agreement on examination procedures and requirements; full consensus, however, has not yet been reached.

Nevertheless, the common examination requirements introduced in the course of the 1970s pertain to almost all subjects, including some that are now being admitted for the first time as subjects in which there is a written examination for the Abitur, such as 'non-conventional' foreign languages and economics. The framework established by these new examination requirements has made it possible to include differences in the syllabuses in the various Länder. At the same time, it makes the examination questions and evaluation of the answers given more comparable and easier to understand in the individual subjects. Thus, even in its present incomplete form, the agreed assessment programme for Abitur examinations can be seen as a compromise between the traditional grading system emphasizing the diversity of given examination situations and the decision-making autonomy of examining teachers, on the one hand, and the approach towards a more standardized examination system which, however, is still far more heterogeneous, compared, for instance, to the French Baccalauréat or the British GCE Advanced Level examinations. In particular, one has to take into consideration that it is the pupil's subject teacher who sets the questions in the oral examination and, in some of the Länder, even determines the three subject topics for the written examination papers, one of which is finally selected by the Minister of Education.

As has been suggested above, it is the revisionist critics among policy-makers, university professors, and the public who thought even this comparatively compact regulation was too open. The Agreement of 4 December 1987 has enacted the following regulations regarding the Abitur:

1   Among the four subjects, one of the traditional main subjects, namely German, mathematics, and one foreign language (started not later than grade 9), must be represented.
2   Contrary to the current rule which gives the pupils a certain freedom to collect credits (Punkte) for their chosen subjects in the Abitur certificate, this freedom will be restricted with regard to the aforementioned reintroduction of compulsory subjects.
3   Contrary to the current rule, the basic courses will be given greater weight which, consequently, will lead to a certain loss in weighting of the specialist courses (a ratio of 2:1 instead of 3:1).

It is obvious that the recent Agreement has not led to a definitive resolution of the controversy. After all, its complexity is rooted in the absence of a consensus on what general education consists of, and the fact that there are no satisfactorily defined and institutionalized criteria for a general ability for higher education. The Agreement having produced a compromise between reform and revision of the reform has, up to now, not ended in the abandonment of the opening which had been initiated by the reform of 1972. Nevertheless, the revisionist features of the Agreement cannot be overlooked. Above all, the philosophy of the formal equality of all subjects as prerequisites for the Abitur has been abandoned in favour of the re-establishment of the traditional major subjects: German, foreign languages, and mathematics to which history has now been added.

The revision of the reform must be related to the unbroken philosophy of the Abitur as the overall prerequisite for entry to all university faculties. Acknowledgement of this philosophy is rooted far beyond conservative groupings. As a powerful organization, the West German Rectors' Conference, while pleading for the restoration of the traditional core, has repeatedly underlined the need for maintaining the Abitur as the main criterion certificating access to higher education, the Allgemeine Hochschulreife, mentioned on p.33.

NO RETURN TO THE PAST

Can the recent changes in educational structures and syllabuses be interpreted as a return to the past? This is the question which must now be answered. It is not necessary to be a follower of Ivan Illich's deschooling philosophy to admit that all the associations related to de-comprehensivization of lower secondary education and to consolidation at the upper stage of the Gymnasium are two crucial components of the revision of reform, which cannot be dismissed as ephemeral crazes. They must be taken seriously, the more so as these revisionist tendencies are inter alia reinforced by corresponding policies in teacher education. They are characterized, on the one hand, by readjusting the training goals to the requirements of the vertical school-types (instead of the horizontal school-levels) and, on the other hand, by reaffirming the academic, university discipline-oriented courses against the more general educational components in the curricula.

This consideration, in its turn, entails another question: Can the stabilization in the structural and curricular dimension of education be blamed on political conservatism in a simplistic way? It seems that the search for an explanation must be more open and multi-faceted. Otherwise it would be hard to explain why the revisionist trend as a whole extends far into the political groupings of the moderate left. The picture becomes even more complex, when one relates the stabilization in the development of educational structures and syllabuses to developments outside the educational system which indicate the complexity of the current socio-political situation. The following considerations are based on the thesis that the revival of traditional structures and syllabuses can neither be traced back to political conservatism nor identified as a return to the past in a simplistic way. To justify this thesis one can hardly fail to pinpoint the following two crucial observations.

1   The first observation deals with the ideological position of those politicians and educationalists who support policies in favour of decomprehensivizing secondary education. Looking at current developments in the Federal Republic of Germany one can notice that preference for, or at least tolerance of, the maintenance or re-establishment of separate (parallel) schools is spread not only among Conservatives, but also among Liberals and Social Democrats. This widening of the spectrum has certainly been affected by the growing insight into the importance of new technologies on content, method, and process of education and, consequently, by the increasing attention paid to selection instead of support, which culminates in individual promotion of highly gifted youngsters. Moreover, there has emerged an overall and increasing appreciation of positive factual knowledge to be produced by subject-bound syllabuses. In view of this overarching trend adherents of different ideological and political positions may turn out to be allied under the umbrella of modernization. On the other hand, one should not overlook that traditional conservatives, who, though liking the renascence of their Gymnasien, are not in favour of standardized testing and the other

objective selection mechanisms which have begun to invade these educational institutions. In matters of regular pupil assessment, however, the subject teacher is still the main arbiter, despite moves to compare results across different schools.

2   The second observation deals with changes and expectations of schools and teachers in the context of this overarching trend. It is true that parameters of expectations are predominantly determined by the responsible politicians and are evident in legal ordinances emanating at different levels: from general school laws to detailed instructions explaining procedures at the grassroots level. Beyond this, however, there are at all levels of society explicit and latent expectations of the characteristics which schools should exhibit and possess. Among those articulating such non-formal expectations, special attention has to be paid to parents and to various representatives of the employment market in their capacity as recipients of school-leavers.

The recent developments in the Federal Republic of germany indicate the tendency for the ministers of education and cultural affairs in the various Länder to attempt to use their powers in a much more explicit and distinct way than they used to do two decades (or even one decade) ago. As against that there is evidence that there is among parents and the general public a widespread drive crystallizing into a changing conception of schools, a change from governmental institutions to service agencies. Among the social groups whose members in particular voice their expectations, one must not forget the young people themselves who seem, compared to their ancestors, to have learned to express their attitudes and aspirations more clearly, including critical judgements and statements of protest. In this respect, pupils attending Gymnasien today have little in common with those of previous generations.

To what extent does the emerging demand for service functions to be provided by formal education affect the structural and curricular dimensions of the education system? When answering this question one has to take into account primarily that this topical demand is rooted in the change of societal position that school has assumed in the current period of mass education and labour market mobility. The widespread increase in citizens' political awareness in modern democracy needs to be considered in this context also. People have become less ready to accept formal education as the monopoly of a hierarchically structured bureaucracy, with the minister at the top of the ladder, and want to make their own choices as far as their children's school careers are concerned. Since the labour market as well as the political system are increasingly dominated by plurality and diversity, diversification becomes more and more regarded as a value in educational policy, with regard not only to content and method of teaching and learning, but also to structure.

It may suffice to note this development and conclude that one of its impacts on educational policy can be regarded as an apparent aversion against comprehensive concepts. This is why the Gymnasium has become so attractive again; it has maintained its position as the direct path to higher education on the one hand, and, at the same time, it offers ample opportunities for a good start in advanced vocational education or even for on-the-job training, with prospects for entering university courses later. On the other hand, the Hauptschule has more and more drifted into a marginal position, that means into a 'school for the remainder'. Special attention has to be paid, therefore, to its becoming the main place of schooling for children of immigrants, a problem which is beyond the scope of this chapter. Conservatives (in the widest sense) appreciate, on the one hand, the Gymnasium very much, while, on the other hand, they want to restrict the number of enrolments and to revalue the function of the Hauptschule which in former times recruited the majority of the younger generation. In most areas it now enrols well under half the school population. The Realschule has proved and even reinforced its position as the school for preparing for the service professions. It finds itself in the most solidly confirmed state. However, the response of parents, youngsters, and the general public signalizes that such a development is unlikely to end in success.

While the Federal Republic of Germany is characterized by a de facto revival of Gymnasien, one should also pay attention to the remarkable number of multifarious pilot schemes and innovatory activities within this traditional school type. One can even point out that headteachers and teaching staff of Gymnasien have fewer scruples about becoming involved in such schemes, because the existence of their schools as such, contrary to that of the Gesamtschulen (comprehensive schools), is not endangered or contested. There is similar evidence from upper secondary education that Gymnasien successfully compete with advanced vocational institutions, in spite of the greater flexibility which has recently emerged at this level of education.

CONCLUDING CONSIDERATIONS

If we had finished our considerations at this point, we might have created this impression: it is true that the structure of the education system in the Federal Republic has moved away from comprehensive schooling. Considering the activities and initiatives in individual schools, however, the revision of the reform need not raise undue alarm. After all, human as well as cognitive values, social and affective educational objectives can be attained in comprehensive as well as in separate (parallel) schools or in various in-between forms of integration, such as multilateral school centres, co-operating and other linked schools. On the other hand, it must be borne in mind that experience has shown that school reforms aimed at comprehensivization of the lower secondary level fail or cause social discord if they are not supported by the vast majority of the public. While acknowledging this experience as proven, it should not conceal the possibility that a new change may occur in majority opinion. At the same time, reforms enacted by small parliamentary majorities and carried through against significant resistance do not provide a motivating climate for innovations at the grassroots level. It seems that this thesis can also be applied to revisions of reforms in general.

The recent revival of selective schools in the Federal Republic of Germany, in open or concealed form, has to be regarded as an earnest of the growing interest in quality of education. In a sense this trend was inevitable since in the past decades quality seems to have been overtaken by equality. However, suspicion is aroused by the unrestricted use of the term quality observed in political spheres. In the actual contest the plea for quality may originate from a disguised attempt to maintain traditional hierarchical structures in the social system by strengthening academic achievement and creativity. Therefore, this claim must be put forth as a pretext for misusing selection for socio-political reasons -- even if such selective schools strongly deny social selection and justify their existence by only emphasizing the need to promote educational excellence. The present Gymnasien in the Federal Republic of Germany, having developed from elitist to mass education schools catering for half the total school population in the country or more, are far from falling back into their former status. This observation justifies, in an exemplary way, the overall conclusion that a return to the past is unlikely to happen.

Chapter Three

TEACHER PREPARATION AND THE REFORM OF COLLEGES IN FRANCE

Raymond Bourdoncle and Françoise Cros

Since 1959 the restructuring of the organization of secondary schooling has resulted in a comprehensive school system in France. After leaving primary school at 11, all children attend the same type of school throughout the country in mixed ability classes. The teachers have not been prepared or trained for such a heterogeneous school population, nor were special educational methods set up for them to follow. However, certain suggestions have been formulated and measures instituted concerned with change in the education of teachers.

THE INSTITUTIONAL CHANGES

Before 1959 there existed two separate types of school with different employment prospects for their pupils. Teachers were recruited, on the whole, from different social groups, and they used different teaching methods in the different types of school. (1) For children who were not leaving compulsory primary school to go directly into employment, there were the cours complémentaires and, with some restrictions, classes providing technical and vocational subjects. They recruited their pupils in the main from the working and lower-middle classes and prepared them for clerical work in offices or as skilled or semi-skilled workers in industry. The teachers of the cours complémentaires had been former primary-school teachers, who had not studied at university and as teachers had taught several different subjects. They were imbued with the philosophy of primary-school teaching methods, relying largely on rote-learning and memory.

The lycées (grammar schools), which had their own preparatory level classes and were the independent schools of the time, prepared their pupils who came predominantly from the upper-middle classes for the baccalauréat, a general school examination which did not prepare them for a particular type of employment but enabled them to go on to university. The long period of time necessary for such studies to prepare the students for a specific job proved a serious obstacle, particularly for pupils from the working classes. The teachers in these schools had been trained at university in one single-subject discipline, and they aimed at getting their pupils to acquire a mastery of the subject through the example of their own mastery of the discipline, in lessons where their knowledge and reasoning were put to the test. Teaching programmes were made up essentially of subjects that encouraged the use of formal reasoning skills and logic, such as grammar, Latin, and mathematics.

In the late 1950s sociological studies on technological functionalism were developed on the economic theory of human capital potential, later taken up by the Organization of Economic Co-operation and Development. (2) This led politicians and administrators to become aware of the contradiction that existed between the need for a skilled, flexible work-force, able to adapt to the needs of modern industry, and the need for a higher level of education and training for the population as a whole, on the one hand, and on the other hand, the wastage of talent and the social injustice that was brought about by the operation of these two socially distinct educational networks.

In 1959 a decision was taken to extend compulsory schooling to the age of 16. This meant that some 900,000 young people, who would have left school under the previous system, were gradually retained in the school system. In 1963 the creation of collèges (junior high schools) enabled three different types of pupil population to start attending the same schools, but by three distinct routes: the school-pupils, who would have left school at the age of 14; those who went to the cours complémentaires; and third, those who went to the lower forms of the lycées.

In 1977 these three distinct educational routes were abolished, since when almost the entire school population, after leaving primary school, has been accommodated in the same classes during the first two years of schooling. Then about a quarter of these pupils, the weakest, are sent to

Figure 1 The French educational system

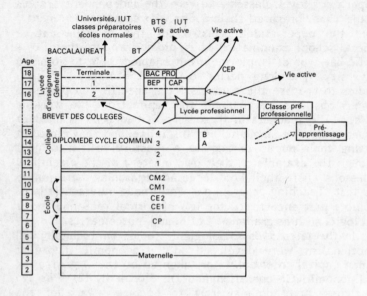

CP : Cours préparatoire
CE1 : Cours élémentaire 1ère année
CE2 : Cours élémentaire 2ème année
CM1 : Cours moyen 1ère année
CM2 : Cours moyen 2ème année
1 : Sixième
2 : Cinquième
3 : Quatrième
4 : Troisième
A : Quatrième technologique
B : Troisième technologique
CEP : Certificat d'éducation professionnelle
CAP : Certificat d'aptitude professionnelle
BEP : Brevet d'études professionnel
BAC PRO : Baccalauréat professionnel
BT : Brevet de technicien
BTS : Brevet de technicien
IUT : Institut universitaire de technologie

vocational streams, while three-quarters of the pupils stay on in the collèges for two further years of study before being allocated to the lycées, the professional training institutions or work at 16 (see Figure 1).

THE PUPILS

As a result of these institutional changes a deep unease was registered by the teachers. This was due to two compounded factors: the dramatic changes in the school population coupled with the fact that the imposed teaching syllabuses and methods were the same as those used previously in traditional tripartite, academically differentiated, teaching. At the moment more than 90 per cent of the pupils in the last year of primary school proceed to a class called the sixième which is the first year of the collège. As the pupils' learning reactions differ the teachers can no longer continue to rely on teaching styles which they had used before. The children in all classes are so radically different, intellectually and emotionally, that the traditional methods, practised in rather more homogeneous classes, are no longer effective. The system previous to 1977, based on a great variety of types of school and stream, has been changed to a system which accommodates a variety of different intellectual and maturity levels, options and teaching modalities imposed by the presence of pupils of mixed abilities within the same classroom of the collège.

The characteristics of this diversified and wide school population can be analysed from four different aspects: the cognitive, the psycho-sociological, the emotional, and the physiological.

The cognitive level

Teachers no longer encounter a single image, the yardstick, as it were, of the same type of pupil intelligence, but different types of intelligence: discursive intelligence which is associated with the learning of mathematics or linguistics is found alongside a more practical intelligence whose representatives are particularly good at solving complex technical problems. These pupils, with different types of intelligence, do not behave in the same way while learning the same subject. Certain pupils are better in verbal

47

activities, others in activities involving a conception of space, while others are better with numbers.

In the past, the teacher used more abstract methods based on deductive reasoning. These methods no longer seem applicable to all the pupils. There are among them some who are more intuitive and think in a more concrete fashion. The teacher too would refer to a universe structured on pure intelligence independent of immediate sense experience. However, today, there are pupils in schools who cannot approach an intellectual task without referring to the environment or making use of social contacts. They are said to be dependent on context compared to those in the category described above who are not so dependent. (3)

A study carried out by Cros, with a cohort of 1,600 school-children in the sixième, based on Piaget's structuralist theory of cognitive development, in the form of a written examination showed the following: (4)

1   about 44 per cent of the students at the concrete stage of cognitive development had not reached the level where they could reason with concepts or carry out operational operations;
2   about 50 per cent of the pupils were at an intermediate stage, a transitory period, the basis of which is firmly rooted in concrete operations;
3   about 6 per cent of the pupils were at the formal stage, that of hypothetical deductive reasoning and abstract thought, corresponding to formal and abstract subject contents taught particularly in modern mathematics and linguistic analysis.

For more than three-quarters of the pupils the formal content of the subjects, which are meant to be taught at school, proved inappropriate. More than half the pupils were in a transitory period undergoing change, uncertain and requiring firm and concrete points of reference. This same population of school-children was subjected to a further written test based on a multifactorial theory of intelligence. In the spatial domain boys seemed to succeed much better than girls. Thus in terms of ensuring success, the areas of enquiry and interests do not seem to be the same. For this population, which was representative of the pupil cohort of France in their first year of collège in 1978, it was observed that differences in functional development varied by more than three years. In the past teachers used the blackboard, books, diagrams, and drawings without any difficulty. Above all, they used visual methods. Now, however, school-children seem to have difficulty forming mental structures from visual stimuli. They need supplementary explanations based on auditory reinforcement through the use of the spoken word and repetition.

On the cognitive level teachers were faced with pupils who did not correspond to the image they had of pupils in the past, who had been through a selection process earlier on, and whose thinking was based on deductive formal reasoning which was stable and structured logically in a linear fashion.

The psycho-sociological level

A short study carried out by Bruner illustrates this variety in groups coming from all the different social classes of the country. (5) For the same intellectual performance the socio-emotional commitment is different depending on the content given. School-children were asked to reproduce the size of a round token. All the school-children succeeded in doing so. When the round token was replaced by a coin, the children from the underprivileged classes enlarged the size of the token in a very significant way.

Pupils who now attend the <u>collèges</u> have rarely been brought up on the classical works of Bach or Handel but rather on pop-music, reggae, or Madonna. Their common reading matter is no longer the novels of Alexandre Dumas or Marcel Pagnol but comic strips. They no longer understand the intellectual benefits of learning Latin or Greek. For them school is no longer an object of strong interest or attraction. In certain <u>collèges</u> classes take place in an atmosphere of constant turmoil and noise, and in some cases, open confrontation. The teachers try to reproduce the kind of teaching they themselves received and which is deeply engrained in them. They believe that the pupils are like the teachers and are utterly confused by the general uproar.

Some of their pupils have already come through negative experiences, as far as school is concerned and, full of anger, refuse to adopt the image given to them by the teacher. They refuse to co-operate with an authority that they do not recognize. After all the pupils have not chosen to go to school, but have been forced to attend by society.

Membership of gangs, especially in the suburbs, is a protection against school and accounts for the growing difficulty in school of working with and managing working groups. Relationships amongst peer groups are rarely harmonious and reflect the situation in society as a whole. We pointed out that not one but many types of intelligence exist. In the same way not one but many collèges exist.

Pupils go to the collège located in their immediate neighbourhood. However, since neighbourhoods can be very different, a collège in a working-class suburb will not be like one in a fashionable district. Pupils go to some collèges on tiptoe and show great respect for an atmosphere of silent study where only the voice of the teachers can be heard. But there are other collèges, which one is reluctant to enter, where the buildings are in a state of bad repair, with graffiti scrawled across dirty walls, and where there is a constant, deafening, chaotic noise. The abolition of separate catchment areas, started in 1985, means that the pupils go to the collège of their choice, which will increase the problem of differentiation. In the past the collège bully often came from a well-to-do family, which believed in the value of school and the classical teaching it provided. The ill-behaved pupil today comes from a working-class council house (an HLM or habitation à loyer modéré) and has been called a 'concrete teenager'. (6)

The emotional level

In addition to this disparity on the intellectual and sociological levels there are also the problems of relationships with other adults and, in particular, with teachers. Teachers can no longer control the pupils and their authority and power have become weakened. The pupils' mental blocks, which in the past resulted in sullen silence, a refusal to talk, now break out in forms of verbal violence and, in some cases, even physical violence. In some collèges, in outer Paris suburbs, teachers are often attacked outside the school by a gang of teenagers. There is an enormous gap between the teachers' own adolescence and that of the present generation of teenagers. Their systems of value are brought out in the clothes they wear, their relationships with their peers, their parents, or with other adults, and have nothing to do with school. The teenagers' culture is formed outside the school and what it stands for. Space for free activity and free expression in schools to offset this trend must be found.

The physiological level

Today collègiens are sexually aware very early. The rapid biological changes in their bodies make them mature from a child in the first year of collège to a fully developed teenager by the time they have reached their fourth year. This enormous physiological change is accompanied by moments of great lassitude, of inattentiveness, frequent mind-wanderings and day-dreaming, and tiredness, when they are forced to sit still. They find that their desks are often too low and too narrow for their long arms and legs. A rapid glance at a class during the last year of collège is very revealing as to the great disparity in the pupils' physical development. Some still seem to be children, whereas others are fully developed young men or women.

To sum up: the present-day population in the collège is characterized by its great heterogeneity in all aspects. Teachers have to teach the kind of pupil whom they have never met before in their own life and teaching experience. The new school, no longer closed in on itself, a school fundamentally intellectual and verbal, has been forced to accommodate pupils who are proud of their own culture, their own specific cognitive style and have attitudes not at all invariably well-disposed towards their place of learning.

THE TEACHERS

In 1985 there were some 181,000 teachers coping with this heterogeneous population of collège pupils. The teachers themselves were divided into two very distinct halves. On the one hand, there were the lycée-type teachers, that is those who had taught exclusively in lycées before the reforms of the last thirty years, and some of whom still do post-16 lycée teaching. They fall into three distinct types according to the special competitive examinations they have passed: the agrégés account for 2.4 per cent of all collège teachers; the certifiés 31.2 per cent; the adjoints d'enseignement or maîtres auxiliaires, who are the least well-qualified in the formal sense, make up 15.1 per cent of the total. On the other hand, there are those teachers who teach only in collèges, the Professeurs d'Enseignement Général des Collèges (PEGC) (50.3 per cent). Most of these have come from primary schools. The reforms which placed in collèges pupils from previously separate schools in the same classes were responsible for doing the same thing with their teachers. However, these teachers, too, did not all enjoy the same status or conditions of service: fifteen to eighteen hours of teaching required of the lycée-type teacher and twenty-one hours of the others. The former taught only one school subject; the latter had to teach two. Above all their academic education and pedagogical preparation differed greatly as well.

Initial teacher training

The academic education of today's lycée-type teacher, in every respect, is the same as that of the lycée teacher before 1959. The same four-year university course of study - in one area of studies - and the same degree and teaching qualification (licentia docendi) are required. They sit the same special competitive examinations to obtain a teaching position, the Certificat d'Aptitude à l'Enseignement du Second Degré or the coveted Agrégation, after a master's degree (maîtrise). Two-thirds of the collège-type teachers started their professional career as primary-school teachers, instituteurs, who received a multidisciplinary training in the écoles normales (primary-school teacher-training institutions). Having previously taught in some type of primary school, they now have the title Professeurs d'Enseignement Général des Collèges (PEGC). Younger, differently trained teachers have joined this second group. They must now possess a certificate of a completed first year of university studies plus two years of special training, including one year of educational theory in two teaching subjects.

There are clearly great differences in subject training for teaching in a collège. As the press, teachers' unions, and even an official commission of inquiry in 1981 were at pains to point out, a short multidisciplinary training or a two-year training in two subjects cannot possibly equal a four-year education in a single academic discipline. (7) But, allowing for this, is the four-year university education really fitted to equip a graduate for teaching collège pupils? Louis Legrand says that such an academic education is too subject-oriented; based too much on content, knowledge for knowledge's sake, and not closely enough linked to the concrete world of the adolescent to be of interest to him. (8) Prost points out that the method of teaching a particular subject, which would facilitate the presentation or acquisition of the subject matter by the pupils, has been seriously neglected in this type of teacher education. (9) Despite these criticisms, the long, monodisciplinary training system - the most widely acclaimed of the three - has been recently adopted as the one to be followed by all future teachers.

The difference in pedagogical preparation among the different types of teacher is even greater than the difference in their academic education. Among the lycée-type teachers, the maîtres auxiliaires who are recruited on a temporary basis without being selected as a result of a competitive examination, and the adjoints d'enseignement, who are former maîtres auxiliaires who have been granted tenure, have had no specific initial teacher education before being appointed to a post. Only the certifiés teachers, and to a lesser degree, the agrégés have had any such preparation.

Since 1952, teacher education for the certifiés has consisted of three training periods spread over one year. Each training period is made up of a series of lesson observations, some class duties, such as keeping order, and finally teaching, all supervised by pedagogical advisers: experienced teacher-tutors. This training also includes an introduction to the life and activities in school, lectures on educational psychology, some general personal education, subject method, and general teaching problems. Preparation classes for the special competitive examination, the Agrégation, were also set up at that time. In 1982 the provision of courses in pedagogical studies was substantially increased, which now consist of at least eighty-four hours of lectures, professional assignments, or observation visits followed by a special test for the final examination. However, as Tixeront and Leselbaum point out, the official programmes and their application differ from one teacher-preparation centre to another. (10) This, of course, is hardly surprising because the centres have no permanent staff who could develop common criteria and concepts for the content of teacher education. They are staffed by university lecturers, administrators, inspectors, headteachers, and other experienced professional colleagues. The final examination includes the candidate's model lesson which tests the subject matter studied and the examinee's verbal skills, which, of course, had already been tested during the entrance examination. What the final examination does not test is the examinee's ability to adapt their teaching style to the pupils' level or to organize and follow up on their pupils' work.

Most of the PEGCs had received their initial training as instituteurs. In their case practical training sessions and courses in educational psychology had always had pride of place. In their present preparation the same emphasis is placed on practical training sessions and professional and subject method studies to suit the education of collège pupils. This training takes two years and the staff are experienced teacher-educators who have come from the écoles normales or universities.

In spite of certain similarities, there are two main differences in the preparation that PEGCs and certifiés receive. The first is that not the same use is made of teaching practice in the training sessions. The certifiés work essentially through their teacher-tutors and very little with anyone else, who might naturally be concerned with such work. Everything depends on the teacher-tutors, who have been appointed to their jobs by the school inspectors, not for their abilities as teacher-trainers - which are unknown to the inspectors - but for their own school-teaching abilities, which the inspectorate had judged as good. This procedure shows to what extent teaching is regarded as an art and not a profession, and that teacher-training means imitating a preconceived model and not being given the chance to reflect on teaching and developing new pedagogical and didactic skills. The PEGCs, on the other hand, discuss and analyse their on-the-job training in the light of their general pedagogical knowledge not only with teacher-tutors, but also with other trainees and the teachers from their training centre. There, by contrast, teaching is considered a profession where a practical apprenticeship must be completed with pedagogical know-how, thus marrying theory with practice. The second main difference in the two types of teacher preparation has to do with the amount of time allocated to the training period itself; over 300 hours for the PEGCs and fewer than 100 hours for the certifiés. This further underlines the two different conceptions of teaching.

The subject matter is the basis of the professional

identity of single-discipline teachers. They have mastered an academic subject in university and this mastery alone has given them access to a teaching position. Brought up on a method of inquiry peculiar to a university discipline, as Legrand points out, (11) they believe it their duty to transmit their subject knowledge to their pupils in the same way. This may be easily accessible to some pupils but they neglect trying to make it accessible to all. Professional training which helps develop a better understanding of the different types of pupil, their learning problems, and the types of study programme best suited to them does not interest these teachers. They do not care that modern teaching experience focuses the teacher's interest on the pupil, and persuades him or her to adopt a less subject-dominated, more interdisciplinary style of teaching, which is of greater benefit to the pupil. They are unaware of the advantages of teacher education which would acquaint them with the findings of the professional discipline of teaching.

To summarize, we may say that the PEGCs in their initial teacher education have been well trained in pedagogy and less well educated in the subject matter they are to teach, whereas with the certifiés and agrégés, we have the opposite case. At the start, new teachers confirm this view themselves. (12) PEGCs complain about insufficient knowledge in one of the two subject areas they are called upon to teach in their lessons. Certifiés and agrégés at the beginning of their careers complain that they were unprepared for establishing progress objectives, coming down to their pupils' level from the heights of their university disciplines, a feeling of lack of understanding about exactly who the pupils are and what the class level is. Their training sessions, in many cases with well-motivated, disciplined pupils, failed to prepare them for school life in the raw. Teaching method and certain psychological aspects of teaching were totally neglected in their studies.

Recently, the recruitment of PEGCs was stopped, and the question arises, whether the poor teacher preparation and method training of the certifiés and the agrégés will allow them to adapt their expectations to the realities of their profession. The recent past would lead us to doubt this.

Teachers and their profession

For a long time teaching was considered a vocation, a deep commitment of service to a caring profession. Today, few teachers speak of their professional choice in these terms. (13) There was a time when some, particularly good students from the working class, were encouraged by their own teachers to continue their studies and go into teaching, which represented a kind of social ladder for them. Many others did not choose teaching as a career, but wanted to continue their studies in a discipline they particularly liked and did well in, and which offered no other professional outlet but teaching. Still others chose the profession because of its compatibility with family life, with time to spend at home. Few actually said that they chose teaching because of their interest in young people or pedagogy.

Perhaps it is not surprising that teachers experience difficulties in a profession where they must deal with school pupils so different from what they were as pupils, in schools which are vastly different from the schools they themselves have known. One of their main complaints is the falling academic standard of the pupils. This is nothing new, as de Peretti points out; teachers always seem to have complained of this. (14) Nevertheless it is true that since 1975 many teachers have faced pupils in the first years of 'collège' who have not acquired the basics in the three Rs, which should have been learned in primary school. A teacher of Spanish interviewed by Navarro remarked, 'My colleagues in the primary school are being confronted by more and more pupils whom they do not understand and cannot communicate with because they do not understand their language'. (15) Since these pupils lack the basics, 'the teachers feel they have nothing to build on. They are teaching pupils who have little ability to understand the teaching syllabus they have to work from.' They regret the heterogeneous scholastic ability levels they find in their classroom even more. According to Navarro all the pupils suffer from this state of affairs: 'Good pupils slip or stagnate, average pupils are practically left to their own devices, and the least fortunate (the poor readers and spellers, the unmotivated ones) make no progress at all' (editors' translation). The teachers suffer too, of course. They feel helpless watching some fail and others becoming uninterested. They cannot risk boring the good or average pupils by constantly repeating everything for the benefit of the weaker ones. They cannot concentrate on pushing the better pupils, because that would leave the others far behind disappointed and discouraged. When they make a choice the result seems to aggravate the position. The pupils' lack of interest in the teaching they receive is manifested in many ways: talking during class, fidgeting, acting in a manner contrary to what the teacher expects, withdrawal or outright rule-breaking and violent class disruption, all have an exhausting effect on teachers and may even prevent them from doing any teaching at all.

How can one teach pupils who do not want to learn? For many teachers the passing on of knowledge, widening pupils' horizons, is the <u>raison d'être</u> of their profession. Thus they are deeply disillusioned. They feel inefficient as if they are only filling up the pupils' time until they leave school. Faced with these difficulties, which they attribute to the drastic change in the pupil population, teachers have found themselves alone and helpless. Alone because they rarely could or dared share their problems with their colleagues and because of an almost total lack of support from their administrative superiors. Helpless, because their initial training had not prepared them for the situation and with no in-service training available, they had no concrete answers to the problems constantly facing them in the classroom.

Louis Legrand's proposals, addressing themselves to these problems, attempt to answer the following questions. How are the teachers to adapt the teaching of their subject matter to pupils' interests and their intellectual levels? How can they offer the most to every type of pupil? How are they to evaluate their pupils' work and their own efficiency at the same time? How are they to enforce the rules governing classroom life, while at the same time fulfilling the educational and social training role that according to Prost is so misunderstood by some teachers, if we are to believe the numerous pamphlets published soon after the <u>collège</u> reforms were introduced. (16)

LEGRAND'S PROPOSALS AND COLLEGE REFORM

Four years after the application of the 1975 <u>collège</u> reform programme the situation is worrying to say the least. The principle of mixed ability classes, applied without any accompanying genuine policy of pedagogical support for poorer pupils or training suited to the teachers' new needs, has lost its viability.

This in itself seems sufficiently serious to demand the effort of deep reflection which I should like to entrust you with, given your long history of work and interest in the subject. (17) (editors' translation)

Thus spoke the Minister of National Education to Louis Legrand on 13 November 1981. The minister had set up a national commission and regional consultation groups. A series of proposals concerning collège reform were the result of their deliberation, some of which were accepted immediately, some were thrown out, while others were put aside for later consideration. Here we shall examine:

1   Louis Legrand's proposals in general terms
2   the proposals retained for the official reform of the collèges in particular.

Legrand's proposals

The proposals of the national commission chaired by Louis Legrand aim at:

1   abolishing internal selection, due to early streaming, and creating an atmosphere of communal life conducive to mutual respect and understanding among all the members of the school;
2   fighting scholastic failure, such as having to 'stay down' or repeating a year of school and thus making pupils fall behind in educational progress;
3   developing the pupils' sense of autonomy, responsibility, and proper use of their freedom;
4   getting the collège to make its contribution to meeting the new social demands, culturally and professionally, in order to raise national levels of education.

Specifically the proposals must be looked at as a package. First, for the sixième and cinquième (the first two years of collège) four main suggestions were made.

1   All pupils of 11 years of age must leave elementary school, thus providing secondary education for all pupils.
2   The curriculum will include interdisciplinary and

optional activities.
3   Teaching periods will vary in length.
4   A pedagogical unit will be created on the basis of mixed ability groups of 104 pupils maximum. A pedagogical team will be responsible for the unit, with four divisions of twenty-six pupils each.

These divisions can be further broken down into homogeneous subject-matter sets according to pupils' standard of attainment levels in the three basic subjects: French mother-tongue, mathematics, and in the second trimester, modern foreign languages. In the other subjects, according to teaching objectives set by teachers throughout the duration of the school year, there will be provided homogeneous or semi-homogeneous attainment-level groups (that is 'sets') on a temporary or permanent basis, the semi-homogeneity decided by the teachers in accordance with learning activities arranged for the pupils. This procedure has been tried out in the social and economic sciences, in the natural sciences, physical education, and sports. During the second year of <u>collège</u> (<u>cinquième</u>) in order to ensure follow-up on the pupils' work, this structure and the pedagogical team in charge of it will remain the same. In addition, a tutor system will be set up where a teacher will look after twelve to fifteen pupils individually. The pupils will choose the teachers they want to be their tutors in this case. Diagnostic assessment will replace all kinds of summary assessment at the end of year or term. Pupils will no longer have to repeat a year of school. They will simply be placed in the groups corresponding to their achievement levels. The allocation of interdisciplinary activities and options and the length of teaching periods is flexible.

Second, for the <u>quatrième</u> and <u>troisième</u> (the last two years of <u>collège</u>) three main proposals were made:

1   streaming at the end of the <u>cinquième</u> directing pupils towards short vocational studies would be the exception; any such streaming must be on a voluntary basis established at the end of the <u>troisième</u>;
2   the basic educational unit and attainment levels set would be available in mathematics, first and second modern foreign languages, and for part of the timetable for French as the mother tongue. A new pedagogical team, not the same as that of the <u>sixième</u> and <u>cinquième</u>, would be established for the two years

(<u>quatrième</u> and <u>troisième</u>) which would look after the pupils for those two years.

3   More options in modern languages, technology (three hours a week), experimental sciences, the arts, physical education, sports, and regional languages would be offered.

Third, on a more general level there was a proposal to alter the school timetables and organization:

1   The length of teaching periods would depend on the activities expected of the pupils. It is well known that a 12-year-old child has an attention span of only about twenty minutes; thus the hour-long class period should not be the rule.
2   More time must be allocated to those subjects which contribute to a pupil's overall, general development, and less time devoted to the other subjects. Sport and physical education, art courses, experimental sciences, and technology are among those subjects which should have a more generous time allocation devoted to them in the week.

Collège reform in detail

Two decisive steps were taken after these proposals were made. First, all the Commission's proposals were accepted by the minister, Alain Savory, indicative of his political strategy, with a slight change made regarding the tutor system and the length of the teaching periods. It was pointed out that a closer relationship should develop between the tutor and the pupils if this methodological and pedagogical innovation were to fulfil its role of helping the pupils, and for this reason both parties were to be asked to give their opinion. The fact that the pupils could choose their tutors deeply affected the teaching body and the teachers' unions, which explains the minister's cautious attitude. To give the pedagogical teams the time to consult with one another between lessons, the one-hour-long periods were shortened. The different number of hours required to be taught by teachers of different professional status greatly complicated the introduction of these proposals. The new minister of education, Réné Monory, took up the main points of the solutions proposed by his predecessor, emphasizing in each case the need for each collège clearly to define its policies regarding the introduction of the proposals across the whole institution, the issues in particular of 'opening up' the collèges to the community: establishing links between the school and local industry and setting up in-service training opportunities linking the different schools in the same region in order to produce centres of quality as far as the proposed teacher preparation is concerned.

Second, the adoption and implementation of the proposals within the collèges depends on goodwill and voluntary acceptance of the principles. No law or decree can force their acceptance. They can at most encourage the teachers and show to what extent the central authorities believe in the need for reform. On the other hand, if the public education system is not to break down, a minimum of homogeneity must be respected. These are the reasons why the last four years have seen fluctuation between official imposition of the proposals and respect for autonomous individual choices. The setting up of a support network and in-service training centres have constituted a way of measuring the effects of this reform. It was out of the question that every collège should start reform immediately in the first year. A five-year plan was agreed on, gradually to include all collèges. For a collège to start reforming itself it had to present a valid scheme, with variations according to regional needs, but containing the following common elements:

1   groups created according to pupils' achievement level in the sixième at least
2   one or more pedagogical teams available
3   a well-supplied library (resource) centre run by a certificated librarian/technician
4   a wide range of specialized pedagogical approaches (individual help, tutor-led group-study programmes, differentiated pupil groups, and so forth)
5   several projects for educational activities
6   adequate technological equipment

We can see in collèges undergoing reform different variations in the way the proposals suggested by Louis Legrand have been introduced. Sometimes the passage from theory to practice and the variations proposed have led to undesirable effects, as in the case of grouping according to achievement level. Originally it was intended to put pupils of the same form, but with different learning capacities in basic subjects, into homogeneous groups for a short time necessary to bring them up to date. What resulted was the creation of new, rigid groups (good, average, poor) which lasted throughout the school year, hardly the hoped-for goal of the group-by-attainment-level proposal.

The school inspectors had therefore to insist on a more subtle differentiated teaching system, allowing for a greater variety of pedagogical methods, pupil groupings, teachers' employment, and teaching hours. This particular 'undesirable effect' referred to took place in a collège voluntarily undergoing reform. It is not difficult to imagine what might happen in the more reluctant collèges, which would insist on continuing to stream their pupils.

Furthermore parental involvement and support in the reorganization of collège practice had always presented problems. There are two ways in which parents can become involved:

1 the formal participation of parents across the full range of statutory consultative bodies (school, management, and class councils), in which they represent the associations of pupils' parents;
2 the informal participation in a variety of multilateral groups and committees established on the occasion of setting out new policies adopted, following ministerial decree, by each collège. Parents are encouraged to participate in such meetings, but only those interested or knowledgeable about the matter to be discussed would attend.

PROFESSIONAL IN-SERVICE TRAINING FOR TEACHERS AND COLLEGE REFORM

The creation of new institutions

The adoption of the reform programme in a number of French collèges was accompanied by professional in-service training opportunities for the personnel already teaching so as to make them aware of the changes and to train them in the new practices. This was, of course, costly to the state and, moreover, needed a co-ordinating agency with the collèges. According to suggestions made by de Peretti the ministry created an in-service centre (Mission Académique à la Formation des Personnels de l'Education Nationale (MAFPEN)) in each educational region (académie). (18) A member of the académie, known for his educational experience and expertise, was appointed head of each Mission, which was allotted several teaching posts and a budget. The idea behind the creation of these Missions was twofold:

1   To separate teacher assessment from training: up to that time, the inspectors who assessed and graded the teachers also provided their further professional training. (19)

2   To incorporate in a structured fashion in the same académie the different, limited, and hitherto scattered types of training provided: this training was available not only for collège teachers, but for teachers and lecturers at all levels of teaching. Now the Chef de Mission, along with the Recteur, the head of the académie, was to define a regional training policy. (20)

Each year these Missions publish a regional training plan, a comprehensive register of courses offered, drawn up in consultation with teachers' representatives. In the beginning, however, the lists contained mainly proposals suggested by the training institutions themselves. But the Missions quickly increased the procedures for analysing and identifying needs and training, so that the content of the courses was a result of negotiation between the teacher-trainers and the trainee teachers. These training courses, advertized in all the collèges, quickly became known to the teachers. By 1984, 80 per cent of all collège teachers were aware of them and half of them had asked to be enrolled on courses functioning during school time. (21)

In addition, summer training sessions in the universities were established from 1982 onwards. According to the official definition, these were in-service summer seminars, professional training preceding or accompanying the most significant changes and innovations in the educational system: the introduction of information technology and other new technologies, preparation for collège reform, creating education priority areas, and other topics. In 1983 more than 800 people attended these summer courses; in 1984 the number exceeded 3,000. The university summer sessions also aim to reinforce the regional training networks which are responsible for setting up national objectives for teacher-training in each académie. All the costs of these are agreed and met by the authorities. No charges are imposed except by a special decision of the minister.

Teacher attitudes, behaviour, and expectations

The great majority of collège teachers have a very positive attitude towards professional in-service training: 75 per cent feel the need to learn to practise new pedagogical methods, in order to maintain the quality of their teaching and to benefit from the experience of others. (22) Over 60 per cent disagree with views that further professional training is useless because teaching is not a profession that can be learned, or it is of no help in trying to assess pupils, or that teachers can learn new methods on their own, or because professional training is only an excuse to spread ideas about what is new and fashionable in pedagogy.

This positive attitude of three-quarters of collège teachers has manifested itself in several ways, either by personal training initiatives, especially through reading, but also by their attendance at university classes, or by enrolling on short training sessions dealing either with additional subject discipline knowledge or methods and techniques of teaching them. In 1984-6, 60 per cent of collège teachers attended professional in-service training courses designed especially for their needs.

Teachers' own priorities for these training sessions centre on improving their knowledge of their taught subject disciplines. They either want to learn more about the less well-known aspects of a discipline or want to be brought up to date in disciplines that are evolving. They want to widen their knowledge of their own disciplines and advance beyond the level expected of them in teaching at collège level. New methods and techniques of teaching (information technology and audio-visual methods in particular), although not the first among priorities, do have a high score, probably because schools are trying to equip themselves as quickly as possible with computers. Among the proposals put forward by Legrand, only the problematic one concerning the tutoring programme did not receive strong acceptance. (23) Apart from this, the teachers showed considerable interest, and gave up their time to attend training sessions to help them to adapt to the other proposals: the new attainment level pupil groupings, the single and multidisciplinary curriculum education units, new methods of pupil assessment and teacher involvement in this, psychological factors affecting pupil behaviour. Rather fewer showed interest in the new division of teachers' work time and its use.

It is important to note that teachers were not so much interested in the content of their subject discipline, as in its organization and teacher preparation for it. Concerning the structure and length of training sessions, more than 75 per cent of teachers questioned wanted sessions of more than one week's duration, that is much longer than what they had attended previously. Furthermore, their interest was strong in matters concerning the organization of teacher training, the allocation of responsibility for this, the training of the educators themselves, and the actual location of teacher preparation.

At the top of their demands were subject specialist associations and the opportunity for pedagogical development, affecting their own institutions, that is associations organized by the teachers themselves according to their subject or their educational ideas, which would give them the confidence to organize their own professional development in their own <u>collèges</u>. This was followed by demands for local, regional, and national training services from the Ministry of Education's own instructors in the appropriate centres. Next came universities with their own teaching on university premises, and finally the demand for <u>collège</u> teachers themselves, who would be responsible for taking the initiative for their own school-based training. The <u>collège</u> teachers clearly demonstrated sufficient confidence in themselves and their in-service training by their own organizations. The inspectorate, which previously used to take care of such training, and institutions outside of the National Education Ministry, definitely took a back seat.

A new conception in training

Professional in-service training concerns all <u>collège</u> personnel. It must be centred on the <u>collège</u> itself. It is important to instigate, define and gradually set up the reform programme according to the Ministry's priorities. (24)

Table 1 Old and new systems of teacher preparation

Professional development	Traditional professional training	In-service training linked to the collège reform project
Responsible initiator	Hierarchic superior; e.g. recteur, inspecteur	Staff and teaching teams from the collège or other school
Length	Short sessions of half to one day	Alternating periods of professional work and 2-3 day group work for reflection and exchanging views
Place	Training institute or inspection (inspector's office)	The collège itself, or inter-collèges groupings
Content	Single subject	Several subjects combined (interdisciplinary)
Method	Traditional teacher presiding over class: theory teaching	Theoretical findings based on practical work exchanges leading to attempts at formulating proposals
Time	At specific times set aside from normal working-day	Ongoing and during normal working time

Participants	Teachers of same subject/same status or both	Teachers from same collège in groups teaching different subjects and of different status
Professional training personnel	Hierarchic superiors, normally from the inspectorate	Part-time trainers with recent school experience along with university staff and non-educational professionals
Assessment	Summative assessment by inspectors (examination)	Formative, collective, and self-assessment
Objectives	Mastering a subject, a teaching programme, and well-tried traditional pedagogy	Initiating research, innovation, and reflection of a professional nature

The main objective of this training is to instil a spirit of research, initiative, and coherence in the teachers. The training must be in line with the projet d'établissement (the general reform programme for the institution): it is an ongoing training parallel with the actual changeover in the collège and worked out collectively. There may be specific individual undertakings, but they must agree with the overall functioning of the collège. The training is no longer only subject-oriented. It must develop along with the development of those participating in the actual job of teaching. Examples of teacher-education include assessment in attainment level groups, pupil observation, team work, formulation of teaching objectives, and project work.

The different types of training will change as increased reflection and practical experience are devoted to them. For example, initially, the concern may have been directed at pupils' achievement at different subject attainment levels, in French, mathematics, and English (compare the Assessment of Performance Unit in the UK). Now teachers are more likely to enquire in more personal terms: who are the pupils? How can we develop a personal, individualized follow-up on each pupil? What pedagogical approach is best? Finally, how can we do research on teaching quality? How can it be evaluated? Such changes have taken place between 1982 and 1987, at the same time as questions have been asked concerning the democratization, decentralization, and autonomy of the collèges and the importance of the syllabuses' content to be taught.

In Table 1, the comparisons between the old and new systems of teacher preparation offer at a glance some grasp of their differences. As a matter of fact, much of the training offered today is a mixture of the two approaches.

To sum up: the same proposals that Louis Legrand had offered to the pupils are being offered to teachers on in-service pedagogical and professional training courses. Indeed how can pupils be helped to acquire autonomy, if their teachers have not been taught according to the principles of autonomy themselves? School reform requires a reform of teacher preparation.

The institutional reforms have broken down the networks of old and their patterns. It has not been easy for the teachers, as Hamon and Rotman point out. (25) They had not been equipped, in their initial preparation, to deal with the demands of a rapidly changing world. The reform measures and accompanying new professional training, especially in-service opportunities, have reduced the number of pupils repeating a year or dropping out early. There also seems to be less of an exodus from disadvantaged schools on the part of the teachers. Learning problems, previously ignored or disregarded, are now often dealt with collectively.

New problems, however, have arisen. Resistance to solutions suggested by the reform has become more acute now that it is no longer voluntary. The heads of schools, who used to be the keystone in this type of undertaking, are now insufficiently prepared themselves to deal with the problems arising; instead, professional training sessions provide the help needed. The <u>collège</u> seems to be perceived as an enterprise in a competitive market. Its achievements are judged by the quality of its products. The question may be asked: just how far will this analogy go?

Chapter Four

TEACHERS' EXPECTATIONS IN THE PRESENT EDUCATIONAL CONTEXT OF ISRAEL

Devorah Kalekin-Fishman

INTRODUCTION

In Israel today teaching is an occupation that is constantly in the public eye. Teachers are civil service employees who are supposed to be capable of reconstructing society. One may well ask whether these expectations are based on reality and whether this is what teachers expect of themselves. By examining teachers' orientations to the organization of education, the nature of learners, and school norms and goals, we can draw conclusions about these issues.

In what follows, I will first describe briefly the structure of the Israeli school system and its social context. I will then raise some questions that touch on the structure of teaching and teacher preparation. These issues will be illustrated by findings from a study of the expectations of secondary-school teachers, headmasters, and inspectors. Finally, I will draw conclusions that imply a need for changes in approaches to teacher-preparation programmes.

STRUCTURE OF THE ISRAELI SCHOOL SYSTEM

The Israeli school system serves a total of 1,356,075 students, among them 1,144,956 Jews and 211,119 Arabs. (1) Altogether 267,400 children attend pre-school kindergartens, 621,858 study in primary schools, and 330,207 study in post-primary, that is intermediate and secondary schools. (2)

Administration is centralized in Jerusalem where the Ministry of Education and Culture supervises budget

70

allocations, personnel, formal and informal curricula, and methods for evaluating students' achievements. Projections of future schooling are elaborated by the ministry and implemented through regional offices directly accountable to it. Municipal offices of education are responsible for the construction of educational facilities, and their maintenance, but all facilities and equipment must meet ministry standards.

Deputies of the Director General supervise recognized parts of the education service. There is a deputy for state education; one for state religious education, that is schools that impose religious observances and emphasize the study of religious lore; and a deputy who administers public education for the Arab minority of the population.

Some private school systems enjoy partial government support. These are sub-groups defined in terms of life-style (kibbutzim, for example), or in terms of their religious orientation - church schools and schools for children from ultra-orthodox Jewish circles.

Parents are required by law to enrol children who have reached the age of 5 in school; but they are free to choose the sub-system that is most congenial to their way of life. (3) Students attend several school organizations over the decade of compulsory schooling. Kindergartens are the independent educational and administrative units in which children are prepared for schooling and literacy. At the age of 6, children are admitted to grade I. There is at least one state kindergarten and a state primary school in every neighbourhood.

A little under half of the primary schools in the country provide an eight-year course of study, following which students are eligible for the ninth grade in a secondary school. In a little more than half of the primary schools, students follow a six-year programme, and complete their studies in relatively large schools that accept students from several neighbourhoods: an intermediate school (grades VII to IX) and a secondary school (grades X to XII). Table 2 shows the framework of a school career.

Of the 200,000-odd students in secondary schools, about 50 per cent study in 'general academic' programmes; 43 per cent in vocational courses; and about 3 per cent in agricultural schools. A further 3.7 per cent of the students in secondary education study part-time in frameworks defined as 'continuation classes'. Streaming and grouping are decided by the school staff in consultation with the

Table 2 Distribution of ages and grades in types of school as applied universally (Grades I to VI), and differentiated in the traditional system and according to the reform

Age	Grade	Type of School		
5	–	(Universal) Kindergarten		
6	I	primary school		
7	II	primary school		
8	III	primary school		
9	IV	primary school		
10	V	primary school		
11	VI	primary school		
		(Traditional)		(Reform)
12	VII	primary		intermediate (post-primary, junior division)
13	VIII	primary		
14	IX	secondary		
15	X	secondary		secondary (post-primary, upper division)
16	XI	secondary		
17	XII	secondary		

counsellors of available secondary schools, or of the relevant intermediate school in those areas where the reform has been implemented. Express wishes of parents and students are weighed in relation to institutionalized, 'objective' standards. Students are assigned to streams on the basis of achievement marks, scores on an accepted intelligence test, and general comportment. (4)

About 40 per cent of the students in post-elementary education study in 'mixed-ability' comprehensive schools; while about 60 per cent study in single-stream, general academic or vocational schools. (5)

TEACHER PREPARATION

During the school year 1984/85, there were 84,459 teaching posts in the public educational system. These were distributed between Hebrew education (74,708 posts) and Arab education (9,751) posts. This number includes the posts of headteachers in the total of 24,999 primary and secondary schools. Approximately 1,500 new teachers graduate annually from teacher-training departments in the country's ten universities and forty teachers' colleges. (6)

In the universities students can prepare themselves for teaching a given subject only if they are, or will shortly be, eligible for an academic degree in the related discipline. Study in a university teacher-training department includes general courses in the philosophy of education, educational and developmental psychology, sociology of education, and general pedagogy. In addition, teaching methods are taught in workshops and tutorials. Programmes at different institutions differ only slightly in the allocation of time to in-school experience.

Various experiments for integrating subjects of study have been undertaken. In three universities (the Hebrew University, the University of Tel Aviv, and Ben Gurion), practice in the craft of teaching is integrated with the study of pedagogy and in-school experience. This is possible because the tutors employed by the university teach at least half-time in a post-primary school. In one university (Ben Gurion) general topics in education are taught as an integrated unit in the Faculty of the Behavioural Sciences. At the University of Haifa students are encouraged to enhance their training with courses that prepare them for initiating projects in education for values, extra-curricular programmes, adult education, and so on.

Teachers' colleges are responsible above all for preparing 'general teachers' for one of the three subdivisions of primary education: kindergarten, grades I to III, or grades IV to VI. The topics studied in the colleges are not very different from those covered in the university programmes. However, the approach is radically different.

Students are grouped in classes that share a weekly schedule throughout a two- or three-year period. A major focus is teaching as a craft, and the students spend a great deal of time practising techniques in workshops and in actual school situations. It is agreed that a 'general' teacher has to have control of the basics of a broad spectrum of subject matter as well as 'receipt knowledge' of a large array of technical skills. Students who have a special aptitude or interest can specialize in a field like teaching English as a foreign language, nature study, or the humanities. Those who choose to specialize earn an additional certificate for teaching in an intermediate school.

EDUCATION IN THE SOCIAL CONTEXT

During the last century educational institutions have undergone many changes in response to political and social developments.

Pre-state education

Until the middle of the nineteenth century education in Palestine was almost exclusively the province of church institutions. Under the terms of capitulation of the Ottoman Empire, a system of treaties with foreign governments which allowed them relative autonomy over their nationals residing on Ottoman territory, European consulates set up schools with courses of study oriented to the mother country, its language, and culture. (7) After the First World War the Department of Education of the British mandatory government provided overall supervision and support for separate networks of Jewish and Arab schools. (8)

The few Arab schools were then sponsored by religious authorities. At the outset of the Mandate in 1918, less than 14 per cent of the school-age population of the Arab minority had had any schooling. The mandatory government set up a considerable number of government schools and by 1948, when the Mandate expired, about one-third of the school-age population in the Arab sector attended primary school for at least part of the seven-year course. (9)

The Jewish educational system was strongly supported by the local community and sponsored by the World Zionist Organization. It reflected the political divisions of the latter. Thus during the 1920s there were several relatively independent school networks, each under the auspices of a prominent political party. One was sponsored by the middle-of-the-road General Zionist party, one by the orthodox Mizrahi party, and one under the auspices of the Labour Federation. (10) These systems withstood the British government's pressure for co-ordinating activities and goals. Despite the system's inefficiencies, by 1948 primary schooling was available to over 90 per cent of the Jewish children between the ages of 6 and 14.

Systems and sub-systems in both the Jewish and the Arab sectors were informed by a single educational idea, namely that the aim of educational institutions is to winnow out the talented elite from the chaff destined for commerce and industry. In line with this idea, curricula were heavily weighted with academic subjects, knowledge of which was presumed to indicate intellectual prowess. (11) Yet in 1948 there were approximately only 10,000 Jewish students in post-primary institutions: vocational schools (2,000), continuation classes (1,000), preparatory classes of teacher-training colleges (750), as well as academic secondary schools (6,500). At the same time there were fourteen (sic!) Arab students in the one academic secondary school recognized by the government. (12)

Education in the State of Israel

In 1948 when the State of Israel was founded, the school system was not immediately reorganized. The separate networks in the Jewish sector were preserved. Jewish and Arab systems of education remained segregated in their administration as well as in the language of instruction. But the Law for Compulsory Free Education, passed in 1949, applied to the entire population. (13) The immediate effect of the law was to cause dislocations. Its enactment coincided with the massive immigration of Jews from North

Africa and the Near East. The various networks competed to attract the new students. (14) Schools were inundated with students who did not know Hebrew (the language of instruction) and whose families had no experience of the country. Three-month teacher-training courses were organized in order to equip potential teachers with some minimal knowledge of pedagogic principles. (15)

As far as the Arab minority is concerned many of their intellectuals had left the country during the 1948 war, and there were not enough educated people in the villages to teach the school population designated by law. Teachers were appointed on the basis of their political affiliations, or non-affiliation. Furthermore, schools were too small and too few to accommodate the large numbers of students that were obliged to enrol. Vacant buildings of all kinds were used as classrooms. (16)

Meagre scholastic attainments showed that the existing institutions and their courses of study were ill-adapted to pupils' needs and abilities. To deal with the new situation, both the structure and the content of schooling had to be revised. This was attempted in the enactment of the Law for State Education, passed in 1953, which placed full responsibility for public schooling in the hands of the central government, (17) and relegated political and religious sectarian education to the private sphere. Apart from the shift in their legal status, however, schools did not undergo significant changes, and the expectations for major advances in academic achievement were not realized.

During the 1960s therefore, educational strategies were altered. (18) These were embodied in the complex of laws, rules, and regulations that bear the name of the Reform in Education. (19) Although to date fewer than half the schools in the country have in fact 'reformed', (20) the ideology of the reform permeates the entire educational system.

THE REFORM IN ISRAELI EDUCATION

Two essential aims governed the reform in Israeli education: first, the goal of improving the scholastic attainments of underprivileged children, and second, achieving social integration in the school system. Changes in administration, curriculum, and the structures of teaching were accordingly introduced. In the stormy public debates that preceded the institution of the reform, it was argued that these changes would in fact raise the level of education provided for all students. (21)

Administration

To provide improved education for deprived populations, primary school education was shortened by two years. The seventh grade became the first year in post-primary education with courses designed to accord with standards required for matriculation - the school-leaving certificate which allows students to go on to university education.

By re-zoning catchment areas so as to ensure the enrolment of students from several neighbourhoods, the Ministry of Education created a situation in which inter-ethnic encounters would be inevitable in the intermediate school. In practice, this meant that children from families of different countries of origin, and those from families with different cultures and religious traditions in both the Arab and Jewish sectors might be educated together. Because of the geographic distribution of Arab and Jewish communities, however, these administrative measures did not mean that Jewish and Arab children would be constrained to register for the same schools. (22)

The administration of learning: mixed-ability grouping

Mixed-ability grouping has taken on new significance because of the changes in administration. In the neighbourhood kindergartens and primary schools, classes are always heterogeneous. Secondary education, on the other hand, has traditionally differentiated student groups on the basis of achievement. Students in academic secondary school programmes who are preparing for university entrance enjoy the highest rank, while programmes of vocational training reflect lower attainments. (23)

The reform has confirmed the hierarchical ranking of types of knowledge. Streaming according to ability is the policy in the intermediate schools for the 'more important' subjects such as mathematics, the mother tongue, and English as a foreign language. Mixed-ability classes were allowed only in 'peripheral' areas, such as social studies, the life sciences, and physical education, topics that are not

77

Table 3 Pupils in secondary education by grade (1983/4)

	Jewish	Annual decline (%)	Arab	Annual decline (%)	Total	Annual decline (%)
IX	55,799	-	12,701	-	68,500	-
X	50,885	9.1	9,322	7.3	60,277	8.7
XI	44,274	8.7	6,841	7.3	51,115	8.5
XII	40,879	9.2	5,945	8.6	46,824	9.1
Overall decline	14,920	26.7	6,757	53.2	21,677	31.6

taken into consideration when the academic potential of the student is evaluated. (24) Thus the importance of academic disciplines is determined by the administrative decision on the number of ability groups allotted to a given school subject.

This policy has had far-reaching effects in retarding the realization of the social goal of integration. Students from a given neighbourhood, as graduates of the same neighbourhood elementary school, often have similar levels of academic achievement. In the relatively large intermediate school, populations of students from different socio-economic backgrounds are placed together in the 'less important' areas of study, and separated out again in subjects that are crucial. Ability grouping, therefore, leads to a resegregation of (sub)cultural groups. The ironic message is that meaningful social integration in daily life at school can be promoted only at the expense of conditions that ensure true academic achievement.

There is no doubt that more students are enrolled for post-primary education than ever before. (25) Under the reform, the introduction of the comprehensive school with its varied facilities has made possible increasing the numbers of 15- to 18-year-olds who complete a secondary education. This, too, is a measure of successful social integration. However, this has not meant that gaps in academic standards have been eliminated. The trend shows that there is a decline in the student population after the age of the kindergarten, where 99 per cent of the eligible Jewish and more than 80 per cent of the eligible Arab populations are enrolled. We can trace this trend in the percentages of school attendance in the age groups defined by the Statistical Yearbook. Whereas 19.3 per cent of the population aged 5-9 attend grade I, only 16.4 per cent of the relevant age group (10-14) attend grade IX. Moreover, as Table 3 shows, this decline is accelerated throughout the years of secondary education. The number of Jewish students attending secondary schools between grade IX and grade XII declines by more than 26 per cent. In Arab education the overall decline is 53 per cent. Moreover, of the 30,697 students who sat for matriculation in 1983 (excluding those enrolled in technological courses of study), fewer than 18,000, or 57.6 per cent succeeded in the country-wide matriculation examinations and could claim the right to enter an institution of higher learning. (26)

Currently the government's demands for cutbacks in

education has turned mixed-ability grouping from an interesting theoretical issue into a pressing practical problem. The economics of streaming is in the limelight. In the streamed subjects three relatively small classes are constructed out of two age-grouped classes. Three teachers are employed instead of two. In addition, difficulties in timetabling arise because teachers of all three streams must work in parallel. The expense is increasingly difficult to justify. Researchers have shown that gifted students lose very little if at all when they learn in mixed-ability groups, while weaker students gain a great deal from not being segregated. (27) In the 1980s mixed-ability grouping is being revived in the intermediate school as the ruling organizational strategy. (28)

The reform and the curriculum: integration and atomization

In the area of curriculum development, the reform has led to more centralization in the intermediate school, and to decentralized differentiation in the secondary school. When the reform was introduced, the Ministry of Education set up a National Curriculum Centre staffed by specialists. Their brief was to elaborate more advanced courses of study, especially for the intermediate school, and to transmit modern conceptions of pedagogy to teaching staffs by detailed specification of what was to be taught in each subject. The teams at the Curriculum Centre articulated operational aims and objectives as well as detailed teaching materials and workbooks for the use of students in subjects as diverse as geography, Bible study, grammar, and composition in the mother tongue, English as a foreign language, the life sciences, physics, and so on. Materials from abroad were revised, extended, or reconstructed in terms of the particular needs of the Israeli intermediate school. (29)

Although there are some interdisciplinary curricula for special topics, such as the study of Jewish-Arab relations, or Family Education, the conception of subjects as separate specialized areas of study has generally remained stable. In fact it was considered worthwhile to divide the teaching of the mother tongue into two subjects: language and literature. Here, too, a paradoxical situation has arisen. The rationale for the investment in curricula for the intermediate school is the aim of enabling increasing numbers of graduates to go on to desirable secondary school programmes. In the meantime, however, curricula in the secondary schools have become more open. No longer are there uniform standards. The secondary-school curriculum has in effect been atomized.

A secondary-school student may compile a matriculation programme that uniquely suits him or her. In the traditional forms of the Bagrut (matriculation) requirements, students were required to sit for at least six examinations. The subjects were defined specifically for the physics-mathematics, biology, humanities, and social science 'tracks'. Under the system adopted in the 1970s students are free to choose the subjects in which they will be examined, and the level of difficulty.

Thus in almost all subjects, there are separate examinations for weights of 3, 4, 5, or even 6 points towards Bagrut. The students are advised to plan the examinations they will sit for, to enable them to collect the minimum total of twenty-two points that is required for acceptance to a university. It is, therefore, possible for a science student to choose to study literature at the five-point level, and for a student interested in sociology to choose mathematics at the three- or four-point level. Furthermore students are encouraged to substitute independent study in an area they are interested in, or a piece of creative work, for one of the matriculation examinations. Variously graded school-leaving certificates are available for students who stay in school for twelve years. Some students take a few matriculation examinations. Students in vocational schools may be examined for an external evaluation of their achievement in the field of work they have chosen. Pluralism of school-leaving certificates is a symptom of an increasingly credentialist system for allocating work. Each type of certificate has a redemption value in the form of salaries and opportunities for advancement.

STRUCTURING TEACHING

The laws that regulate the organization of the schools and methods of devising curricula determine demands that influence teacher preparation, teaching tasks and teacher-student relations. In intermediate schools the role of the teacher is defined in terms of subject expertise rather than in terms of pastoral responsibilities. Initially 'academization' was accepted on faith as a means for raising teachers' professional potential. At the outset of the reform, teachers in primary schools who wished to go on working with students beyond the first six grades were obliged to read for a university degree. The Ministry of Education promoted academization by allowing teachers time off from teaching, and providing partial grants for advanced study. (30)

In 1978 a commission appointed by the Minister of Education examined the status of teachers and the profession of teaching. The commission heard evidence from people in different branches of the educational system as well as the universities and the 'community'. The inquiry concluded that an academic education is the key to raising the level of teaching and the prestige of teachers throughout the educational system. (31) It was stated that teachers who have an adequate background of relevant knowledge are likely to be fully professional: autonomous in their ways of thinking, able to find authoritative solutions to problems that come up in their work, and to preserve sensitivity and empathy.

The recommendations of the commission were not entirely new. In teachers' employment contracts, increments were awarded for academic degrees as well as for years of teaching experience since the 1950s. The decisiveness of the commission's report, however, has encouraged teachers' colleges to insist on advanced degrees for their own lecturing staffs; as well as to revise their programmes of study to enable them to make a claim to award academic degrees such as that of Bachelor of Education. Referring to the teachers' roles and relations with others in the school system, the commission insisted that the professional teacher must undergo suitable training ('humanization') to 'develop an ethical concern for clients and colleagues'. The report defines 'humanization' operationally in a Code of Ethics with guidelines for dealing with students and their parents, as well as with members of the school staff, headteachers, and inspectors.

In sum, the reform in education has led to a redefinition of teaching as a humane, academic profession. Questions that are of interest are first, whether teachers currently active in post-primary schools are indeed professionals in a meaningful sense of the word, and second, whether their involvement with others in the schools is 'humanized'. The answers to these questions can shed light on the ways in which the system and its values are transmitted in classroom encounters. We undertook to construct a bridge between the classroom and the system, by analysing teachers' points of view as disclosed in talk based on self-reflection.

THE RESEARCH

A research project on the professional identity of teachers was set up to discover what Israeli post-primary school-teachers' thoughts are on issues deemed central to the profession. (32) Teachers were interviewed and encouraged to discuss school curricula and subject knowledge, their students' and their own relations with them, as well as long-range issues of education in their areas. A focal question was that of the compatibility of teachers' views on curriculum development with their approaches to subject matter, on the one hand, and to the learner, on the other. The working hypothesis was that teachers' points of view would be differentiated according to the location and organization of the schools with which they were associated, and the education sub-system (Arab or Jewish, religious or secular) in which they were situated. These are precisely the elements affected by the socio-historical formation of education in Israel.

Method

The sample consisted of ninety-six 'workers in education' in the north of Israel, comprising seven inspectors, six headteachers, and eighty-three teachers, all holding academic degrees and certificates to teach in post-primary schools, grades VII to XII. Of the respondents, fifty-six were men (twenty Arabs and thirty-six Jews) and forty were women (three Arabs and thirty-seven Jews); of the inspectors and headteachers only two were women. There were thirty-nine interviewees who worked in villages or kibbutzim, and fifty from areas defined as townships or cities. A sample of schools stratified according to nationality: Jewish or Arab; location: urban or rural; religious affiliation: state secular or state religious, was selected from the official lists of schools published by the Ministry of Education. Interviewees were chosen from the staff of each school in the sample to represent different areas of subject matter and different levels of experience in teaching. One hundred and twenty people were contacted. Of those who did not participate, ten were prevented from taking part because of technical problems, and fourteen refused, saying that they did not wish to be quoted.

The project co-ordinator made initial contact with all the interviewees. He introduced the project, and notified those who agreed to be interviewed that a member of the staff would arrange a meeting with him or her. Five interviewers - three Jews (two women, one man) and two Arabs (one woman, one man) - who were trained in a preliminary workshop, carried out the study. Interviews with teachers usually took place in their homes, sometimes with small children present; while interviews with inspectors and principals took place, at their request, in their offices, though they were conducted after office hours. Each interview lasted between an hour and a half to four hours.

A semi-structured interview schedule was employed, with interviewers being given a list of topics which were to be raised in the course of a relatively free-flowing conversation. For each topic, the interviewer was instructed to inquire about the respondent's knowledge of the issue, and then to use probing questions to elicit the interviewee's interpretation, application, evaluation, and expectations regarding the topic. In relation to the curriculum, for example, interviewees were asked for information on how the curriculum is developed and how teachers learn about it. Probes included questions on how teachers implemented the curriculum, how they evaluated it, what changes they expected, and how in their opinion curricula should be processed. Further questions related to educational values and to problems of the classroom.

Results

In the research my assumption was that educators' talk about pedagogical themes reflects the social context, defines the nature of pedagogy, and reveals the types of orientation and expectation that inform teachers' actions. The tool of analysis was adopted from the 'dilemma language' described by Berlak and Berlak. In their study of schools in Britain the Berlaks observed how teachers' practice is oriented to the resolution of general problems. (33) They demonstrated that the types of learning task assigned, the kinds of evaluation and feedback applied, the relationships cultivated with students, and so on, represent each teacher's own resolution of the interrelated and inescapable dilemmas presented by problems of 'control', 'curriculum', and the social context shaped by the system. The dilemmas delineated are in fact themes of pedagogy that are dealt with in teacher-education courses. Viable resolutions are often taught as professional maxims. Among these are maxims related to the nature of knowledge, the nature of the learner, the learner's socio-cultural context, and school norms.

Views of knowledge were analysed as being 'given' or 'problematic', and thus 'public and objective' or 'private and subjective'; and views of gaining knowledge as 'acquiring items of content', or 'experiencing a learning process'. A second line of analysis was to see if learners are thought of in terms of their shared traits, or their uniqueness; whether society is understood in terms of a dominant culture, or as a complex of sub-cultures; and whether classroom events were thought to require treatment in accordance with a 'universal law' or in accordance with ad hoc criteria arising from the events that develop in each situation.

Categories were tabulated for each interview, and a point of view attributed when a categorization was made at least twice in the course of the interview. One rater analysed all the interviews. Reliability was tested in forty interviews with a different rater for each area categorized. The proportions of agreement were knowledge: 93 per cent; the learner: 85 per cent; society: 96 per cent; school norms: 81 per cent.

Curriculum development and knowledge: in the investigation of their views of knowledge, teachers and headteachers were asked what they know about who develops curricula and who in their opinion should have that responsibility; as well as about the enforcement of their implementation in school, and the degree to which curricula had to be implemented. Respondents were also asked how they evaluated existing curricula.

Procedures in developing curricula

Most of the interviewees identified more than one source as 'originator' of the curriculum. On the whole, teachers gave only sketchy details about the actual procedures used before the material is distributed to the schools. Information about curriculum dissemination was more specific: 64 per cent agreed that the headteacher receives 'pamphlets', passes them on to department heads and the latter instruct the teachers. When asked about who should develop curricula, all the interviewees except the inspectors claimed that teachers should have a central role; 87 per cent of those who thought that curricula should be developed in schools cited teachers as the only ones who should be involved. Fewer than 20 per cent suggested that teachers should co-operate with 'people' from the Ministry. In the Arab sub-system respondents insisted that since relevance is of the utmost importance, students and parents should also have a say.

Enforcing curriculum implementation in school

Altogether 75 per cent of the respondents thought that most of the curriculum had to be carried out as written. In general, programmes for subjects in which students sit for matriculation were considered unalterable. 'The teacher can deviate neither to the right nor to the left'. Syllabuses of subjects for which there are no external examinations were generally thought of as open to improvisation. Yet for teachers of English as a foreign language, the teaching syllabus based on school television is most rigid; while the matriculation programme itself is far more flexible. Teachers in the Arabic medium schools and in the state religious schools felt most strongly that the syllabus must be carried out in every detail. The first group said that they adhered to the syllabus in order to forestall disagreements over political issues. Those who taught in religious schools felt that the syllabus reflects the teaching goals very well.

Proportionately more teachers of arts, crafts, and physical education assumed that they had the right to pick and choose among the items of the syllabus, than did teachers of academic subjects. A teacher of art in one of the kibbutz schools went furthest, saying she had never 'even looked at' the officially presented syllabus for her subject. Work experience apparently has an effect on teachers' interpretations of the syllabus details as binding. Two teachers of chemistry (one in a kibbutz school and one in an Arab school) who work in industry and teach part time, and a teacher of mathematics who has been teaching for more than twenty-five years, maintained that the teacher may in good conscience manipulate the syllabus to suit the perceived abilities and interest of each class.

Teachers' evaluation of the curriculum
About 60 per cent of the interviewees volunteered the opinion that some syllabuses are indeed 'rather good', praising especially those that explicitly allow teachers to exercise options, take pupils' needs into consideration, and are suited to the existing conditions in the schools. The curricula designed for above-average pupils were judged to be better than those for pupils with learning disabilities. But many syllabuses are difficult to translate into classroom practice, and they make unrealistic demands on pupils and teachers. In the teachers' views, well-designed curricula have some relevance to the world outside the school, the world of the students. But they are rare. By the time a curriculum has been developed and tested in schools, it is already out-of-date; and by then it has little to do with the needs of either the students or the community.

Knowledge and the student
Most of the interviewees thought of knowledge as given, public, universal, and objective, a content that persons in the role of 'student' must acquire. Only 20 per cent of those interviewed were found to think of knowledge in terms of a problematic, private, and subjective process. Those who could see a mutual interdependence of the person who knows and the subject matter to be known in this way, were more likely to view learners as unique persons who are likely to be identified with distinct sub-cultures each with its own interpretation of the world.

Types of norms that govern teaching
More than half (58 per cent) of the 81 respondents who raised the issue of school norms, opted for a flexible application of ad hoc rules to classroom situations. About 42 per cent spoke of applying universal laws in order to find solutions to problems that arise in the classroom. Significantly more teachers and headteachers in the Arab sector asserted that there were unalterable laws that had to be applied (61 per cent versus 35 per cent).

Expected outcomes of teaching

The individual student rather than society is the focus of most teachers' goals and expectations. Most interviewees (87 per cent) cited personal values and goals, such as honesty, enthusiasm for study, a willingness to work hard, and some general educational aims such as: 'I expect them to be good human beings!' A minority of the respondents stressed the importance of goals embodying national or collective values. These were usually recalled as an afterthought. No one elaborated group values in concrete detail.

Disposition of teachers to preserve the status quo

Teachers were generally conservative in their consideration of alternative frameworks in the school system. Only a third of those interviewed expressed the opinion that changes were worthwhile. Of these only a handful entertained the notion that more learning could be done outside schools than within them. People associated with kibbutz schools stated that their schools were not, in any case, conventional, and that was why they were satisfied with the existing framework. Those teachers who did suggest changes proposed technical adjustments at most. Teachers' disposition to conform was highlighted in discussions of the distribution of authority in schools. None of the interviewees thought that a school should be managed by an unknown, untried system. All the Arab interviewees and teachers from urban schools in the Jewish sector confirmed the efficacy and usefulness of chains of command. Interviewees in kibbutz schools sided with reaching decisions through staff discussion, because this was the way their schools were run and that was the right way. Inspectors and headmasters generally expressed views that justified the imposition of authority. In no case were there differences of approach related to gender.

Discussion

I have outlined the background and development of Israeli education during the last century, and discusssed at some length the reform that was introduced in the late 1960s. For teachers in post-primary schools, the reform has meant basic changes in their working conditions and increased demands for professionalization. Findings from a research project on teachers' professional identity have been cited to show how teachers view education today. In this section some implications for teacher preparation will be considered.

The Ministry of Education has insistently called on teachers to be professionals in the full sense of the term. This is usually taken to mean that teachers should be in possession of a unique body of knowledge and skills on the basis of which they should be capable of making autonomous decisions, finding authoritative solutions to classroom problems, demonstrating sensitivity to the needs of their clients, and developing the empathy that will enable them to choose the approaches that are most suitable to each individual. Above all, professional teaching is conceived of as an ethical undertaking in the service of the individual student and of the community. (34) In analysing statements of teachers who were encouraged to reflect on themselves and their work, it was possible to draw some conclusions about the extent to which professionalism is salient in teachers' approaches to schools and classrooms.

Most of the interviewees saw themselves as the possessors of knowledge and skills without which it is impossible to get along in the schools. These are the store of information which can be acquired in schools. But this special stock of knowledge does not seem to be the key to an ability to make autonomous decisions. Interestingly enough, all of the respondents interviewed stressed the advantages of the authority structure as they know it in their own schools and had no objections to the ideology that is conveyed in publications of the Ministry of Education. Except for the teachers who work in kibbutz schools, almost all the respondents regretted the lack of authoritative guidelines to apply even when they complained of organizational, administrative, and curricular pressures.

A desire for autonomy was shown in the almost unanimous agreement that teachers should be active in formulating and developing curricula. On the surface this is a sensible stand and a view that is compatible with progressive trends of curriculum development. (35) However, according to their own evidence, teachers' involvement would not by itself ensure novelty.

In line with traditional terminology, teachers classify their students in their different roles as academic achievers, that is according to the marks they get in examinations.

There was mention of legitimate individual differences only in connection with physical education and art. The view of teaching as a service is also hemmed in by conventions. Here, there was unanimous agreement. Teaching was considered important because it is a service to the community and because it meets students' needs. When probed, teachers revealed their willingness to fulfil the tasks that society sets. The upshot is that the rhetoric of independence is overweighed by the prevailing 'intuition' that teachers must fit into the existing system. In the circumstances it is difficult to conclude that teachers expect teaching to be a profession.

This situation can be attributed to two groups of factors: the contradictory situation of the teacher in the school, on the one hand, and the impact of teacher-training programmes on the other. As has been shown, the centralized administration of education in Israel has made it possible for the state to undertake co-ordinated measures for the improvement of the system. Administrative co-ordination, however, has in fact intensified contradictions in the school system. For one thing, the practice of streaming for improving the academic achievements of a variegated student population has worked against the aim of social integration. For another, the intermediate school that was designed for children from several neighbourhoods and was meant to provide serious, formal academic training for 12-year-olds, insists on holding everyone to a universally measurable level of excellence. But its dimension and complexity make it difficult for teachers to monitor the progress of individual children, or to attend to psychological blocks that may impede their advancement in their studies. Teachers hold themselves responsible for developing the abilities of each and every student; yet teaching is structured in such a way that this is in effect an impossible task.

Our analyses of teachers' perceptions demonstrate that among Israeli teachers in post-primary schools, the views of problems and of possible solutions are related to structural distortions that contradict explicit social goals. Structurally generated contradictions reflected in teachers' views do not support the presumption that teachers are the most suitable agents of change - even though educators state that they are highly motivated to serve in that capacity. The fact that teachers of unstreamed subjects such as physical education and art are the only ones who see their tasks as relatively unconstrained is highly significant evidence in this context. There are indications that pre-service training programmes prepare student-teachers for the rather dependent condition that prevails in schools. The mode of 'academization' demanded of teachers undermines the possibility of turning teaching into an autonomous profession. Moreover, the very organization of the pre-service programme does not encourage the development of autonomy in the budding teacher.

To all intents and purposes, academization means the intensive study of education as a discipline, or the study of an academic discipline in the humanities or the sciences, or both. Thus academization involves the fostering of a commitment to a body of knowledge, a point of view and a culture that is far removed from the dynamic pace of classroom processes. (36) In a class of learners, knowledge is constantly on trial; it must be reshaped to overcome the unique obstacles raised by novices; and the teacher must be flexible enough to respect unorthodox approaches and conclusions. The teacher who holds a first academic degree is at best likely to have acquired the 'given, objective and public content' of a discipline, as a stock in trade. Burdened with the responsibility of bringing students to a level of competence demanded by external examinations, the teacher thus 'academicized' is ill-prepared to allow the expenditure of time for flights into uncertainty that may lead to disagreement with accepted perceptions of the subject matter.

On the other hand, students of teaching are inculcated with basic principles of pedagogy as well. An implicit contradiction exists between the two kinds of knowledge demanded of the teacher and this is echoed in the perceptions of secondary-school teachers. Students are taught to commit themselves to maxims of child-centred pedagogy, to make use of sensitivity and feeling. These ideals of professional practice inculcated in teacher-preparation courses demand that teachers relate to pupils' learning problems on an individual basis and examine knowledge through the prism of the act of learning. To do this, however, teachers must place themselves in the position of dealing with knowledge as a subjective, problematic, and personal process. Thus teachers who accept maxims of good pedagogy find themselves consistently in conflict with the objectivist conception of disciplinary knowledge that both academe and the school system foster.

An additional constraint on budding professionalism is the fact that teacher-preparation programmes are as a rule planned as a series of required courses. Although there are doubts as to the possibility of defining the professional content of teaching, (37) and avowed difficulties in delimiting the specific practices that might characterize the profession; teachers' colleges and university departments of education impose programmes 'as if' the status and the content were well known and generally accepted. There are no opportunities for making autonomous choices among most of the courses offered. In the dynamic multicultural context of Israel, these confusions undermine teachers' potential contribution to the formation of society. The many problems attending the distribution of educational goods (and educational good) in a pluralistic society require that teachers be indeed capable of functioning as autonomous, competent, capable, and critical professionals. Current training programmes however socialize them into dependency. Furthermore, their work conditions are responsible for perpetuating this dependent stance. Proclamations of professionalism and calls for self-examination are not enough.

A strategic point of departure would be to revise teacher-training programmes. Student teachers should be encouraged to exercise options in choosing courses, projects, seeking experienced advisers throughout their pre-service education. It is important to help the teacher-candidate achieve an understanding of the limits of care and concern (learner-centredness), that is the degree to which pastoral care can work to the advantages of the learner. Practice teaching should not be limited to gaining skill in didactic techniques and classroom management. It is perhaps more important for the student to gain insight into the organizational culture of the school and to learn how to preserve individuality in the face of grinding bureaucratic controls.

Finally, the aim of academization must be the development of critical thinking in the widest sense. To this end, institutions engaged in teacher education must be prepared to help the student re-analyse and resynthesize the disciplines of academic training. Academicized teachers may not need to increase their stock of knowledge, but they must be aware of the excitement that attends the constant reprocessing of that stock. This is usually the focus of post-graduate study, (38) but, because of the demands of the classroom situation, the practising teacher should not be forced to postpone this experience. The current contradictory situation of the teacher in the school structures is underlined by a contradictory relation to the curriculum, the learner, and the school organization. Our findings suggest that educators must analyse the paradoxes inherent in their relation to the students in the classroom, to the norms that regulate school behaviours, to knowledge and to society. A clarification of goals and values and a conscious resolution of dilemmas must precede a successful attempt to penetrate the circles of planning and policy-making. A more refined analysis of the relationships discussed here through further research should provide the tools for tracing processes and thus provide a dynamic explanation for how education contributes to social reproduction over time.

Chapter Five

TEACHERS' EXPECTATIONS, TEACHING REALITY, AND TEACHER PREPARATION IN EASTERN CANADA

Patrick Dias

In what follows, I discuss how teacher-preparation programmes can take fuller account of teachers' expectations, particularly in the light of the actualities that schools represent. While I speak primarily from my own situation as a member of the Faculty of Education at McGill University in Montreal, that situation is not unrepresentative of the situation of most Eastern Canadian institutions concerned with teacher preparation. Since the early 1970s with one exception, teacher-preparation programmes in Canada have been housed entirely within university departments, schools, or faculties of education; they are available either within a three- or four-year Bachelor of Education degree programme or a one-year post-graduate diploma programme. Differences among the various university teacher-preparation programmes lie primarily in the time assigned to the in-school practice, in how that teaching practice is organized, and in particular curriculum requirements dictated by provincial certification criteria - one of many instances of provinces exercising control over education in Canada, a jurisdiction which constitutionally is strictly a provincial matter.

Such differences among teacher-education programmes, however, do not affect the general applicability of the discussion that follows. Neither, as it should become clear below, does the fact that McGill is situated in a bilingual community in which two systems of education operate side-by-side.

TEACHER EDUCATION IN A BILINGUAL COMMUNITY

McGill University is one of three English-language universities in Quebec, a province whose population is approximately 80 per cent French-speaking, though in Montreal, where McGill is located, the ratio of French to non-French (mainly English) speakers is roughly 60:40. The two language communities are served largely by two parallel public education systems linked at the top by supervisory governmental and quasi-governmental bodies but with little contact of major significance at other levels. To take a prime instance: while the centrally mandated curriculum for English language schools is largely a translation of the curriculum for French language schools, and while this curriculum was planned by committees drawn proportionately from both major language communities, there is little evidence of any further exchange of ideas or information across the two systems, or any coming together of personnel to resolve common sets of problems. Thus, while teachers in the two school systems will jointly negotiate with the government on employment conditions and wages, such joint deliberations do not extend to a common front on curriculum matters.

The fact is that though both school systems follow a common centrally mandated curriculum, in practice each language group's cultural attitudes and concerns override common content and objectives. For instance the curriculum in history tends in French-language schools to consider events primarily in terms of their relevance to Quebec; the approach in English-language schools might consider the same events in the larger Canadian (albeit English-speaking) context. Another instance of the extent to which cultural values and attitudes prevail in implementing curricular objectives is apparent in the differing approaches to teaching the mother tongue. While the programme for French as a first language does not differ radically in its overall orientations from the programme for English as a first language, fears of anglicization ('an island of French in a sea of English') provoke concerns for basic skills, concerns to conserve and protect. Such concerns tend generally to subvert those goals of the French programme which de-emphasize formal accuracy and dwell largely on 'communicative competence' as a central goal of the programme.

Such division historically brought about by the

organization of the public school system along denominational lines (Catholic-French and Protestant-English) is however not institutionally enforced at the tertiary levels. Thus, at least 22 per cent of McGill's student population is French-speaking. On the other hand, what occurs in teacher education is more in keeping with the linguistic divisions prevalent in the school system. McGill's Faculty of Education is mandated by the provincial government to prepare teachers to teach in the province's English-medium schools, and thus the students who enrol in its programme are largely English-speaking. Given the continuing reduction of the school population in English-language schools, which by law are permitted to enrol only English-speaking Canadians (children of immigrants, by whose influx Quebec's English schools had in the past managed steady growth, must by law enrol in the province's French-language schools), McGill's qualifying teachers generally hope to find teaching positions in the northern reaches of Quebec, in those provinces of Canada that still continue to employ new teachers, and more recently, in the USA. Thus the faculty has become increasingly aware of the need to meet extra-provincial certification requirements as well and has adjusted its programme to take account of such requirements. In other words, the faculty's outlook is just as much national and international as it is provincial.

It is primarily in the area of second-language teaching, both French and English, that one is aware of significant gains in bridging the gap between the French and English school systems. Students at McGill preparing to teach English as a second language are placed as student teachers largely in French-language schools. At the same time, French-speaking students enrol in large numbers in the teaching of French as a second language programme and are placed in English-language schools and expect to find employment in the growing number of schools across the country that operate French 'immersion' programmes. It should be said that the popularity of French immersion programmes outside Quebec is attributable not to any new-found love for the French language, but to a growing realization that job opportunities, especially in the federal civil service, increase considerably when one is bilingual.

These are relatively small developments, however; it will take the coming generation of largely bilingual teacher candidates to set the ground for exchanges that energize teaching in both languages. At present, with the exception of those students enrolled in the English as a Second Language programme, the French-language school system does not figure largely as a teaching reality in the preparation of teachers at McGill. A more potent reality is the effect of declining enrolments both in schools and university on the resources that are now available to teacher education.

EFFECTS OF DECLINING ENROLMENTS AND BUDGET CONSTRAINTS

The question of the extent to which teacher-preparation programmes take account of teachers' expectations and school realities, in itself quite problematical, is further confounded by developments that over the last decade or so have overtaken both teacher-preparation institutions and the schools they prepare teachers for. Such developments have been occasioned primarily by a prolonged decline in pupil enrolment in school and university, and consequent budget restraints.

In university faculties and departments of education, measures to overcome such constraints have generally meant a freeze on hiring, a policy to encourage early retirement, a growing emphasis on post-graduate education and in-service courses for teachers, some branching into new areas of educational training, and an increasing pressure to fill out an expectedly reduced teaching workload with research activity and publication. As teacher-preparation institutions and faculty members have attempted to work out new roles for themselves, teacher-preparation programmes have had generally to settle for a reduced importance and the kinds of reorganization that would bring the effort and resources expended on them more in line with their reduced circumstances. Even so, the will to innovate is apparent in new programmes designed to retain potential school dropouts and to retrain unemployed youth and adults.

The straitened circumstances brought about by enrolment decline and budgetary restriction are also apparent in the reality of the schools. Schools have responded in different ways; however, an ever-present reality is an ageing teacher population generally quite set in the ways it perceives teaching and curriculum, an increased teaching load that discourages experimentation, and even the merest keeping up with developments in the field, and a growing tendency to fill new openings with tenured but under-employed teachers who are not necessarily qualified for the posts.

I have raised the issue of constrained circumstances for both teacher-training institutions and schools not as a mere backdrop for the discussion that follows; rather my contention is that one prevailing expectation must be that resources for teacher education and for schools will certainly be limited for the coming decade and that schools will tend to expect, from newly trained entrants, at the secondary level at least, a lesser degree of subject specialization and yet a wider range of expertise to deal, say, with new technology and the 'mainstreaming' 'integration' of students normally assigned to 'special education' classes.

THE CHANGING SCHOOLS

The early 1980s have also seen in most of the provincial jurisdictions in Canada the emergence of mandated school curricula that are current with newer understandings of teaching and learning processes, of group processes, of the nature of language and language for learning, of what is fundamental to learning in each of the subject area disciplines, and of child and adolescent development. One might say school curricula and teaching methodologies have finally narrowed what was until recently a wide gap between theory and practice. While I can speak knowledgeably only about developments in 'Language Arts' theory and practice, I am assured by my colleagues that there have been similar developments in other subject disciplines as well. In practical terms, such new understandings represent a growing emphasis on helping pupils acquire autonomy and authority as learners and dictate classrooms that stress independent learning within the collaborative framework of the small group.

Not all changes in schools and teaching are a result entirely of newer understandings of learning and learners. Enrolment declines have pressed school-teachers into considering more holistic notions of learning and moving away from subject specialist teaching towards finding integrated 'common cores' in the curriculum, especially at the lower levels of the secondary school. Teachers' jobs and schools have also altered to take account of high levels of youth unemployment in Canada, and, it follows, a higher pupil retention rate in schools and the returning to school of a large number of early school-leavers. Special schools in less traditional settings have emerged to accommodate such students and, as well, older members of the local community who have decided to acquire new skills or assert their claim on free public education. Not all such students can be accommodated within special schools; thus Quebec's classrooms, organized generally on a mixed-ability basis with a set of common final examinations for all pupils, may need to become mixed-age as well.

It is ironic that as some long desired changes are finally achieving official sanction, the resources to implement them, both material and human, may not be adequate to the task. For institutions preparing teachers for the coming decade, the challenge could not have come at a worse time. I may be developing a far bleaker picture than I intended to or than is generally true. My intention is to argue that even within the constraints I have described (and few politicians in power and without are likely to effect any real increase in educational expenditures over the next decade) it is possible to prepare teachers for the changing schools and the changed roles they must all too soon assume.

TAKING ACCOUNT OF TEACHERS' EXPECTATIONS

When I refer to teachers here, I mean primarily those student-teachers preparing to become teachers in university faculties or departments of education, though I shall refer later to school-teachers already established in the field. When I consider student-teachers' expectations and their relevance for programmes of teacher preparation, I have in mind specifically their expectations with regard to 'teaching reality'.

It is a habit of mind to speak of 'teaching reality' as though it were something 'out there' in schools - a reality defined by the activities of pupils and teachers, the controls of administration, and exigencies of government and society. It is such a reality that looms large in the minds of those preparing to teach and directs the thinking of experienced teachers. Such a reality is also uppermost in the minds of those of us involved in teacher preparation. I have suggested in the early part of this chapter that such

99

teaching reality is in flux and not as easily defined or demarcated for teacher preparation to take fuller account of it. I have also pointed out how the limited resources of teacher-education institutions are also part of that reality that one must take account of in prescribing solutions to the perceived gap between preparation and reality.

Given our institutions' straitened circumstances and the changing circumstances of schools and school curricula, I would like to suggest that we shift our attention from the reality 'out there' to the reality 'in here': the set of beliefs, assumptions, and expectations that to a large extent govern our behaviour, that determine to a considerable degree what and how we teach and with what degree of success. In what follows I consider some of these assumptions and expectations and the realities they define. I go on then to suggest how teacher-education courses and programmes can take full account of them. In a subsequent section, I shall discuss the problems and possibilities for teacher preparation represented by the realities 'out there'.

THE 'REALITY' OF THE STUDENT-TEACHER

In defining the assumptions and expectations of student-teachers as a reality, I am not merely pointing to their existence; I am asserting that they exert in fact a considerable influence on the student-teachers' learning and practice, and that they are all the more influential because they tend to go unrecognized in the minds of those who plan teacher-education programmes and design and teach courses for these programmes.

In the initial stages of the student-teachers' development these assumptions and expectations represent a 'world view' of teaching reality constructed from, among other things, their own experiences as pupils, their experiences as children and as adults interacting with children, their reading, and often their acquaintanceship with experienced teachers and sets of injunctions thus derived, such as: 'Never smile until Christmas', or 'Don't ever turn your back on a new class'. Initially at least, these sets of assumptions and expectations constitute the working knowledge which new teachers operate from. New knowledge, new understandings, new theories of teaching may force a re-examination and a reformulation of 'teaching reality'; however, unless these constructions from their past experience and ingrained habits of thinking are continually articulated and open to discussion and examination, new teachers are less likely to be influenced by what is said and heard in lecture room and seminar session. In other words, what is 'taught' in teacher-training institutions is not necessarily learned and is less likely to have significant impact on teaching activity.

Put another way, my argument is that new information, new ways of perceiving and interpreting teaching reality may be considered and held by student-teachers without in any way altering the construction they put on teaching reality. The new 'inputs', even when they are convincing and make sense, may be recognized as far too disruptive of set ways of thinking and acting for them to be given immediate consideration. 'This is all well in theory', is a familiar way of opting out of the need to question one's habitual ways of thinking and acting.

How then do we overcome the inertia of set ways, of classroom folklore and prejudices, for instance about the aptitudes of certain groups or classes of students, ingrained habits of perceiving teaching reality? A necessary start, as I said above, is to draw to the surface the sets of beliefs and assumptions that direct one's ways of perceiving the world of teaching and working in it. I have found it useful, for example, to have my students keep a journal: a weekly written record of observations, reflections, anecdotes, questions, and explorations occasioned generally by what the students have heard in class or read. I have responded with comments and questions, suggested further reading, and generally acted as a sounding board to stimulate further exploration. There are other uses for the journal to which I will refer below. The point here is that we find several means of helping our students realize what 'baggage' they carry with them as they enter the classroom.

We must allow as well time and create opportunities for dwelling on 'new knowledge' - further reading, reflecting, discussing, writing, observing, and trying out - a realization of what must shift in one's view of 'teaching reality' before 'working hypothesis' becomes 'working knowledge', which in turn is again open to reworking and change. In our haste to 'cover our programme' we may be unwittingly countering this process of becoming a teacher. We may, in fact, be reinforcing a tendency to keep apart what one learns in initial training in university and what one learns on the job, to maintain a gap between the self that studies and the self that teaches. We may be ensuring that these selves work from different sets of criteria and to different purposes. Consider these two instances of disjunction. First, the initial teaching experience is perceived by most student-teachers as fraught with risk. The need to work through that period with the least amount of disruption for teacher and pupils and to confirm oneself as a teacher (in control, well-prepared, and at ease) predominates at the expense of tentativeness, experimentation, and risk-taking. Much of what has been learned about teaching now appears to be new and unconfirmed and merely academic (particularly if one has been greeted in the school common-room, as some of my students have, by the no doubt kindly meant, 'Forget everything you have learned at McGill; this is the real world!'). Under the pressure of the demands of syllabuses, timetables, tests, immediate ends, and the need, above all, to survive in the classroom, new and informed educational theory is shelved, and the tried and the true strategies of survival come to the fore. The disjunction between theory and practice is particularly brought home when some school pupils pressure student-teachers to do things 'the way it spozed to be', to use the title of James Herndon's book. (1)

Second, contrary to expectations and despite all good intentions, teacher-training institutions tend to encourage the development of 'utilitarian teaching perspectives'. Zeichner cites a number of studies to demonstrate that inadvertently

> the universities and schools work in concert to provide a powerful, conservative force for defending existing institutional arrangements from close scrutiny and challenge ... (primarily) because of a focus on procedural rather than substantive issues in supervisory conferences and seminars. (2)

Thus while university tutors in their course work may discount the students' concerns for recipes and bags-of-tricks, these very concerns are reinforced in the field-experience phase and the typical educationalist emphases on ideological questioning, the concern for the 'why' as well as the 'how', are relegated as of secondary importance.

It is not surprising that the student-teacher is unable to make an easy passage from theory into practice. What is unfortunate is that most of us operate as though the passage will occur somehow, and take little account of how the theoretical principles we promote and the practices we advocate are continually subverted by the 'reality' of the student-teachers' world-view and the reality of the school. Somehow we must plan our teaching to take account of these realities; otherwise those deeply set assumptions will have found fertile ground in some aspects of school practice, and a reality exclusively defined by school needs, expediency, and student anxiety will have prevailed.

ENGLISH EDUCATION AT MCGILL

I shall use the example of one particular teacher-education programme to illustrate what might be done to ensure that teacher-preparation programmes take fuller account of teacher expectations and teaching reality. I shall speak entirely in terms of what is popularly called the 'methods' course in the teaching of English. Most Canadian one-year post-graduate teaching diploma programmes for secondary-school teachers allow specialization in one or two school subject areas and offer 'methods' courses in these subjects as well as courses selected from among offerings from educational psychology (e.g. adolescent development, learning theories, testing and measurement), educational foundations (e.g sociology of education, philosophy of education, history of education), and educational administration (e.g. school law, curriculum design). Students are also able to select from among such courses as educational media, reading in the content fields, simulation and gaming in education, and computers in education, to name some of the more popular options. Between one-fifth and two-fifths of course work will be related directly to subject 'methods' work. Between nine and fifteen weeks in a thirty to forty-five week programme is given over to practice teaching. The length of the programme and the time allotted to course work and field work vary from province to province and within provinces as well.

In my own faculty, with the gradual shift away from a shared concern for faculty-wide programmes towards increasing departmental specialization, there has been only a modicum of effort to ensure some degree of coherence among the various courses. Thus the links between courses are often tenuous and often expose multiple contradictions. Again, the general climate in schools is hardly conducive to obtaining appropriate school placements for most of our students. Given such contexts, it becomes even more urgent that we find some ways not only of making up for the inadequacies I have described, but also of ensuring that we meet the challenges of dealing creatively with constraints that will clearly be with us for some considerable time.

I identify below five major concerns that must be taken account of if teachers are to be better prepared to deal with current developments in our school systems. Though I speak specifically about the training of teachers of English for secondary schools, these remarks are intended to apply to teachers at all levels of the school system for all subject areas.

TAKING A THEORETICAL STANCE

Given that new teachers must deal with a changing curriculum and be prepared to work from a theoretical position that is consistent with recent developments in the teaching of English, I would in the first place encourage them to articulate their beliefs and assumptions concerning the teaching of English. I would suggest they seek out hidden assumptions in their own thinking about 'English' as a school subject, to test out their positions against the views of others in the class and against what they are able to observe in school practice. In other words, I wish them to map out a tentative theoretical position on several issues in the field of 'English', a position to be fleshed out through their readings and to be tested in the field.

I have already explained how I would have students keep a weekly journal as a means of drawing to the surface the sets of beliefs and assumptions about what English is and their roles as teachers of English. I hope their writing will help them clarify the positions they hold, the likely conflicts such positions imply, and how their positions might be modified to be consonant with teaching reality as they are now beginning to know it. For instance, to take a common and least problematical issue, I recall the student with an honours degree in English expounding initially on how much he hoped to share his love and understanding of English literature with his pupils, and later recognizing the gap between his expectations and the real needs and capabilities of his pupils and assuming a less directive stance towards their reading. Journals kept during the student-teaching period tend often to be plaintive accounts of failed expectations and resuscitated hopes, a recognition of real needs and a confirmation of real strengths. In coming to terms with their beliefs and expectations, their strengths and weaknesses, the student-teachers have a clearer idea of how they must use the resources of the university in practical and efficient ways. As I often point out to them, they will seldom, as full-time teachers, have the opportunities they now have to reflect and experiment in order to realize and discover what it is they must do and what they really do well.

ALLEVIATING ANXIETY

If we are really attentive to the reality 'in here', we must somehow recognize and acknowledge the anxieties generated among student-teachers in expectation of their first teaching experience and ensure to alleviate these anxieties by helping place them in proper perspective. We might recognize, for instance, that during their first weeks in school, student-teachers are faced with competing demands for their time and attention. They may have to choose, for instance, either to do small group work in a class whose pupils are not used to working in groups and thus risk disruptive behaviour, or to forego the small group work and use a more traditional approach. Given such competing demands, it seems sensible to make the choices that ensure survival, point to predictable outcomes, and do not disrupt the normal routine of the classroom. Such anxiety-ridden teachers are unlikely to recognize that it is often the exploratory and risk-taking activities that invite and promote pupils' involvement and collaboration.

Somehow, student-teachers must have opportunities early in the course to observe and to test, to confirm and to modify, to place in proper perspective and balance those concerns that cause undue anxiety; so that when they do begin an extended period of student-teaching, they will be free to attend to issues of import to their own development as teachers. At McGill we have experimented with assigning student-teachers from the very start of their programme to observe and work in their spare time with a teacher and in a school where they are scheduled to teach later in the semester (another logistical problem for our student-teacher placement office, and therefore more and more a luxury). By the time they begin their formal student-teaching, they have become familiar with school routine and personnel, are recognized by pupils as belonging in some way, and have already had opportunities to work with individual pupils and small groups, to assist with planning, and occasionally to teach whole classes. What is important is that they have come to distinguish between central and peripheral issues. They can identify 'real' questions and therefore avoid considerable floundering around, recognizing what is immediately relevant to their needs and what is, for the time being, at least, merely of academic importance. Thus they are able to call on the resources of the faculty with a judiciousness that is both economical and productive. On the other hand, those who have not had the same preparatory experience cannot help getting ready, despite better advice, to take on the whole world. They dissipate their energies anticipating outcomes that, while in the realm of the possible, are not likely to occur or can easily be anticipated and forestalled.

Thus for many beginners the question of discipline in the classroom (accompanied by visions of pupils running riot, flying chalk, and paper aeroplanes) provokes a thought-crippling anxiety. Those student-teachers who have spent some time observing how competent teachers 'manage' their classes are aware that discipline is not the central issue, that while these teachers' management behaviours can be elaborated as sets of rules, the teachers do not operate as such. The 'focal point' of their attention, in Michael Polanyi's sense of the phrase, (3) is maintaining involvement and interest, anticipating difficulties of understanding, and respecting pupils as participants in learning rather than seeing them as passive receptors of knowledge. Order and consistency (not regimentation) are seen to be valued by pupils as setting guidelines for behaviour. Again, by working with small groups and individuals in this preliminary phase, the student-teachers have broken that anxiety-creating barrier between teacher and pupil: they have come to see pupils as individuals who are just as anxious and insecure as the student-teachers were; they have confirmed for themselves in small but significant recognitions that they can communicate with and be well-received by high school pupils.

BECOMING A PERSON

Beginning teachers must also come to realize the extent to which the act of teaching is the act of a person. The self they present to pupils may not be the self that best promotes learning, quite likely because that self is a role or a persona they may have tried to assume rather than have grown into, an attempt to fit models of successful teachers they may have known or to heed advice about the kind of person they must be to maintain interest and involvement. It is important for them to realize that teaching is not so much role-playing and projecting an image as it is accepting the individuality, the humanness, and the interestingness of others and responding as a person. At the risk of being misunderstood I would say that the most successful teachers are those who are most truly themselves.

I recall the teacher in an in-service course who confessed in the midst of a great deal of enthusiasm from his colleagues about journal writing that he had had little success in getting his 14-year-old pupils to keep a journal. I refrained, at that time, from pointing out that he did not generally present himself as an audience one would want to write for (particularly if the writers were as vulnerable as I knew his pupils were). Moreover, his pupils had never themselves seen him write or heard him reading his writing and take a delight in the kind of personal reflective writing called for in the journal entries he was soliciting.

We believe students can grow in self-awareness, and offer a course, 'Experiences in communication' (for want of a better name), designed to help student-teachers realize, confirm, develop, and extend their resources as communicators and to interact more confidently and more 'personally' with their pupils. We are used to speaking of resources in terms of hardware and software, and ignore the primary resource, 'self-ware'. The course works in a variety of ways, depending on the interests and expertise of the university tutor. Many of the exercises I myself have used are derived mainly from the work of Viola Spolin, (4) and are concerned primarily to strengthen the creative and improvisational aspects of one's teaching: for instance, the extent to which successful actors (and improvisors) are acutely aware of and able to pick up and build on the responses and reactions of their audience. I should say that some of my more successful students have not been, as one might expect, majors in English. The course calls on the creativity and imagination of students and requires that they work collaboratively. Not all students (and even some faculty members) see the value of the course; and sometimes, even some of those we think have derived considerable benefit from the course may say, 'I have enjoyed the course, but what has all this got to do with teaching?'

TEACHING BEYOND SURVIVAL

One aspect of reality for student-teachers is that they expect or are expected to 'become' teachers in an unrealistically short period of time. It would seem sensible therefore to reduce our goals to meet the expectations and demands that are normal for the first few years of teaching, with the reasonable assumption that these beginning teachers are likely to return later for in-service courses or graduate study. I believe, however, that teachers taught only to survive, to meet limited expectations, are less likely to return to university, essentially because survivors quite often learn how to cope, to be self-sufficient, and if it were not for salary incentives, would not feel inclined to undertake further study.

Knowing therefore how relatively limited an eight-month programme can be, those of us involved in the English methods course designed a course that would help students establish for themselves realistic short- and long-term goals so that they are not overwhelmed by the comprehensiveness of the skills and knowledge they must acquire. They must realize, we believed, that their first year in education is only the first step in becoming a teacher.

Thus our course, 'Secondary English curriculum and instruction', is open-ended, outlining in a course booklet the larger area of inquiry and a set of modules that cover major areas of study in the teaching of English. The modules describe each area of inquiry, and prescribe tasks and readings that may be undertaken to complete those tasks. Some tasks invite group inquiry, others may be undertaken individually or under the guidance of a tutor in specially scheduled meetings. Some modules focus on what one might call the subject matter of English, for example linguistic theory pertinent to the teaching of English or current theory and research on the development of writing abilities. Other modules focus on the process of instruction, for example planning a unit on the novel, comparing and assessing textbooks in English, designing a multi-media unit on a particular topic, or taping one's reading of several poems with or without appropriate musical accompaniment. Some modules, 'Microteaching' for instance, are required of all students; others are optional. A minimum number of modules, including the compulsory modules, and a minimum number of tasks in each of the modules undertaken need to be completed to meet course requirements. Where students perceive a particular need not covered by any of the modules and are able to assemble appropriate resources (including resource persons), they are permitted to design their own module.

Thus students will have completed the course very much aware of the introductory nature of their studies, but they will know what the major questions in their field are and what resources they may turn to for useful answers. In choosing their optional modules and tasks they will have had to decide what they need to know for their immediate goals and what they should be picking up once they are settled into their roles as teachers. In any case, because individual backgrounds and needs vary, most students are likely to encounter other students who have studied those areas they have not touched. Weekly meetings of small 'contact groups' allow students to report to each other on the work they are doing and receive feedback. There are built-in demands to share resources and information, to collaborate. A few of the tasks are related directly to observing and working with pupils in schools. Given the limitations of time, we are also very much concerned that student-teachers realize through their own learning processes and strategies the value of some of the instructional procedures they are asked to consider. Thus those who have employed small-group discussion in their own learning are more likely, we expect, to understand the dynamics of that procedure and the advantages and difficulties involved.

I would be less than honest if I did not mention that over recent years, given declining enrolments and staff reductions, the course can no longer offer the number of options and the supervision that were once available. I have provided this account primarily to suggest what, I believe, is essential in taking full account in our courses of the individual needs and expectations of our students and of the developments that are occurring in schools. In brief, the course allows students within certain limits to decide in terms of their own needs and experience what it is they need to study. By laying out an outline of what is encompassed in such an inquiry, the course sets realistic goals and at the same time suggests that the study of English curriculum and instruction must be an ongoing inquiry to be continually taken up as classroom experience suggests modifications in one's position and new directions for study and experimentation. As much of what occurs in the course is not teacher-led or teacher-directed, the course models approaches to teaching that value individual initiative and collaboration in small-group work.

I am obviously idealizing course objectives and procedures. In practice our goals are queered by the demands of other courses; the students are sometimes frustrated by the constant reminder (in the reading lists for the various modules and in the list of tasks they might undertake) of the gap between what they need to know and what they can reasonably accomplish within the year; some individual members make group work difficult, particularly because they cannot reconcile their notions of what teaching and learning are with a process of collaborative learning.

PUPIL-CENTRED TEACHING

If there is one trend that has become firmly established in school curricula (that is at least in the documents that support them) and is often hard to point to in actual practice, it is the notion that teaching should be less subject- or content-centred and more pupil-centred; for as Moffett puts it, 'the subject is in the learner'. (5) Moffett is speaking of English as a school subject, but the notion, I believe, applies to all areas of the curriculum. Students in education who have come through university as subject specialists find it particularly difficult to move away from the centre of the classroom as the dispensers of knowledge, a role that Douglas Barnes describes as that of the 'transmission teacher'. (6) This indeed is the role they have seen generally modelled through their own schooling, especially in university. That the notion of pupil-centred teaching is not exceptional is easily apparent when one considers that most elementary-school teachers tend to see themselves as teachers of pupils, not subjects.

At the heart of such a notion is an understanding that

pupils must be allowed to assume responsibility for their own learning and that the teacher's role is to provide occasions for such learning to occur. Such occasions often involve collaboration in small groups. Some of the more useful classroom applications of the microcomputer, for instance, are just those that promote such collaboration and eventually the autonomous learning that is implicit in the notion of pupil-centred teaching. As pupil-centred practices become more established in schools, as one might notice, for instance, in the increasing use of small-group work and changing perceptions of assessment, teacher-preparation programmes need not only to promote such a notion in theory, but also to demonstrate what pupil-centred teaching represents in practice.

In advancing these five concerns, I have described an approach that addresses teacher education as a process that must take fuller account of the 'reality' of the student-teacher, the expectations and the personal resources that the student-teacher brings to the programme. I have also suggested how there can be greater consonance between what we teach at universities and what school curricula and practice demand of teachers. To that end I have proposed that we focus on helping students establish a coherent theoretical framework that shows a fair understanding of one's subject discipline, of adolescents, and of the process of learning. I had said earlier that we must make clear that a year of teacher preparation is only the first step in becoming a teacher. If we truly believe this, we must not act as though we believe otherwise, and should proceed to state what the other steps are and what our stake is in ensuring that those steps are taken. The system of probation that is currently in place in most provinces should certainly be part of the process of final certification (the one we have in Quebec has not worked that well); it may also provide the wedge that allows a fuller and more realistic programme of teacher preparation to emerge.

THE 'REALITY' OF SCHOOLS AND THE PRACTISING TEACHER

Student-teachers soon find out that teaching in schools is circumscribed, on the one hand, by institutional demands such as administrative directives, school structures, and demands of the syllabus and examinations, and on the other hand by the teachers' views of their own roles and abilities, their perceptions of their pupils' needs, and the pupils' real abilities. I believe that, on the whole, practising teachers are ready to engage theoretical issues and consider the findings of research that would point to radical changes in their own practices; however, such theories and research findings are more often than not seen as inappropriate and inapplicable to these teachers' particular situations and, even when they are appropriate and applicable, they are often judged difficult to implement because of institutional constraints.

I do not believe teachers are being deliberately obstructive; rather, given the prevailing school climate of cutbacks and restraint, the growth in class size and consequent work-load, I can understand why many teachers are loath to experiment and innovate. Moreover, they are likely to suspect that the new approaches proposed are essentially of the moment and likely to pass as newer theories are proposed and new research discounts earlier findings. Yet innovation and experimentation are the very stuff of learning for student-teachers, and, if such attitudes are not modelled and if student-teachers do not see for themselves how the approaches advocated in the university operate in practice, they are quite likely to reject those approaches as inappropriate and out of touch with reality.

In fact, what happens in real classrooms with real teachers must continue to inform what happens in teacher-preparation courses and vice versa. There are several ways in which closer links between university teaching and classroom practice can be established.

First, school-teachers can be co-opted to teach at the university for short periods, and even better, exchange teaching positions with university tutors. University tutors thus not only have an opportunity to test out and demonstrate the usefulness of the ideas they promote, but also can speak to their own students with a higher degree of credibility about schools and pupils. At the same time, student-teachers can benefit directly from the experience of classroom teachers. Moreover, such teachers can now influence the content and style of university courses, and at the same time come to understand the rationale and content of the university programme.

Second, university tutors should seek opportunities to conduct research in schools and involve practising teachers as collaborators. It is my experience that good teachers are also often the ones who maintain a questioning stance towards what and how they teach. There is in fact a great deal of research that is conducted informally by such teachers, though it is seldom labelled research. Teachers need to know that they can be researchers in their own classrooms without having to obtain an institutional seal of approval. Collaborative research efforts often breathe new life into tired teachers and help propagate some of the new theory and research that will otherwise hardly achieve currency. It will not be surprising if such teachers are most willing to have a student-teacher in their classrooms; for they are now more able to speak from a common set of understandings.

Third, since it is not the practice, in my university at least, to compensate school-teachers for taking on student-teachers, university teachers should feel bound to reciprocate in some concrete way. One way that would benefit both university and schools would be to explore with teachers what issues are of most interest to them and how the university can assist teachers in the study of these topics. Such assistance may take the form of workshops, workshops that again help implement some of the practices that are advocated in university classes. I had said earlier that, in general, the new government-mandated curricula in many provinces were fairly consistent with current theory and research in the various areas of the curriculum. School-teachers have often sought help in adjusting to the demands of such new curricula, and it would certainly be in the interest of the university to offer such help.

Fourth, in order to narrow further the gap between what is taught in university and what is practised in schools, university tutors should seek an active role in local, provincial, and national professional organizations of teachers in their particular field. At McGill, for instance, we have been able to provide office space and secretarial help to several professional associations such as the Association of Teachers of English in Quebec and the Quebec Reading Council. University teachers should also make an effort to contribute to the professional journals and other publications that are most accessible to teachers.

Fifth, as the notion of Teacher Centres has not caught on in most Canadian provinces and due to financial constraints is unlikely to, universities might serve such a function at little additional cost to the services they already offer their own students. Library, curriculum lab, media and computer centre resources should certainly be made more accessible to practising teachers.

I have suggested various ways in which the gap between teacher-preparation institutions and schools may be reduced. Enrolment in regularly scheduled in-service courses and graduate programmes is not in itself a sufficient means of maintaining productive links between practising teachers and the university. What must be perceived by teachers is that the university's interest in teachers and schools goes much beyond its concern for the initial preparation of teachers. Teachers need to know that the university has a considerable stake in the continuing education of teachers, and is a natural ally in curriculum development and the improvement of classroom practice.

I had said earlier that it has become increasingly clear that a year's preparation for teaching is inadequate, that it is only a first step in the process of becoming a teacher. But my main point is not that the initial year of teacher training needs to be extended. What does matter to the process of becoming a teacher is that such teachers find employment and begin teaching. It does matter that these initial years on the job are perceived not as years 'on probation' but as an internship with a well-organized programme of support from the university and the school. It does matter also that such interns are able to return, within some formal arrangement for part-time study, to take up those questions that have now come to matter. I have taught long enough to have met several teachers both as beginning teachers and some years later when they have enrolled in in-service courses and post-graduate programmes. I have then found out that much of what I thought they had learned in that qualifying year does not seem to have registered in any way that matters. This is particularly apparent when such teachers read as though they are reading it for the first time a key text they had read in their qualifying year. They realize that their teaching experience has added a perspective that has made the book a very different book.

I realize I may be understood as proposing a means of keeping teacher-education institutions in business; that too, but only in the sense that teacher-education institutions need to be working with teachers if they are truly to be about their business.

Part II

THE CLASSROOM REALITY

Chapter Six

'AND GLADLY TEACH': THE ENGLISH MOTHER-TONGUE CURRICULUM

Anthony Adams

The teaching of English in England is currently a matter of wide-ranging debate. In the immediate post-war years there had developed what came to be described as the 'progressive consensus', (1) which culminated in the publication of the Bullock Report, entitled A Language for Life. (2) Much of the foundation for this had been laid at a month-long Anglo-American seminar held at Dartmouth College in the summer of 1966, which gave rise to the publication of John Dixon's influential book, Growth through English, which provided a pattern for much of the work that was being developed in the then relatively new comprehensive schools. (3) Effectively this led to a separation of much of the work done in schools up to the school-leaving age, shortly to be raised to 16, from that done in the universities and in the education of 16-19-year-olds. In the days of a selective education system there had been a tendency for the secondary modern schools (for the bulk of the population) to concentrate in their English teaching on what Dixon called a 'skills model' of English, providing the basics of literacy and communication, while the grammar schools (catering for the academically able) provided an English curriculum modelled on university English teaching concerned mainly with the teaching and appreciation of great literature, called by Dixon 'the cultural inheritance model'. Growth through English rejected both of these approaches. In the dominant egalitarian climate of the 1960s the move was towards mixed-ability teaching and a view of English teaching that focused upon personal development through increasing mastery of language. The period saw, therefore, a move from 'great' to 'contemporary' ('relevant') literature, dealing

117

Anthony Adams

mainly with social issues, and to an increased emphasis on personal writing (as opposed to more formal traditional essay writing) and on the role of talk. Indeed, it was in this period that the term 'oracy' was coined on the analogy of 'literacy' to emphasize the equal importance of talking and listening alongside reading and writing skills. (4)

With modifications this view of English teaching has continued to inform good practice until almost the present day. It is certainly the model of English which most current trainers of potential English teachers espoused in the 1960s and which still influences much of their thinking today. I have elsewhere made clear some of the ways in which I differ from this 'consensus' (which was never simple or complete of course) but, as is the case with most of my fellow teacher-trainers, it comes close to the actual practice of what I do. (5)

The crisis in English studies that is now upon us has its origins in a number of quite different places. In the first instance there is a populist fallacy that there is something wrong with the standards of literacy in our schools. This is a familiar enough cry to be found in all cultures going back even to the days of Plato: there seems to be an enduring folk-belief in a golden age when everyone could read and write and 'standards' were miraculously higher. So firmly held is this view that the fact that all the evidence assembled by, for example, the Assessment of Performance Unit, set up after the publication of the Bullock Report, especially to monitor standards, is consistently ignored; the popular view remains that there is a crisis of literacy in our schools. In establishing a national curriculum, therefore, English has become quickly identified as one of the 'foundation subjects' alongside mathematics and science. It is already clear, from statements made by the Prime Minister and her Secretary of State for Education and Science, that what is looked for in English teaching will be a return to more in the way of rigour, a restoration of the older tradition, combining education in basic skills with education in and through great literature. (6) 'Personal growth' is no longer seen as an end in itself.

There is some conflict, therefore, between the beliefs and practices of many teacher-educators in universities and colleges of higher education, and amongst the Inspectorate and advisory services, and the expectations of the public and central government as to what the schools ought to be doing in English teaching. This conflict, for reasons to be explored later, finds particular focus in the area of initial training for teaching.

As a consequence of this public concern the government set up in 1987 a Committee of Inquiry into the Teaching of English Language under the chairmanship of Sir John Kingman. This committee reported in April 1988, (7) and its conclusions are to be taken note of in the discussions of the English Curriculum Working Group, chaired by Professor Brian Cox of Manchester University, himself a member of the Kingman Committee. Indeed the Cox Committee and its membership was announced on the very same day as the Kingman Report was published.

The Kingman Committee was wide-ranging in its composition; it was, however, notably short of professionals from the schools or from teacher education. Such professionals as it included were mainly drawn from the field of linguistics and it is clear that they had a considerable influence on the form taken by the final report. However, the committee refused to come up with the easy answers that may have been hoped for by those who commissioned it. For example it was insistent that there should be no return to traditional formal grammar teaching; it did, however, believe that teachers of English do not know enough about the language and argued cogently for more 'knowledge about language' on the part of both teachers and pupils. There appears to have been some confusion and division of opinion about whether such 'knowledge' is desirable for its own sake or whether it will actually lead to improved performance in pupils' use of language. The question remains unresolved and will doubtless underlie much of the discussion going on in the Cox Committee which is due to complete its work by April 1989.

More than half of the eighteen recommendations of the Kingman Report are concerned with teacher education at both initial and in-service stages. The members are anxious to educate all teachers in knowledge about language and potential teachers of English in secondary schools in particular. They are also critical of many university degree courses in English for their lack of any systematic study of language at all, a point to which we return later. The report as a whole can certainly be seen as very critical of the preparation of teachers, seeing it as deficient in what it has identified as an important area of concern.

But the crisis in English studies is much more complex than this. The reform of the examination system at 16-plus,

119

and the move to the largely course-work-based English programme for the General Certificate of Secondary Education, mirrored much that was best in the 'progressive consensus'. This can be seen in its stress on individual choice of topics on which to write, its inclusion of oracy as a compulsory component of the examination, and its valuation of 'response' as the way to examine the study of literature. However, English studies post-16 remained, at least until relatively recently, largely unchanged. The reasons for this have been explored elsewhere. (8) But it is a fact that 'English', the most widely studied of all GCE A Level subjects, has remained virtually unchanged as an A Level subject in the post-war years (A Levels themselves were established in 1951), and, for most of the pupils who take it, it is an examination exclusively in English literature based upon a canon of set texts. Similarly, in most British universities, until recently the study of 'English' has been the study of English literature, using the tools of critical analysis as a means of study. Pressures from outside, however, are forcing changes both in the 16-19 curriculum and in the universities.

To begin with we can no longer talk about the education of the 16-19-year-old in terms synonymous with 'the sixth form'. Much of that education now goes on outside traditional schools, in sixth form and tertiary colleges, and in colleges of further education. Because these institutions are free of the older, still grammar-school-based ethos of the traditional sixth form, they have often proved more willing to experiment with other forms of English than that of pure literature study. A Level syllabuses in communication studies, in media studies, and in English language have been introduced and are seen by many students as more appropriate to their needs than what has been studied in the past. Similarly in much, though by no means all, higher education the new critical approaches deriving from post-structuralism and linguistics are making themselves felt alongside Marxist, feminist, and other new ideologically based critical approaches. (9) Such new approaches are more likely to be found in the polytechnics and colleges of higher education, in the public sector, than in the universities.

The paradox is that many recruits to teacher training themselves come from the more traditional sixth form and university background. Their own education is rooted in a tradition that has not changed very much from the days of the grammar school; many of them will be unaware of much that is going on in the 'new English studies'. In the present climate they are also likely to share the popular view that something is wrong with 'standards' and that there is a need for a return to the older mixture of skills and tradition. When they are interviewed about their motive for teaching the answer is nearly always the same. They have been successful in the sixth form at school, they have chosen to do an Honours degree in English because they 'love their subject'. Many of them hope that teaching will be a means of enabling them to keep contact with the subject; for some, secondary-school English teaching is seen as a poor substitute for teaching in the tertiary field. Many are obviously most interested in obtaining a post in a sixth-form college. Such students, who necessarily form the majority of those recruited, contrast with those who have come into teaching through more unusual routes, having done their degree with, say, the Open University or in a polytechnic, mature students with a work record in a profession other than teaching, or sometimes, those who have done a degree in a subject other than English. Such students, often amongst the very best, frequently do not fit the firmly expressed view of the Secretary of State for Education that teachers should have had at least two years of formal academic study in the subject that they are going to teach. Even those who have done a traditional English degree are likely to be at odds with what the Kingman Committee felt such a degree should entail.

It is thus a very heterogeneous collection of people that one finds on an initial course of training for secondary-school English teaching, much more so than in most other subjects. There is, in practice, no one 'reality' that can be described as the university discipline of English, for some of the reasons discussed above. The students will come with their expectations dependent upon their own construction of that reality as defined by the courses they have undertaken in their studies so far. The one thing, however, that they all have in common is the considerable gap between that reality and whatever it is that they will meet in the schools, being trained, as most of them will be, with the needs of the comprehensive school in mind. Even in the schools there may well be little agreement about what constitutes the curriculum in English, a disagreement that is likely to persist long after the Cox Committee has delivered its report. However, in most schools, however variously it may

Anthony Adams

be delivered, there is likely to be some agreement about the need for the experience of literature and the development of the skills of communication. So much, at least, of a consensus remains.

The major difference that such student-teachers will later encounter in school from their own experience will be, of course, that in school up to age 16, English (whatever it may consist of) is a compulsory subject for everyone, not an option as it had been for them in sixth form and university. This means (and it is to be hoped that the Cox Committee will recognize this) that the subject has to be more popularist in its stance; it has to offer something for everybody. For many of their pupils and their parents (as well as with most other members of the school staff outside the English department), English will be valued for its instrumental uses; if they have other values to promote in their English teaching, the onus will be upon them to sell these to their pupils. They cannot take for granted an easy acceptance of their world in this respect. It is the relatively amorphous nature of English as a school and university discipline, the fact that it is a subject area about which everyone feels entitled to have an opinion (as they would not do in the other foundation areas of science and mathematics), that makes the subject so crucial a one for considering questions of teacher education and training.

The first task of a programme of teacher preparation and education must, therefore, include an element of reorientation on the part of the students. They are at the beginning of that transition stage where they will cease to see themselves as educational consumers and come to see themselves as responsible for the provision of education for others. This transition becomes especially acute if the view of the curriculum for which they are being prepared is one which is very different from their previous experience and their present expectations. Much that needs to be done will lie as much in the area of the affective as well as the cognitive domain, it will be concerned, above all, as in the account given above of the English teaching of the 1960s in schools, with personal development. Without this, any amount of educational theory and practical advice will remain inert when the student is actually faced with pupils in the classroom. Teacher education is essentially personal education or it is nothing.

Alongside the more formal programme of study, therefore, we may frequently include (as was done over some years at Cambridge) film material in which issues of childhood and adolescence are raised in the context of works of art which allow for a different, perhaps more holistic, approach from the orthodoxies of psychology and sociology. Indeed a strong case can be made out for the inclusion of more materials from the arts, especially novels and films, in teacher education, particularly for those students who have not dealt with such subjects in their degree courses. For example, in Cambridge, a local drama specialist runs a drama workshop course (aimed in part at self-discovery and understanding) for all those students interested in attending, irrespective of their subject discipline. Many of them later describe such activity as a central part of the course as a whole, though it is certainly not perceived as such by the orthodoxy of the university department of education.

When students begin their period of one-year teacher preparation for English teaching at Cambridge (the Post-Graduate Certificate of Education, PGCE) there are three immediate steps we take to begin the reorientation process. (10)

First, we seek to help them to redefine what it is that they mean by English literature. In the first few days of the course we expose them (mainly by reading aloud to them) to a great deal of children's literature, including picture books originally intended for very young children, and to a good deal of literature in English drawn from cultures other than the western European one with which they are most familiar. We try to demonstrate by example the importance of hearing stories read well aloud, and to show that this is a pleasure that does not cease with the primary school. At the same time we are enlarging the repertoire of material that they have available to them. Significantly enough, this is often the first time for many years that some of the students have enjoyed the experience of story for no other reason than to enjoy and engage with it. They are not going to have to write essays on these works, to 'compare and contrast', or analyse them. Part of the purpose behind this phase of the course is to reorientate them to both books and school students so that they may later be able to do a better job of bringing them together.

Second, we urge them all to keep a personal journal in which they are asked to record their experience of the course while it is taking place and to set this alongside their earlier experiences and expectations of teaching. For many of them this is the first time they have done any personal writing since they were in the lower secondary school. They often find it difficult to make their journal writing honest and reflective and to escape from the 'safer' format of the formal essay. They are told from the outset that the journal is a confidential document that no one will see except themselves: they can of course share it with us, or each other, if they wish but there is no pressure on them to do so. (This whole notion of writing for oneself as audience is fundamental to English teaching in schools but one that comes as a surprise to many of our students.) We see the journal as a way of using writing as a means of coming to terms with new experience, integrating it into oneself, and as fundamental to their own development as persons and their growth as beginning teachers. (11)

Finally, there is our characteristic 'workshop' way of working with the students. We are fortunate that main methods courses in Cambridge provide about two and a half days of methods time for work with the students. One full day is spent working with them in school in a carefully planned programme of induction into the realities of the classroom, one or two one-and-a-half-hour sessions are spent in looking at some aspects of theory; the other whole day is spent in a methods workshop, in which we generally involve also a local serving teacher (a teacher-tutor) who works alongside ourselves and the students. The work done in these sessions is closely related to the theoretical input but is based essentially upon asking the students themselves (characteristically working in groups) to carry out much the same kind of activity as they may be asking of their own students when they work with them in school, though necessarily they will be working with material drawn at an appropriate level for them as adults. The purpose of this is to provide a concrete focus for their growing understanding of the theoretical ideas and, at the same time, to ensure that they learn something of the value and difficulties of group work. Such work is not only intellectually but also emotionally and physically demanding; it entails working very closely with others, being dependent on them for your own success, and (equally) having them depend upon you. It is far removed from the lecture room and the writing of the weekly essay, which will have been the staple diet of most of them until now. Part of the intention is to make them aware of teaching and learning as essentially a collaborative activity, not something in which one engages in protected isolation. In our schools most teachers are still not used to this idea; many good teachers hate being observed in the classroom, and even those who embrace 'open' styles of teaching may have an irrational dislike of the 'open-plan' classroom. We still often train teachers on the assumption that they are going to lead solitary lives. In the complexities of the late 1980s and beyond this will no longer prove sufficient. Our teachers and students will need to become much more consciously aware of how dependent they are upon others for much of the learning process. This will be especially so as a consequence of the micro-electronics revolution on society outside school. As the range of information becomes ever greater and ever more available from more sources, our dependence upon others outside the school (as information providers) and others inside the school (as those who can help us turn this information into knowledge) will also become even greater. No solitary person will any longer be capable of making sense of it all. As the world collapses into MacLuhan's 'global village', the days of Goldsmith's 'Village Schoolmaster' will come to an end. (12)

The workshops referred to embrace such fundamental topics for the English teacher as the teaching of poetry, the short story, drama, reading development, and many others. They lead, however, to an ultimate workshop at the end of the first term, the presentation to their peers by the students (again working in groups) of a programme which they have put together and which has some application to the teaching of English.

These presentations often take the form of multi-media productions which we encourage since they provide an opportunity for the students to practise basic skills in the handling of audio-visual equipment. (13) Recent presentations have included one group which investigated primary education in Cambridge, making a tape/slide programme from playground interviews, which they counterpointed with autobiographical and literary extracts to show contrasts between growing up in Cambridge today and earlier times. Another group wrote and acted their own pastiche of a 1930s detective story and created a work-sheet of language activities around the performance for the audience to carry out. A third group took a well-known children's novel and articulated a series of activities, including a computer-based game, around it.

The above examples illustrate the wide range of possibilities open to the students. We give them some starting-points but deliberately refuse to give them too much direction. Finding out what they want to do as a group is, in itself, part of the activity. We provide practically no class time for this very time-demanding project. One of the things that students in training need to learn is how to organize themselves and how to use their own time properly. Most of them will have come from backgrounds where they have had all their time allocated for them in terms of lecture lists and due dates for essays; even in a university, the space for free negotiation of time in undergraduate courses is often very limited. In an age when more people will have on their hands 'negotiable time' (Watts' term for the enforced leisure that results from under-employment), (14) it becomes an urgent priority in education to help young people to plan and organize their own lives, something that in conventional schools we generally fail to do. It is all part of that process of helping people to become autonomous which we see as a fundamental educational end. The end-of-term presentations are one way in which we seek to enable students to become self-programming, but in a way that accepts the dependence of the individual upon the group, that recognizes that true autonomy can best be achieved through an element of collectivism.

Enough has been said to illustrate the essential marriage of theory and practice that underlies the course. Indeed, we would hope to make the distinction between the two as meaningless in the experience of the students as it is in reality. It is a truism that we cannot do anything in a classroom without some theory of education underlying it. The question is whether or not we are always aware of the theory that informs our practice. We hope, by such methods as have been described, to make students more aware of theory in practice as well as to give them resources which will stand them in good stead when they go into school. Such resources will, of course, include materials (we are always struck by the number of occasions when we see the same materials that we have used in student workshops being used on teaching practice); it will also include skills (the ability to handle audio-visual equipment and microcomputers (for example); it will (and must if the rest is to be of any use to them) also include intellectual understanding. But the fulcrum of the activity must be the response of the student as a whole person to what is going on, it must include an affective engagement and an excitement with the business of teaching and learning in the student-teachers as well as in their prospective school-students if it is to be of any real and lasting value to them.

Of course to have this amount of time for 'methods work' could be seen as something of a luxury. But the primary reason why students are with us is because they want to become teachers of a subject and, therefore, their education in the wider business of teaching can best be done within a subject context. This, in itself, means that subjects must not be conceived in too narrow a sense. We believe that our programme is a fully educational one that, working in this case through the medium of English, develops all the faculties and personalities of our students; other programmes in other subjects, though they may have a different focus depending upon the needs and structures of the subjects themselves, may very properly have the same end in view.

It is a universal experience that students in training as teachers are generally very hostile to educational theory and, in particular, to the specific disciplines of philosophy, psychology, sociology, and the history of education. Such areas are important, but the question necessarily arises as to how we teach them and how students are to be motivated to learn them. We would argue that much of what needs to be known can be learned through the medium of methods work and that many of the relevant areas of theory will be covered there, provided that the subject boundary of the methods course is not too narrowly interpreted. We have found this to be (for example) by far the most effective way of raising some of the theoretical issues concerned with topics such as multicultural education, social class and education, learning theory, and the like.

The Cambridge University Department of Education many years ago abandoned the formal teaching of the educational disciplines to PGCE students as separate lecture courses. It characteristically teaches educational theory in an integrated course (known as 'Situations and themes') which is team-taught by all members of the department. The lecturers concerned generally work in pairs, a 'methods' lecturer being teamed with a 'foundations' (educational theory) lecturer. Part of the intention here is to break down the idea in the minds of the students of a false separation between the two sides of our work, to integrate them in the experience of the student. Apart from proving to be more highly motivating (and less time-consuming) than the separate courses formally taught, the involvement in this course of all methods lecturers has brought about a significant shift of focus to the problems and possibilities of the classroom. It also makes for the real integration in the mind of the student which takes place, at least ideally, in the methods course itself which is intended to draw out the relevance of the 'Situations and themes' course for the theory and practice of education in the various methods areas.

A further element of what goes on in the first term of the PGCE course is the time spent in school visits. The idea here is not to provide an early experience of teaching practice but to set up a series of structured experiences that will be helpful to the beginning teacher in developing his or her repertoire of classroom skills and techniques. We like each of them to work for a time, for example, with a school-student with reading difficulties, which involves taking an informal reading inventory, diagnosing difficulties, and preparing and teaching appropriate materials. It therefore gives an opportunity for the students to put into practice some of the ideas explored both in the reading development workshop session and in the theoretical seminars on the teaching of reading, as well as some of the work in the 'Situations and themes' course on motivation and cognitive psychology.

Ideally in a further attempt to integrate the various elements of the course, we like to send the students in batches of about six into not more than four or five schools so that we, as lecturing staff, are able to work closely with them in the school situation. We also try to use some of the teachers with whom they will be working in schools as part of our team of teacher-tutors.

Naturally such a course evolves and changes over the years. In some ways it is unfortunate that government policy as represented in Circular 3/84, (15) and the establishment of the Council for the Accreditation of Teacher Education (CATE), has imposed change and sought to establish a greater uniformity across the whole field of initial teacher education. For example it is now mandatory that all PGCE courses must consist of a minimum of thirty-six weeks. At the same time little consideration has been given to the extra demands on staff as well as student time that such courses entail. This, along with such demands as that all lecturers engaged in methods work shall have 'recent and relevant' experience of teaching in schools, makes inroads on the time such staff have available for their other university work such as research and writing. Few would disagree that PGCE courses in the past have been too crowded and too short. The real solution to the problem might have been an extension of such courses to two years rather than attempting to crowd more into a single year of thirty-six working weeks which, in fact, provides even less time for reading and reflection on the part of the student.

The attempt to salvage some remaining time for other academic pursuits has led, in Cambridge at least, to the establishment of a new feature of the course that has proved to be very successful, the notion of 'extended professional experience'. Students in the final three weeks of the course (having already successfully completed teaching practice) are attached to an educational institution, which may be a school but may also sometimes be quite different, for an enlargement of their experience. Although students are given guidance and counselling, what they will do is left very much in the hands of the students themselves. Our experience of having worked this system in its first year is that it has been a most valuable one for the students, enabling them to see the educational world in a wider perspective than school. For example in the past year, one of the students worked in a children's bookshop; another worked with adult illiterates in a women's prison. Although many stuck to more conventional experience in schools or sixth-form colleges it is already clear that those who gained the most were those who sought to work outside the formal institution of the school. It is likely that their forthcoming professional work in schools will be enhanced by an ability to relate the classroom reality to a wider educational reality.

The purpose of this chapter so far has been to describe some of the considerations we feel to be important in the initial stages of preparing to teach in schools, particularly with the demands of the classroom-based curriculum in mind. The term 'classroom-based' is used here in preference to the more commonly used 'student' or 'pupil-based' because I wish to emphasize the reciprocal nature of what is being undertaken in this form of curriculum construction. The teacher certainly has a voice (and by no means a negligible one) in determining the nature and content of the learning that will take place. But the teacher's voice is one amongst others in the classroom. If the teaching is to be successful, if motivation to learn is to be established and maintained, that voice will have to engage in a constant process of discussion with other voices also. My purpose has been to show that very special approaches are needed in initial teacher education to enable beginning teachers to cope with the demands such a curriculum and such a classroom entail. Once the teacher ceases to be the sole arbiter of the agenda in the classroom, once a more open classroom concept replaces the teacher-dominated class, new qualities become needed alongside traditional teaching skills. These can most properly be described as dispositions which will include such qualities as flexibility, a willingness to take risks, adaptability, and the capacity to learn alongside the student.

Characteristically in such a classroom the teacher may become more an organizer of resources than a provider of knowledge. Knowledge itself comes to be seen as something that is constantly being remade in the learning process, not something that can be handed over ready-packaged to the learner. Indeed teachers may often be co-explorers with their students of areas of knowledge of which they are not the master, a concept explored in the 'support teaching' of children with special educational needs. The emphasis will be upon how to learn rather than upon what to learn; as already suggested a major goal will be the development of students as autonomous learners, ones capable of taking increasing responsibility for their own learning. (16)

It follows that such a notion of curriculum and of the learning process is far removed from a system-based curriculum which entails a syllabus laid down from outside the school by central or local government authority, such as the one with which English schools are currently threatened. Such a concept of education, which is essential if we are to prepare school-students to live in the year 2000 and beyond, is still rare enough in practice, although its base in learning theory, and especially in our understanding of language in the learning process, has long been with us. (17) It is also very much unlike the ways in which most trainee-teachers themselves received their own education in school or (regrettably) in university. They are still likely to have been brought up on a diet of a commodity-based view of knowledge. This is why such tactics as those that have been described above are needed to reorientate not just their performance as teachers but their whole understanding of education.

There is always a tension in teacher education between whether we are preparing students for the world of schools as they are now, or for schools as we believe they should become. Those who take the former view will see teacher education as simply the task of preparing students for their first job in teaching, giving them an assembly kit that will enable them to get by in their initial forays into the classroom.

However, the kind of approach to a negotiated curriculum just described - the notion of consent being the basis for what happens in the classroom, the dethronement of the teacher from the role of omnipotent authority, the development of a genuine autonomy on the part of students (not a spurious autonomy where they are, in fact, only free to choose to do what the teacher has already pre-ordained), the cultivation of a critical scepticism as a major purpose of education - all of these elements (many of which are commonplace within the alternative schools movement) come, in the end, to provide a challenge to the whole of the way in which we organize our society. A reason for more effective teacher education is to enable young teachers to challenge with authority the ways in which their schools are run and to lead their school-students, in their turn, to challenge the ways in which society is run, to empower students in fact.

It is worth quoting Brian Simon:

It is the acceptance of the existing social structure as the natural environment of the human animal ... that promotes ideas, directly at odds with the educationist's intention of equipping human beings to think and act in and upon society. (18)

There is an important distinction to be made between this position and that of classical liberal humanism. The latter emphasizes consistently the value of the individual and individual goals of aspiration. This had been, in essence, the approach to English teaching implicit in Growth through English in 1967. In a later edition Dixon makes it clear that he had failed at that time to take sufficient account of the social element of language. (19) It is political empowerment through a control over language rather than purely individual growth with which a relevant English curriculum for the 1980s is likely to be concerned as was emphasized in a further international seminar, the successor to Dartmouth, in 1981. (20) Similarly Simon places more emphasis upon social goals: it becomes necessary to see the individual as one element in a more complex pattern. This is to elevate co-operation above competition, to lead in the direction of a pattern of teacher education that stresses the interdependence of students upon each other in the kind of programme that has been described.

To implement such a programme with the beginning English teacher is of particular importance since English, being fundamentally concerned with language, is fundamental also to the learning process in all other subjects. Teachers of English, especially, need to learn self-awareness and self-determination so that they may be equipped to pass these lessons on to their pupils. Such a course of teacher preparation will also prepare them for the teaching reality that most students will face when they take up their first teaching appointment.

To equip them to face such a reality it is necessary for them to be armed with such a view of English teaching as will enable them to face intellectual challenges; with such pedagogical skills as will enable them to gain the respect of their peers and their students; and with such sensibilities as will enable them to work together comfortably with others. Such a programme for teacher education is in the end a programme for fundamental and far-reaching change in the students as people and as educators.

Chapter Seven

TEACHING THE MOTHER-TONGUE CURRICULUM IN GERMANY

Hans-Werner Eroms

The shift to linguistics in universities in the Federal Republic of Germany in the 1960s had very important repercussions on mother-tongue teaching in schools. It introduced a new concern with linguistic and, in particular, grammatical theory which, because linguistic science enjoyed the prestige of being recognized as a university discipline, left school concerns out of immediate consideration. However, it was possible to observe how the concept of grammar widened from one of a study of syntax to the development of a set of rules for effective communication. However the question whether school-students need a knowledge of grammar, even within this widened definition, has not been satisfactorily answered to this day.

This chapter looks first at how the understanding of what constitutes mother-tongue teaching in schools has developed in the Federal Republic. Next, two models are presented for teaching the mother tongue: one might be described as theoretical, while the other is more practical. The latter is clearly much more directly concerned with the everyday aspects of the school. However, the theoretical model is also important since the very rigidly defined school syllabus in the Federal Republic is considerably affected by its tenets. In what follows we will try to emphasize the positive impulses which flow from the two models rather than stress the points of friction.

GRAMMAR-ORIENTED TEACHING OF GERMAN AS THE MOTHER TONGUE

Mother-tongue teaching in the Federal Republic has been exposed in the last few years to an extraordinary number of conflicting pressures and demands for innovation. This could be said to be true for all kinds of schools and all age groups. (1) The first impact of this new view of mother-tongue language teaching came as a result of the interest in generative transformational grammar as pioneered by Chomsky in the 1960s. (2) In this context the possibility of reducing syntax to a few clear principles which could be easily formulated had a great fascination. At first, this applied especially to the universities. With generative transformational grammar, so it seemed, one could link the already established concern with grammar to international developments in linguistics. For all non-transformational grammars the term 'tradgram' was coined with a clearly dismissive connotation. Alongside this more general, theoretical development which did not much concern the school, transformational grammar could also be linked with a particular pattern of teaching which very much affected schooling. Chomsky with his concept of grammar had wanted to do justice to the aspect of creativity, albeit within a rather formal grammatical and theoretical framework: that is he believed that it was possible to conceive, within a finite number of rules, of the total set of all possible sentences in a language, from the simplest to the most complex, by the simple expedient of using suitable modifications, that is transformations. Sentences already expressed could be analysed in this way, and new ones, never before heard or written, could be created. It was obvious that such a somewhat formal interpretation of linguistic creativity could easily be applied to a concept of individual personal creativity. It is as a result of this that in the 1960s and 1970s in manuals intended for school use we find, on the one hand, mechanistic applications of the principles of transformational grammar and, on the other, a more strongly ideological belief that students' creativity could be extended by their working with transformational grammar. (3)

How hurriedly this development was carried out is made clear by the fact that transformational grammar itself did not find an established place in all universities and could not displace the old traditional grammar even there. This shows particularly the absurdity of a direct application of theoretical grammars to school-teaching. At the same time a purely student-centred approach is likely to imply a lower position for grammar in the priorities of the school syllabus, with it being seen not as an end in itself, but as a means to an end. But what should be the purpose of mother-tongue teaching? Surely not to equip students with arguments to engage directly in discussions towards a better grammar theory. More likely, it is to improve their linguistic competence if by that we mean, referring to Chomsky, the skill to produce sentences in a language in accordance with rules. The jump from this still rather theoretical, grammar-tied concept into the activity of language use cannot be made, even allowing for the realization that competence can be seen only in terms of language acts (that is performance) and must not be taken to mean the quantity of language rules mastered by an individual. (4) Strong interests emerging in the course of the further development of transformational grammar to use this grammar as proof for the existence of universal inborn rule dispositions, that is rules which extend beyond individual languages, have to this day received no ready acceptance in schools. (5)

In the universities the intrusion of transformational methods of description created alternative grammar models, especially the so-called dependence-oriented represent-ations, (6) in which the structures of a sentence are not represented through part/whole relations but by dependency relations of words amongst each other. The valency concept contained therein which accords a central place to the verb was quickly introduced into school-teaching and has had the pride of place there to this day. (7) The necessary reflection, however, about the use of grammar for the school-student, was delayed even more because of this. Moreover there emerged, again starting with the universities, a point of view which wished to reduce the concern with 'grammar' generally to its auxiliary character within broader linguistic disciplines. Here also there were important influences from outside the Federal Republic. We refer in particular to the socio-linguistic theories of Bernstein, (8) which had a great impact in the Federal Republic, (9) where, however, Bernstein's pair of opposites (elaborated and restricted codes) was applied less directly to class differences (middle class and working class) but rather to the distinctions between standard and non-standard language. This concept was also directly introduced into

135

schools. (10) Even though its introduction into the schools again happened too quickly and too directly, it had important methodological consequences: already the theoretical knowledge findings are characterized by an emancipatory element. The obvious chance inequalities between speakers who can use the elaborated code and those who have only the restricted code at their disposal clearly needed to be taken account of. Thus, not the exclusive preoccupation with the theoretical position of the discipline, but the needs of the student were to be taken as the point of departure. The linguistically less endowed student should be offered a deliberate programme of advancement, that is one of linguistic compensation. (11)

On the one hand, however, the effects of attempts at linguistic compensation proved to be insignificant because the programmes of student advancement themselves had to be developed completely independently of diagnostic theory and thus received no help from that quarter; on the other hand, it was soon realized that language varieties could, indeed, be evaluated positively. (12) What can be said is that the theoretical dialogue among specialists with the theses of Bernstein (13) and Oevermann (14) led to a reappraisal of regional languages and dialects and, at the same time, to a recognition of other functional codes.

Further new linguistic theories, in particular in the area of pragmatics, hardly affected schools. (15) And yet the 'speech-act' theory, (16) which can be easily reduced for teaching purposes to its essential progressive findings, would be especially suited to an understanding and, above all, a practice of basic linguistic performances and of functional varieties. Speech-act theory takes the activity character of language as its point of departure, thus preventing a reduction of linguistic considerations to a concern with 'pure grammar'. Also, the varied linguistic ideas which occupy themselves with spoken language have been insufficiently applied to schooling, (17) although they would be particularly suitable in divorcing mother-tongue teaching from too strong a concern with written texts.

To be sure, it is precisely the use of texts instead of an exclusive preoccupation with paradigmatic sentence patterns or even isolated vocabulary exercises that can be regarded as progress. For rather than the more or less unreflecting practice of grammar exercises, it is the practice of essay writing which requires a thorough concern with texts as the natural occurrences of language. (18) Here we wish to quote the example of Beisbart/Dobnig-Jülch/Eroms and Koss, (19) who attempted to make the discoveries achieved by university linguistics, to wit that language utterances are text bound, more widely known. Their main concern was to perceive texts as communicatively complete units. In lessons which they quoted in their book they showed that those procedures were most successful in which a start was made with the analysis of a (written) text that was available. They exploited texts of stylistically various kinds, not only sport reports, articles from youth newspapers, and advertising sheets, but also literary texts. The analysis procedures had as their first objective to assimilate the whole text unit by means of formal ('textual-grammatical') and content criteria. In a second objective the nuclear information and intentions inherent in the text were to be teased out. For this, use was made of different procedures of text reduction, using parts of the total text and the discovery of implicit patterns of cohesion. We will not go into details; we wish, however, to emphasize that it is precisely through the discovery of textual-grammatical links that the functional character of grammar can be seen particularly clearly: the various steps taken towards achieving an understanding of the content totality of the text can be retraced in grammar form. Reports from school experience with the book were positive throughout. However the procedure, which was meant to be complementary to others already in existence, did not claim to place mother-tongue teaching on a completely new basis because the authors believed that a measured application of linguistic procedures alongside existing teaching approaches had a better chance of acceptance than more radical proposals for change. Their method tried especially to strengthen student motivation. Since, on the one hand, complete language activity situations were taken as the point of departure while, on the other hand, texts were used which were of real interest to the students, motivation was achieved in a perfectly natural way. Allowance was made for the fact that the variety of language activity modes was presented only in excerpts. Insight into the contextual base of language activity, and the development of an awareness of the processes involved, especially those necessary for the understanding of texts was the main concern while the simulation of complete language discourse, that is language production, took a back seat.

The making conscious of language processes, which was

also the main principle of other projects of the second half of the 1970s, (20) was the main learning objective, in this case with the result that the cognitive side of education was dominant. If necessary, a direct practical productive application could be added in later steps. However, the project of Haas also demonstrates attempts to accept work with textual linguistics as a preliminary step to an integrated teaching approach in which not only the cognitive side, but also the moral and spiritual, can be linked with social demands. (21) 'Integration' it would seem, was the magic word for the pedagogical justification of methodological decisions to present mother-tongue teaching as student oriented, on the one hand, while, on the other, making it possible to avoid syllabus constraints in so far, at least, that the prescribed teaching syllabus objectives and materials, did not have to be introduced atomistically. (22) For we note a regrettably increasingly more rigid scheme of work being prescribed in all the Länder (states) of the Federal Republic at that time, a reaction of the cultural bureaucracy to the changing reception of linguistic models into schools. (23) Official syllabuses are being guided again by the traditional learning objectives in which linguistic and, above all, grammatical concepts are accorded an exclusively subordinate function in the development of language skills of students. (24) Integrated models are the ones which can most easily be reconciled with rigid prescriptions.

SITUATION-ORIENTED MOTHER-TONGUE TEACHING

Before we go into details of this model, we wish to present another one which was bound to develop as a reaction, so to speak, against the ideas outlined above. On the one hand, it challenged their theoretical assumptions, and, on the other, it also challenged the rushed adoption of linguistic models into the schools. It is surprising that a concept which set out to link language learning with the real experience of students met with an extraordinary interest despite the existing bureaucratic hurdles. Undoubtedly below the surface, there is a strong desire to escape from an exclusive, or at least predominant, concern with grammar as a means of illuminating texts.

What is now to be discussed, then, is the concept of a 'situation-oriented' German mother-tongue teaching as it was presented by Boettcher and Sitta:

> The main plank of a situation-oriented German language teaching can be summarized in so far that it uses the existing and accessible school-based life situations and experiences of the students as paradigmatic model learning situations. (25)
>
> (editors' translation)

The examples analysed by Boettcher and Sitta show particularly that communicative breakdowns in everyday school life can be taken as a starting-point for lessons and that, by solving such linguistic problems, communicative competencies can be developed.

The authors criticize the classical grammar teaching approach. They regret, in particular, that the grammatical concepts and the answers used have no links with the students' everyday experience, (26) and further that the new developments in linguistics had only led to shifting the emphasis on such elements as syntax, semantics, and pragmatics, while taking no account of the complexities of genuine utterances and understandings. (27) The concept of language that students receive from such grammar teaching is often one of something formal, something abstract, something that does not include their own language, but is confined to school, with the additional feeling that their own language is not a proper language at all. (28) This widespread view is opposed by those findings of linguistics and its related disciplines which represent the real conditions of language use. (29) Amongst other things, the authors deal with the complementarity of verbal and non-verbal communication, the link between message and the role relationship of the originator, the appropriateness of the situation, the goal orientation of the communicative act, as well as the conflicts between norm and creativity. Of course, consideration of all of these may be necessary but it is not an adequate condition for successful mother-tongue teaching. The decisive condition is the motivation of the students at the moment of learning: the insight that it is their language that is to play an important role in teaching. The everyday world of the students must be introduced directly into the teaching and not merely tolerated alongside the theory-reflecting world of the classroom. In this process the stimulus arising within school, especially, will provide a primary motivation to which experiences from outside school on which the teachers have based their preparation will be added. Such complementary inside and outside school experiences must be understood as the starting-point for the learning process. (30) Important for the authors is the introduction and preservation of the students' own verbal utterances in their original form. It is essential that 'the students' contributions and their linguistic form should not be pre-censored or sanctioned by either teacher or fellow students'. (31) It is further necessary, to a far greater extent than hitherto, to let the students themselves have a say, to let them argue constructively, to sensitize them to the divergent interests of others. One could call this basing one's teaching on 'communicative ethics'.

The authors make clear that the concept of a situation-centred teaching is diametrically opposed to that of a learning objective one:

> While the learning-objective-centred approach sets out primarily to change the school syllabuses and aims at attaching itself to a post-school life reality analysed by theoreticians, the situation-centred approach sets out to change the school as a situation for the students in order to gain their acceptance to see teaching and learning as something that primarily belongs to and affects them. (32)
>
> (editors' translation)

Particularly drastic is their argument that in the learning-objective-centred approach in an extreme case:

> It may be expected of the student to start grammatical investigations now, that is in the second primary school grade because, so he is told, he will need this skill twelve years later, that is after the Abitur examination. Any rational adult would try to defend himself against such conditions of work: to labour for thirteen years for something the purpose of which for his own life and that of others he cannot appreciate except perhaps to keep himself in his job. (33)
>
> (editors' translation)

Before we move on to an analysis of the situational approaches used by the authors we ought perhaps slightly to correct the scepticism inherent in the statement just quoted. This is because 'imaginary situations' in teaching do not have to be seen exclusively in a negative sense. Indeed they can encourage students to work by appealing to their readiness to take on role-play, an important element in extending their social relations as such. The anticipation of adult roles or being put into other communicative roles need not necessarily lead to a failure of the lesson unit. On the contrary an all too direct and, to boot, too regular a reference to reality could lead to inhibitory measures on the part of the teacher which could have just as negative an effect on motivation as the feared elimination of the students' real experience.

These remarks are not intended as a general criticism of situation-centred German mother-tongue teaching, although Boettcher and Sitta's book presents such far-reaching possibilities for this type of teaching, endowing it with the potential of cross-curricular application, that one can almost hear voices calling for a moderation of the whole exercise. The book presents in detail some three dozen examples of their situational approach. We will take three of them and examine them for their potential to link grammar teaching directly with the students' world.

> The students are angry about a circular letter from the school headteacher in which they are forbidden to play football during break in the school playground, written in what they think are too rigid tones. A rather long inquiry follows this letter. Students collect in the next few weeks all sorts of written and oral utterances which in their opinion contain something like a prohibition or command. There follows an examination of the spectrum of grammatical and other linguistic devices which are used to command or forbid people to do something.
>
> Directed analysis: Students' attention is drawn to the difference between the formal grammatical distinction of different sentence types (statement, question, command), on the one hand, and the pragmatic distinction between commanding, requesting, instructing, pleading, questioning utterances on the other hand. They find the choice of an appropriate grammatical form for a command situation clearly depends upon a range of hierarchical relations and norms. (34)

This indeed is a genuine situational impulse: the students are directly affected. The directed analysis is aimed at

141

syntactical, speech act, theoretical, textual, and other pragmatical features. It could indeed be extended. There are two problems here: first, is the situation such as it occurs in real life lost in this process of analysis? Surely, in actual fact, the orders of the headteacher are intended to be carried out (or, at best, discussed). In other words, the speech act 'prohibition', or the text variety 'instruction' is to be experienced in a primary sense by the students, that is it is to be carried out by them rather than to become an object of reflection. It is doubtful, moreover, whether the tensions arising out of this could be sustained in class. (We do not, of course, wish to deny the students' right to be critical, even if it involves criticism of their headteacher's actions). On the other hand, the directed analysis sketched in by the authors requires a thorough command of linguistic concepts on the teacher's part. This is in principle a very positive development. It assumes a thorough elaboration of linguistic expertise in the process of education by the teacher. It also fundamentally requires pedagogically responsible teachers who are free to plan their lessons and are not subject to syllabus constraints.

> In a biology lesson students have learned that a slow-worm is not a worm but a kind of lizard; in the mother-tongue lesson meanwhile they are reading a story about a slow-worm and they complain about the imprecision of language used.
> Directed analysis: the students' attention is drawn to the difference between technical language and everyday language and the evidence for the relative appropriateness of each sociolect for its area of application. (35)

This example is rather an obvious one as far as its choice of subject is concerned. Introducing it into teaching, however, evokes a different kind of reservation from the previous one. Obviously the students would quickly lose their motivation and interest if such examples were used too often. This is because they anticipate that the directed analysis will dwell on that and they will soon suspect any source of harmless communicative break-down as a pretext for a piece of didactic teaching.

> Students in the third grade are making fun of the speech of a new Turkish fellow student who omits the

definite article with the noun. The teacher herself, struck by this phenomenon, learns from a colleague who has specialized in German for foreigners that no article exists in the Turkish language and that the Turkish student in learning German analogously to his mother tongue and its grammatical rules is making systematic mistakes. Using the Turkish sentences of the student and their German translation as an illustration, she discusses with the class such instances where Turkish and German sentence structures differ considerably. The students no longer make fun of the language behaviour of their Turkish fellow student because they have understood its origin.

Directed analysis: the students' attention is drawn to contrastive comparison between the two languages. This contrastive analysis is extended by using examples of standard language and dialect; insight is gained into the fact that one regards one's own mother tongue as the most self-evident in the world and suspects all foreign languages and linguistic peculiarities as being wrong or bizarre. Problems of linguistic interference (in unsuitable analogy formations) between mother tongue and foreign language as a source of difficulty when learning foreign languages are discussed. (36)

In this example over and above the linguistic application, an appeal is made to the concept of 'communicative ethics', which was mentioned earlier. It is clear that this is a suitable opportunity to motivate tolerant linguistic behaviour, not only to reflect on it but also to apply it in practice.

We will dispense with a discussion of other examples. However, the examples of communicative situations already given could demonstrate that the extension of the communicative skills of individual students, above all however their communicative socialization, can succeed through situation-centred teaching in which grammar, in the widest sense, is to be taken as a yardstick of communicative activities. A further positive aspect of this mode of teaching is, as already suggested, that professionally competent and pedagogically autonomous teachers are essential. Their freedom of action must on no account be curtailed. There are dangers as the few examples have already made clear - that the situational motivation becomes over-used and that the school experiences that are introduced are too directly close to the bone. Only a tactful exploitation of such incidents will avoid the danger of getting too close to the subject matter itself and away, therefore, from the language study programme. However, Boettcher and Sitta's concept of developing a completely new type of mother-tongue teaching deserves considerable respect, especially when the school reality looks very different in consequence of an imposed rigid set of syllabus constraints.

INTEGRATED MOTHER-TONGUE TEACHING

In the case of the situation-centred mother-tongue teaching the students' real experiences are taken as a tool to eliminate communicative breakdowns. In the last resort, therefore, such teaching is to act as a kind of communication therapy, to obtain from already resolved experiences insights for similar future communicative situations. The integrated mother-tongue teaching approach, by contrast, is explicitly planned with the curriculum in view. This is particularly true when it is linked to a specific course used in the school. This is so because school courses are approved by the ministries of the federal Länder, only if they are geared exactly to the requirements of the curriculum, they are thus the best guarantors for putting the curriculum into practice.

The authors of school courses have gone over more and more to bundling their syllabus suggestions in year or age groups, putting them together in meaningful units and linking them with the experiences of students of the relevant age levels. In this way linguistic objectives are to be integrated into the students' own world. In comparison with situation-centred mother-tongue teaching, which is characterized by its use of genuine experiences, even if they appear only in excerpt form, the integrated mother-tongue teaching is linked with fictitious situations. The best example of this integrative approach, as here understood, is the course book Westermann Sprachbuch Deutsch. Taking Sprachbuch 6 for the Gymnasium which differs only slightly from the corresponding books for other types of school as an example, we propose to analyse the principles of integrated mother-tongue teaching as we understand it more closely.

In the accompanying teachers' book the authors say:

In Sprachbuch Deutsch 6 the attempt is made to
achieve the fullest possible integration of the various
areas of language teaching. In each teaching unit oral
communication, written communication (including text
production), reflection upon language (including
grammar and spelling) are related to each other; the
emphases are, of course, applied in different ways in
different places. (37)

(editors' translation)

The integration is achieved in a twofold way: first, in the
learning areas, that is it is 'curriculum-centred' because it
sets out to achieve a complete assimilation of the syllabus
content by the student.

Through the integration of the various learning areas in
short clear learning units the learning conditions and
learning potential of the students of this age group are
to be satisfied. (38)

(editors' translation)

Second, 'student-centredness' is also to be seen in the fact
that the students' own areas of experience are taken as the
point of departure. Integration is achieved through
structuring the content according to experience areas.
These experience areas, again, are not global fields of
activity but concrete situations culled from age-specific
incidents in which the linguistic situations occur.

Concrete situations are taken over from students'
experiences which provide stimulus for oral
communication through illustrations and/or texts. (39)

(editors' translation)

These are followed by the use of closely topic-related
written communicative exercises.

We must now try to explain what is meant by
'experience areas', 'fields of language activity', and 'oral
communication'.

Experience areas

Experience areas are the incidents through which the
learning areas are integrated with language theory.

> For the purpose of integration content-contexts, thematic foci are needed which correspond to the students' level of understanding. To ensure this understanding, topics are chosen which link directly with students' own experiences. (40)
>
> (editors' translation)

In this way

> it is possible for the students to bring their own experiences into the lessons and to explore them linguistically. This language exploration of one's own experiences can, in turn, facilitate a more linguistically appropriate activity on the part of the students. (41)
>
> (editors' translation)

From what follows it becomes clear that the chosen concrete situations which we shall refer to later are not intended to be stimuli for language work alone, but are also meant to help the students to expand their own areas of experience and, in particular, those in which social relations play an important part. Furthermore the students are to be put into situations calling on them to resolve familiar incidents with greater linguistic efficiency.

> They are also to be prepared to be able to act linguistically efficiently in important incidents not previously experienced by them. (42)
>
> (editors' translation)

We can see from this that language education is in this way combined with the aim of socialization.

Fields of language activity

The authors rightly emphasize that language activities do not appear in isolation but are always embedded in larger situational contexts. Language activity is one part of an ever more complex activity. At the same time communicative activities are distinctive forms of activity in which language plays the dominant part.

The authors now ask the question, how situations filled with language activity can be incorporated into teaching. It seems to them that to wait for real-life situations to occur depends too much on chance and is incapable of continuous planning and thus not practicable in school-teaching. A situation-centred mother-tongue teaching thus does not interest them. Another possibility, that of setting out to create activities filled with linguistic potentials, would be the so-called 'project-centred' teaching, (43) where students and teachers together prepare and carry out a comprehensive work project. In the process a variety of genuine speaking and writing opportunities would occur. In this case, too, the drawbacks are presented as insurmountable. Amongst other things there is an excessive reliance on learning from particular instances and there are

> great difficulties in respect of syllabus completion, planning of a continuous learning progression, and the assessment of individual performance as well as directed individual advancement. (44)
>
> (editors' translation)

Integrated mother-tongue teaching is presented as the happy mean through which writing and speaking stimuli are varied alongside situations and texts being linked, and so occurring in their natural mutual mesh. When active participation is appropriate to motivate the students this can provide a realistic solution. However two reservations must be made. This kind of teaching starts with fictitious incidents and it is very strongly oriented towards the curriculum, subject to the pressure of completing the syllabus.

Oral communication

The primacy of oral before written communication prevails as the point of departure for mother-tongue teaching not merely in the course referred to above. (45) The catalogue of demands presented by the authors for the development of students' communicative competence emphasizes its social role. Amongst other things, it is justified by the fact that the content of the oral communication in mother-tongue teaching also acts as content material in all other subjects across the curriculum. The danger that this entails is that the students play a predominantly receptive role in the lessons. The authors are also aware that efforts to activate the students linguistically are hampered by regional and class specific speech inhibitions which must be weighed up and overcome. This is why appeal is also made here to communicative ethics which is to protect this procedure from too pronounced an egocentricity. (46)

Above we have mentioned several times that fictitious situationality, the use of role-play, in language experience areas, need not be inferior to the concern with real incidents of communicative conflict although their application in out-of-school linguistic reality cannot be guaranteed. On the other hand we must also take into account that schooling cannot be released from this concern with out-of-school. In the course book that we have been discussing the experience areas quoted are doubtlessly also taken from the real-life concerns of students, and the concept of communication which the authors represent is not limited to normative, let alone paradigm drilling, grammar.

One thing must, however, be borne in mind. Since, as put forward, the integrative approach represents a meshing together of all language activity areas (such basic functions of communication as giving information, engaging in verbal quarrels, putting arguments forward, and many others); all forms of communication (written as well as oral utterances); grammatical concerns and spelling; and, since this meshing is organized with the curriculum in mind, it must be feared that education in communication will still lag behind the attempt to complete the syllabus. An example may indicate the dangers which loom. In the authors' chapter, 'Living together - getting along together', the entry into the integrated learning unit occurs through a linguistic conflict case. (47) Illustrations of such conflict situations appear on the first page of the learning unit. There we can see amongst other things how children quarrel about who should take over the washing up. We also read an excerpt from a letter in which the writer reproaches the recipient for something that had happened. This serves as an introduction to a student-led discussion on the learning area theme. In the teacher's book we find sentences of a high pedagogical and communicative ethos, such as:

Only when the presence of conflict in all forms of human relations is accepted and not suppressed, is there a chance of finding collectively a form of relating together which is acceptable to all those concerned. (48)

(editors' translation)

No doubt this statement could start a very lively discussion of this problem area! The exercises provided for this make use in the first instance of all of the motivation involved. After that, however, increasingly, a completely different communicative aim is attempted: 'description' is practised through illustrations and texts. The students are expected to recognize descriptive texts and practise this textual form while they describe their classmates. Because for this kind of description of persons a number of characterizing adjectives necessary, the unit includes a series of comprehensive exercises in which the morphology and functions of adjectives are practised. The change-over to the linguistic exercises is made clear from headings which appear in the list of contents but not in the learning unit itself. For example 'to criticize someone - to react to criticism and reproach', 'to praise someone - to express approval of him', 'describing a person'. Obviously a whole associative sequence ranging from 'commitment' to 'neutrality' is to be attempted here. This may even be successful in this particular case: even learning the use of adjectives and spelling exercises may be a bit more palatable after this! However the communicative stimulus with its much higher demands is thrown overboard. One could ask oneself whether, in this particular case at least. it would not have been more acceptable to use an inductive and constructive approach.

However, apart from these reservations the integrated mother-tongue teaching approach offers the opportunity, in a relatively natural way, to explore linguistic problem areas and to further students' communicative skills. How can teachers adjust to this form of teaching and what sort of preparation do they need? Essential is a thorough linguistic training concerned first of all with grammatical theory, especially analysis; in short, the functional value of all linguistic elements must be mastered. A linguistic course of study such as that produced by Pelz gives a sound grounding in this. (49) Apart from that, it is especially important for the teacher to have assimilated the fundamentally active character of language. The teacher must be in a position to build up language activity contexts, step-by-step, and to recognize and correct communicative disturbances of all kinds, from a spelling mistake to misunderstandings and false linguistic manipulations. So far, there has been no adequate material available to cater for this. However, in the teachers' books accompanying the Sprachbücher courses.

sufficient background information is provided. Once teachers have decided to use the integrated mother-tongue teaching approach, they can control the individual steps of this procedure from a linguistic and pedagogical perspective.

CONCLUSION

The three scenarios sketched above of how to teach in a communicative and grammatical way exhibit both conformist and controversial alternatives. There is no single ideal way to teach the mother tongue. Curriculum objectives are available in the Federal Republic for schools and they are compulsory. It is clear that both models, those which conform to the curriculum plan, as well as alternative ones, require teachers grounded in linguistic science who are pedagogically independent in their teaching so as both to encourage the students' practical communicative actions and to develop their cognitive linguistic skills. (50)

Chapter Eight

FREEDOM AND CONSTRAINT IN TEACHING GERMAN LITERATURE

Karl-Wilhelm Eigenbrodt

This chapter is a practitioner's account based entirely on the author's own classroom experience as a teacher. In order to preserve its empirical character I have deliberately discarded any 'learned' additions, used no quotations, and made no references to secondary literature. These would have done nothing to clarify what I want to say; indeed in some ways their use would be a contradiction in itself. I will confine myself strictly to what my students and I did, thought, and experienced in a sequence of lessons taught during a school summer term two years ago. Using an actual example, I propose to demonstrate that co-operative learning, for personal and social development, can take place in German literature lessons, though it does produce its problems. Before giving my account I wish to give a brief definition of the concept as I understand it in my teaching. Co-operative learning I take to mean is primarily about learning to live with oneself and with not against others in society, recognizing their worth, being able to listen to them. Competitive demands, achievement at all costs, and calls for ideological conformity are its negation. This rather wide definition has proved viable and productive in my pedagogical practice. For the purpose of this chapter I have taken a series of German literature lessons taught by myself to illustrate my intention.

The class was the tenth grade (age 15-16 years) of the classical languages Rabanus Maurus Gymnasium in Mainz. Of the twenty-nine students about half were girls. Though I mention this statistic I have not observed anything which could be interpreted as gender-specific behaviour in the classroom. The majority of parents have themselves taken their Abitur - the upper secondary school leaving examination - many of them have in fact completed a university education. Mainz, the second oldest city in Germany, with well over two thousand years' history, is an interesting bustling city, with some two hundred thousand inhabitants, the capital of the state of Rhineland-Palatinate and the seat of its government, the Johannes Gutenberg University, the second German television station, with a good deal of modern industry. These details may illustrate the context in which I work.

The lessons themselves were given over to the study of Schiller's play Don Carlos for which task, in accordance with the guidelines of the prescribed school curriculum in the Land (state) we had one week with four periods of forty-five minutes duration each. Schiller's Don Carlos is a demanding play in many respects and studying it is by no means a simple or easy task. There is a unity of action of sorts, but it is a complex one, often indirect and hidden. As against that, there is no problem as far as the unities of place and time are concerned. However, if the question is asked concerning the psychological and moral make-up of the various characters implicated in the action, it becomes immediately clear that it is here that the heart of the problem must be sought. Schiller quite deliberately presents a many-sided, multi-layered set of characters capable to some extent of very different interpretations. But this is not our main concern, which is essentially the pedagogical task of teaching Don Carlos. To understand that task more readily, it may help to have a brief outline of the plot.

The play is situated at the royal court of Spain around the middle of the sixteenth century, and the plot is based on two dramatic moments, one essentially political, the other private, which impinge on each other. Don Carlos, the heir to the throne, wants to be given the command of the Spanish forces ordered to hold in check the rebellious Netherlands. Secretly the prince hopes to be able to deal with the Dutch who had been cruelly subjugated until then by the Spanish and prevented from practising their Protestant faith, in a more humane and libertarian way. At the same time Don Carlos cannot come to terms with the fact that his father, King Philip II, had taken away from him his bride, the French princess Elizabeth, and for reasons of state married her himself.

The Marquis of Posa, the prince's friend, a distinguished young officer, becomes involved in this double father-son conflict. Like the prince he too supports the 'modern' ideas of liberty of thought and conscience; his gallantry moreover has also attracted the king's attention. Posa has won the confidence of the old, embittered, and lonely monarch and wants to use this to help Don Carlos and to further the cause of the Dutch. Not least, it is thus the character of Posa which is meant to arouse our interest and which has a particular pedagogic relevance. How is one to judge Posa? Is his courageous siding with the freedom party morally justified or should one condemn his virtual betrayal of the king who has looked upon him almost as his friend? A whole spectrum of psychological, ethical, and political problems light up in this figure which for me has always been a most important reason for studying Don Carlos. For surely adolescent students such as I teach seek to make evaluative judgements even if they lack the necessary maturity and experience. This is my problem as a teacher of literature.

Thus the first step towards learning for social and personal development in German literature lessons is taken when choosing a text for detailed study. Not all texts are equally suitable and it is certainly not unimportant which text is selected. If the text reflects the problem of value-laden action in the midst of manifold complicated social relations clearly and convincingly, then the text is likely to be more suitable for our purpose. Co-operative learning thus begins with the choice of text; in this respect the official school syllabuses do offer a choice. Don Carlos is particularly exemplary for the discussion of the problems mentioned. All, or nearly all, the characters are conceived in such a way that they are implicated in terms of their own individual destinies and relationships as well as those of their social circumstances in which they find themselves. Thus they are tragic figures in the dramatic sense of the term. It should be noted moreover, that the Marquis of Posa reflects this tragic quality which consists in the irreconcilability of contradictions of human existence in a particularly high degree. This figure is therefore of especial interest for classroom purposes: a point to which I shall return later.

The next step towards co-operative learning is a specific way to deal with the text. How do you set about teaching it? It cannot be assumed that this highly suitable text will by itself have an impact on students, nor can one expect them fully to recognize its significance for their own personal and social lives just like that, indeed to the circumstances in which it may affect them. In many cases it is precisely the rational and linguistic analysis of the text which prepares the ground for the desired practical response and confirms it. Though this is but a behavioural means for proceeding to action it is no less necessary for that. It cannot be stressed often enough that however effectively motivated co-operative learning may be in the long run, it must contain an intellectual component too, if it is not to be limited to cursory, uncommitted, and changeable behaviour patterns which quickly lose their impact.

The suggested approach requires 'sacrifices'. The points made earlier make it clear that teachers must establish their own priorities and keep to them. This applies particularly when teaching students who have been used to the traditional teaching style of schemes fixed beforehand and rigidly adhered to according to plan. Changing over to co-operative learning styles requires time and this time must be borrowed from somewhere. This is especially true in view of the fact that the study of a complete text can keep the students' attention alive for only a limited period, which in the case of Don Carlos should probably not exceed a month. Thus teachers must trim some aspects of the syllabus, or give them up altogether, since there is a relatively large number of aspects which may legitimately be considered in literature lessons. Teachers may easily be faced with a dilemma if they concentrate on only a few of these or indeed only one: namely learning for personal and social development. There are important study fields: problems concerning the dating, literary history, philology, formal structure, socio-linguistics and other aspects of the text which I do not wish to underestimate. However, it is just as much a mistake to dwell on these traditional ways when teaching, as it is to raise the concept of co-operative learning to one's exclusive guiding principle. On the contrary, because co-operative learning has its price it must not be used in every case. Besides, teaching methods which are over-used and over-emphasized tend to turn into their opposites.

A further condition of effective co-operative learning is thorough didactic preparation. This meant that the students were given appropriate time to acquaint themselves with the full text by reading the play at home. In fact they had one week for that, during which time they were given no other German homework. Reading was their homework. The four classroom periods at our disposal in that week we used to clear up questions, problems, and difficulties which arose. The literary and linguistic demands posed by the text made such clarification indispensable. A point which teachers must be aware of and prepared for: especially when dealing with a 'classic' author such help is more than necessary. It usually concerns old or obsolete expressions, words which have changed their meaning meanwhile, but also vocabulary peculiarities of the author himself and sometimes sentence structures which are difficult to understand. Moreover, not all scenes and contexts in Don Carlos can be puzzled out on first attempt, especially where plotted intrigues, cleverly concocted secret plans, are concerned, such as Schiller often has recourse to. Since I knew full well that I, too, had to make the effort, among other things, to know all characters, intentions, and strands of plot at all times, I ensured the students' understanding of what they had read by frequent open questioning.

I could also use this opportunity to refer to some preliminary topics. For example it is quite unavoidable to mention Schiller's idiomatic peculiarities, his often complicated sentence structure and word order, his style: his use of pathos, metaphor, rhetoric, and such like in composition. It is also an advantage to consider the structural law of composition, since this can be recognized only by studying the peculiar type of dramatic start of the play itself. Beyond that I asked the students for their first, uncommitted, subjective impressions of the play. What did grip their attention? How dramatically tense was the play? Had they been prepared for the conflicts to come? In short, there are a plethora of possibilities profitably to exploit and diversify the preliminary questioning phase. I might add that a few indispensable bio- and bibliographical details could also be introduced at this stage.

Compared with the alternative didactic approach, to expect the students to read at home one or two scenes or passages at a time for each lesson, for example, I consider the procedure just mentioned as much more appropriate for co-operative learning. For the fundamental essence of real or fictitious characters has to be explored holistically, in the fullness of time or not at all. Especially in dramatic contexts it is inextricably interwoven in the dovetailing and succession of criss-crossing, interpenetrating, contradictory actions and situations, and it cannot be grasped in isolation from them. Indeed, to recognize it, it is necessary to know the entire play beforehand. The piecemeal or 'slicing' technique on the other hand, impedes, prevents, or negates the whole effect of co-operative learning.

The appropriate didactic preparation constituted the second step towards co-operative learning. I will now turn to the third. This consists in the particular use of teaching strategies and begins therefore with the first lesson in class after reading the play at home. The content of this lesson was essentially determined by the elaboration of a complete, lucid 'content' statement of the plot of the play. All students should have a sufficiently clear, precise, and appropriate picture of the action before them. It is a basic condition for successful co-operative learning in this case. You can only judge and evaluate when you are in possession of the necessary facts. In open classroom discussion therefore we complemented and corrected each others' understanding of the play and explored those aspects, hidden or uncertain. In the case of slower or weaker pupils we made sure by using supplementary questions that they too had an adequate and firm base for comprehension.

However, this lesson served another purpose too: we combined the simple summary of the plot with the 'weighting' of the component parts in relation to each other and to the whole of the play, the 'core'. This 'weighting' of different parts for their significance is, as is well known, no simple task for students of this age and is a special achievement when it succeeds. But how is one to evaluate an action, the significance of which escapes one? In this sense 'weighting' of the individual parts (acts, scenes, dialogue, monologues) is not only an indispensable precondition for successful co-operative learning, but also an important contribution in kind made by the students themselves. In our case 'weighting' showed that the struggle for freedom of thought and conscience lies at the centre of the play. Around this central 'theme', which is formulated particularly clearly in a number of dialogues, are ranged some additional problems and conflicts, such as the risk of loss of friendship, the crisis of the raison d'état, the value of religious dogma plus some minor irritations caused by love, striving for personal happiness and so on. Most of this was discovered in the process of classroom discussion, following the students' own interpretation of the play. It was indeed a rich and rewarding period; following its findings we could start in the next lesson with what I wish to call unravelling the 'intention' of the play. By this I mean its 'educational purpose', that students will acknowledge the text or some definite parts of it as a source of relevance to their life's experience. Here too it was necessary to make a choice, and quite deliberately I selected the passage, which illustrates most clearly and convincingly humanity's ethical, moral conflict. The demand for the suitability of a text for successful co-operative learning is met, in my view, best by the transition, extending over several scenes, of Posa's act of winning the king's confidence only to exploit this newly found position of trust for implementing his own ideas and plans. Here the Hegelian moral dichotomy opens up which occurs in the midst of the question of 'good', the question which is at the centre of all ethical thinking. Since students at this age often find themselves in an important value crisis which to a large degree affects their lives and since often they do not even know how to set about to perceive what is good, their concern with moral problems coincides with their intention of finding a meaning for them which can help them with life's problems. It is here that co-operative learning must be firmly anchored.

However, the selection of the textual passage alone is not sufficient. It must be supplemented by an appropriate approach to deal with it. Indeed, there is a particular, most urgent reason for my emphasizing this point. For in recent years in the Federal Republic it has become customary to publish school texts of all kinds, including those by 'classical' authors, in a ready-to-use form, equipped with leading questions, method suggestions, and other teaching aids. This leads to the paradox that the avowed aim, to improve the quality of teaching, that is in the case of co-operative learning at least, is turned into its opposite, and changes the quality decisively for the worse. Quite apart from the fact that there is no such thing as an interpretation 'as such', indeed it is an impossibility, the numerous aids actually deprive the student of that most pregnant of all pedagogic moments, the astonished shock of recognition, the onset of the awareness of the existence of a problem in their own minds and the realization that the fictional character, say that of the Marquis of Posa, has something to say to them too. The use of such guide-books robs the students of the highest thing on offer, the revelation the text itself can provide; and all because of some completely unnecessary ready-made interpretations; a handicap which has the effect of preventing them from letting themselves be affected by their own reading experience. It is no help either that ethical values are 'discussed' and the student's knowledge instantly assessed and awarded marks in a written essay, in many cases obligingly supplied by the publisher. The only efficacious remedy is the method which takes co-operative learning on board and which takes the absolutely personal and independent problem-finding and the search for a sense of purpose by the student as its starting-point.

I earmarked three lessons for the actual 'theme' of co-operative learning and in doing so I was guided by my own, earlier experience. I will now turn to the first of these three lessons. First of all I asked the students for their own opinion of Posa and I referred once more to his duplicity in his relation to Philip II. It soon became clear that there was no unanimity on this point. There were some widely differing, partly divergent and controversial concepts. We decided on letting a number of students who wanted to answer the question make their statements without any comment. I took no position, agreeing with no one, nor did I let on whether I was more inclined towards this or that view. We called this part of the lesson a 'gathering'. First of all you have to gather in what there 'is', and what 'is' does in fact produce a broad and multicoloured canvas. Without the carefully aimed triggering off mechanism at the start of the lesson (the initial question) the whole thing would become vague and diffuse.

Then, in the next part of the lesson, I exploited the yield achieved and thereby set the first concrete operation of co-operative learning in motion. I asked student A if he could imagine the reasons which had prompted student B to present a view contrary to his own. That is if he thought that B too might perhaps not be altogether wrong. Student A answered in the affirmative. Immediately I repeated the procedure with student B and asked her the same question about student A. Here too the answer was in the affirmative. This means it can be argued that something was happening here, that could be called group awareness, a sensitivity to others, which is, in my view, the decisive basis of practical, social, co-operative learning in action. The students learn at the same time how to behave socially, in the sense of social co-operative learning.

What then is this group awareness, this sensitizing to others? It is in fact what social co-operative learning is all about that individuals respect one another, pay attention to them, listen to them, and take them seriously as their partners. Particularly it means that one's neighbour abandons for the duration of the lesson the role of competitor or rival to assume instead that of an interested discussion partner. It represents a turn of 180 degrees in the social perspective you have of your fellow student. Both students experience each other with reversed symptoms, the usual and expected competition (the most advantageous place in battle) is replaced by co-operation in the attempt to discover the highest possible degree of 'truth' by the entire team. This procedure which assumes honest answers and the fullest use of group work, though answers may be supplied by individuals, results in students' revising their opinions in the course of the lesson, enriching them with borrowings from others, and thus differentiating more and providing more subtle and careful solutions. Co-operative learning is impossible without this deliberate, self-critical attempt by means of which one's fellow student ceases to be a rival and becomes a collaborator with respect to one's own opinion-forming. In the following phase then, with due logic, the interaction which had occurred between students A and B was extended to as many as possible, indeed all other students in the class.

I continued therefore, helped by some students, to ask for further comments, and new points of view. It became apparent that the general wish to participate in this open teaching situation increased as we went along. The pattern was to apply model 'A and B' to C, D, E, and so on, so that the interaction network became increasingly tighter and more variegated, since obviously, F for example, referred not only to A and B but also to C and D, E and so on, in order to ponder the situation between them. I might add at this point in the lesson I was not unmoved to experience with the students how these young people argued with each other with tremendous earnestness and manifest honesty in their search for 'truth'. It was a significant emotional experience which only confirmed my resolve to refine further my method of social consciousness formation and students' sensitivity. The lesson ended without any kind of conclusion; instead it resulted in a most interesting restructuring of the entire class. It transpired that four larger groupings came into being, one around student A, one around B, a third which agreed with neither, and a fourth inconclusive one. None of the groups was homogeneous and the boundaries between them were fluid. I could also see that the degree of mutual tolerance quickly increased. The students' preparation for the next lesson was to produce a written record of the one just ended.

This brings me to the second lesson with a co-operative learning theme. Its centre-piece was marked by reflection on and consolidation of all that the students had contributed in the preceding lesson with spontaneous creativity and therefore largely subjectively. We based ourselves especially on the available written records ('minutes'). Unfortunately, because of the rather large number of students in the class, we had to confine ourselves to sampling. For the evaluation of samples I used the same approach as in the previous lesson. Several students wanted to read their version of the minutes. This choice of who should read first was arbitrary, after the first presentation; however, I asked the students whether anyone had produced a completely different account, and I asked that one to read it in turn. This resulted in another dialectical confrontation of thesis and antithesis. I had to be careful however not to ask the same students (those who had been prominent in setting the tone in the previous lesson) but to choose those who were inclined to be somewhat reluctant or retiring. The production of written minutes is an excellent opportunity to entice the quieter students to abandon their reticence, and this is surely an integral part of co-operative learning. I will return to this point later.

The next step was to ask the students once again, which set of minutes reflected the previous lesson better, which was 'right' so to speak. We soon found out that each set of minutes in its own way contained most of the essential information, therefore each included some objective and some subjective elements. We agreed in fact that they complemented each other in a positive way and when taken together provided a kind of super set of minutes. To test this for actual examples I asked if any students thought that their minutes occupied a place somewhere in the middle between the two others which I now proceeded to call T (thesis) and A (antithesis). We quickly found a student who would then be asked to read his version. It confirmed that in a number of important points it agreed with T and A, but it nevertheless betrayed also in some traits the personality of its author. We called the third version S (synthesis) because we felt it combined elements from both T and A. At this juncture I gave the class a brief sketch of Hegel's dialectic principle and referred the students to the didactically as well as pedagogically productive idea that in S, T and A cancel each other out. If we translate this idea into learning method then obviously co-operative learning is the result, quite apart from the insight students gain into one of the most influential ideas of the western world. To illustrate it further I transferred, analogously to the previous lesson, the pattern which had emerged between T, A, and S to other students by taking S as the new T at the next stage and then asking the students to look for a new A (T and A): in short we refined the concept. There was no homework after the lesson. In any case the open class discussion had encouraged most students to continue the discussion. Pedantic insistence on formality and a fully programmed lesson is educationally unsound.

The third lesson, itself an S to the T and A of the previous two, was intended as a résumé of the results so far to provide a statement limited as to content and its interpretatory exploitation. It was the last session given over to the central theme of co-operative learning. It started with a concise statement by me in which I linked together our efforts and findings up to that point without, however, attempting to draw any conclusions. This the students were to do for themselves. A sort of questionnaire was suggested as the best means to achieve this and I dictated to the students the text of a total of seven verdict categories according to which they were to rank the moral behaviour of the Marquis of Posa: (1) impeccable, (2) good, but not without misgiving, (3) plus and minus equal, (4) no opinion, (5) misgivings predominate, (6) I find little that is good, (7) totally reprehensible. Each student could tick only one of these verdict categories. They were given a few minutes in which to consider their verdicts and we collected the voting slips. The result was what I had expected it would be. Some two-thirds of all students voted for category 2 (good, but not without misgivings), a view which I shared. A considerable distance behind in second place came category 3 (plus and minus equal). The rest was divided among the remaining five categories and can be ignored for our purpose. The results were communicated to the class, and only at this point did I give my own opinion. After this I requested the students to compare the end result as announced with the first, uncommitted opinion given in the first lesson of the lessons sequence given over to the theme of co-operative learning. We very quickly concluded that most of us had learned to modify our opinion, and that in two respects: on the one hand under the impression and influence of our fellow students' opinions if these were well supported by argument, and on the other with the growing tendency to differentiate more finely. It also became clear that the more extreme 'radical' positions yielded in favour to the more moderate ones. Thus an important effect of co-operative learning had been not only achieved but also empirically demonstrated. Many of the students had understood it in this way.

The result of the questionnaire, however, also pointed in another direction, important for the evaluation of a work of literature: the author. For surely it was necessary to ask how Schiller succeeded in putting such complicated contents into such a clear form, so that, as proved by the questionnaire, it was possible to arrive at a relatively unambiguous understanding. As is well known, this is the more difficult and rarer, the more demanding and sophisticated the problem. Usually total unanimity of interpretation can be achieved only at the price of total banality. Nor can this question be separated from another one with which it is most closely linked: the psychological one, as to the personality of the author under these conditions. With this part of the lesson sequence completed, our co-operative learning trials returned to more literary specific considerations.

However, I see the theme just mentioned as entirely appropriate and well established within the framework of co-operative learning, for the first question concerns obviously the distance in time which separates Schiller from us and it requires from us the 'imaginative leap' to engage with it and to shed, as far as possible, the prejudices of our own epoch! Whoever has had much to do with such procedures will know how difficult this can be at times, and not just for one's students. But the effect is obvious. Once again it is that it enables one to distance oneself a bit from one's self to find something rather more general, something valid across the times, in another being, and it stands to reason that one distinguishes quite clearly between those elements which are bound to a specific period and those which are free of the constraints of their own time. With that we returned to certain considerations of the first lesson period. I could again latch on to the idiosyncrasies of the text and to ask this aesthetically most productive of questions as to a possible conditioned link between content and form. Adequacy of form (see pp. 154-6, lesson one) in regard to content is one of the decisive criteria for the literary quality of a text, as well as throwing a significant light on its author. Many of the students admitted, as was shown in the lessons, they could easily imagine themselves facing a situation with a similar moral dilemma as the Marquis of Posa. Co-operative learning for social and personal development in this case meant that you assume another person's problem and try to do it justice. The students were practically unanimous on the point that the text, despite the often rather off-putting (for us) exterior appearance, is by no means merely of antiquarian interest.

This attitude of taking things seriously, attentive listening, careful and sustained contemplation, which we have recognized as the basis of successful collaborative learning in class and tried to encourage now extends to the person of the author and thus receives a deeper significance by reference to him. Schiller has become for the students, not just a lesson topic which may even help you get good marks if you work hard at it but, and this is the new element, an important human being, who must be taken seriously and whose work qualifies to be studied, because it has something significant to say to you as a person. If, for example, I reflect Posa's situation then he is reflected in my ego and this makes a number of things more easily comprehensible for me than before. Seen in this way he provides a lifeline for me.

While elaborating these last mentioned points a particular circumstance was of great help to us. In its present form, with its many characters, problems, and plots Schiller's <u>Don Carlos</u> is almost entirely fictional, and it is absolutely marvellous how such a comprehensive work is the product of the mind of a single individual. It is most important to allow the students to arrive at realizing that this is so. (No, it is not self-evident!) It is precisely the fact that Schiller had altered reality to suit his purpose which is especially significant. Come to think of it as far as historical reality is concerned, Schiller had used practically nothing but the external formal conventions (place, time, names); as against that, almost the entire 'interior' circumstances he produced himself. He thus lives himself in this unmistakably autonomous, imaginative world of his own creation, is reflected in it and together with it forms part of the theme. You can see from the struggles of the characters, that it is the author's own struggle; to articulate which, to bring it to the fore, must be seen as the best motivation for writing the play. What we wanted to say is that Schiller tried to gain a sense of purpose for his own life by writing <u>Don Carlos</u> and in so doing he shows that it is possible for others to do the same.

The topic 'sense of purpose' was of course most important for that group of students who needed it most, that is those inclined to self doubt, who were most uncertain, shy, and anxious. Among them there were mostly those who I knew saw no sense any more in making an effort, or exerting themselves to concentrate on anything. These students are often misrepresented, and are labelled 'lazy', 'uninterested', 'untalented'. However, in reality all that has happened is that in the process of growing up, particularly in puberty, they have lost their 'sense of purpose' which at one time used to be provided by their parents. There is the danger that this loss of sense of purpose affects not just their school behaviour, but their future lives beyond that. I will not go into detail, describing symptoms of phenomena which are generally well known, except to mention the dangerously growing incidence of drug-taking and suicide.

We could see that the co-operative learning method which takes the sense of purpose as its point of departure was well suited to thaw out students. It was indeed revealing to see how those students whose 'ice' was 'thickest' would model themselves on those who hesitated less. There was an atmosphere of mutual encouragement: co-operative, personal, and social learning, which became a practical example of a lifeline, self-help. It should be added that diffident students, once they did become active, generally suffered no relapse. On the contrary, their achievements improved as their self-confidence grew and we watched how several managed to overcome their original fears and reticence. They once more saw a sense of purpose in concentrating on a problem they could come to grips with themselves. Personally I was amazed by the speed with which certain individuals had changed their attitudes. It was like a sudden awakening.

A brief note about literature and co-operative learning to conclude this section. Clearly the latter method can be equally successful with other subjects, indeed in the discussion of students' own problems. However, unlike the case of your personal experience, when studying literature you can distance yourself from your own personality and explore yourself without the initial stumbling block of inhibition. The choice of text is crucial.

This report would be incomplete and misleading if I did

not mention the negative experiences I have had with co-operative learning and their main cause is time. Co-operative learning costs time, more time than it takes to recite the ten times table. For someone who rejects this method on principle the time spent on it is time wasted. It is obvious that teachers are faced with the alternative: to use the time at their disposal to dispense as much factual 'information' as possible, or to develop their students' own exploratory capacity. I will demonstrate this briefly with an example.

The result obtained at the end of the third co-operative learning lesson with the active participation and co-operation of a number of students could easily have been anticipated by me at the beginning of the first lesson, 'to save time'. Perhaps the lesson could have started with a remark by me that Posa may indeed want to do good, but in so doing shows a certain lack of fairness towards King Philip. This may not be the right thing to do but is unavoidable in the circumstances. That is life. Or I could have made the comment that Posa's action must be rejected on principle, since in moral terms he has committed an act of breaking faith with the king. Thus all his efforts on behalf of his friend Don Carlos and the freedom of the Netherlands are morally speaking worthless. His action is inexcusable and so on. We could have saved ourselves nearly three hours of time, the more quickly to complete the 'teaching' of Don Carlos or, indeed, to start on another text. I could have said in three minutes what took us three hours of time, almost one full teaching week for the subject. If the co-operative learning approach is replicated over the entire school year, or indeed if it is raised to a paramount teaching principle, then you can easily work out how soon you will fall in arrears compared with colleagues who gain time. For isn't the best teacher the one who has 'taught' most subject matter? There is the further consideration that the results of co-operative learning are difficult, if not impossible, to express in terms of percentage marks. Unfortunately measuring achievement plays a considerable role in educational circles in the Federal Republic and elsewhere where it is said to raise comparability. Many of our educationalists see here a contribution for improving students' opportunities and thus ensuring social equality. And yet it should be obvious that in this way, under the guise of social equality the students are given a dis-service and deprived of education as opposed to training. I regard

165

this link as crucial in any assessment of co-operative learning, for all depends on a detailed, very thorough, and very careful evaluation of the results of upbringing which must be undertaken by those responsible. I would find a full discussion of this last point very tempting, but realize it would take up too much space and anyway it is a topic of its own. I will therefore return once more to the concrete, practical difficulties which I have experienced, when using the co-operative approach, which of course have their own system specific causes. Since co-operative learning does not take place in a vacuum, but must be inserted into an already existing school structure, its opponents turn against an innovation, whose ethos in many ways seems radically to run counter to the traditional trend. What this means is what I have observed: the repudiation of co-operative learning is often justified by an appeal to the emotions. Haven't we had enough reforms in the last few years? This objection is voiced by a sizeable minority of parents. But parents also have another argument to hand: they fear that their child will receive too little tangible instruction. Now this has two drawbacks. On the one hand, teachers who do not know co-operative learning and who have taken over from one who did use the method, expect more in terms of content knowledge, making unjustified demands on the students. They will either cram in all haste what subject matter in their opinion the students have missed and which they consider essential, overloading their students with extra work and ranging themselves self-righteously on the side of enemies of co-operative learning.

It has been my experience that in the last few years the responsibility for this state of affairs at least in the Federal Republic lies with an over-intense preoccupation with centrally prescribed subject syllabuses. The central curricula and syllabuses which have been formulated in the Federal Republic in recent years have shared three main characteristics. First, they have adopted a pedagogical theory based on the taxonomy of educational objectives about which there has been a good deal of specialist literature. Second, there has been the over-zealous aim of doing justice so far as possible to all educational implications of the school subject. Third, within the official syllabus and the outcomes it seeks to assess, such factors as consideration for others and the provision of a relaxed experimental climate find no place. In contrast to this, the patterns of co-operative learning here described assume the use of appropriate 'curricular gaps' rather than rigidly prescribed syllabuses.

The other drawback was seen by some parents who felt that their offspring would be leaving school for the professions or university with too little knowledge. Only a well-constructed pupil-oriented 'theory of knowledge' which the teacher can explain to the parents can help this state of affairs. I wish only briefly to mention that there exists a number of shocking investigations which attempt to show how little 'remains' if one still believes in the reliability of behaviouristic or allied learning theories. The high percentage of 'subject matter' simply forgotten after a short lapse of time is frightening, whereas what has been affectively and socially (indeed co-operatively) acquired is still largely or even entirely proof against forgetting (oblivion resistant). Some students too, it must be said, expressed similar doubts about this style of teaching. They were the ones that are referred to as 'achievement conscious', and inevitably those least inclined to co-operate with their classmates. Opposition to co-operative learning must also be expected from this quarter which sees school as a kind of knowledge supermarket.

The saddest thing of all I will leave till last: it is only fair to warn co-operative learning enthusiasts! To cap it all, I had difficulties with the headteacher of my school. He saw his duty in ensuring that the teaching programme (Lehrplan) was strictly adhered to by all teachers, in as nigh a perfect co-ordination of concerted time and subject matter action in parallel classes. Since in the Federal Republic teachers who neglect their duties can be challenged by an administrative tribunal, and since many headteachers will regard the exact observance of the centrally laid down curricula as one of the more noble of a teacher's duties (to be sure, they too are appraised according to the assessed achievements of their schools) there were not infrequently often unpleasant exchanges between the headteacher and myself. The purpose and the value of co-operative learning cannot be negotiated just like that, without a good deal of enlightened explanation beforehand.

After nearly forty years as a senior teacher in my Gymnasium, I confess to being a convinced adherent of the practice of co-operative learning for personal and social development, as one means to help young people in crises. To those who claim to have overcome problems with puberty and others, I retort: are you sure? Is there not in all of us

167

something that we have failed to come to terms with, something that makes our lives more difficult? Besides, have there not meanwhile been some changes in this world of ours? The general loss of precisely the sense of purpose, not least among adults, has grown: a trend that, alas, is likely to grow still further.

Co-operative learning has come about as a result of the demands of our time; education has always been conditioned by circumstances and has an adapting historical function. This function is first and foremost that of enabling the younger generations to live in a world of change. And I do not share the pessimism of those who claim that the time of 'enlightenment' has passed and that our epoch is characterized by a radical pessimism. A pessimist cannot be a teacher: that is a contradiction. But I believe, following a critical optimistic stance, that co-operative learning is one of the most urgent pedagogical tasks of our time, at the same time much remains to be done to perfect the approach and to carry it through not least in the education and training of new teachers.

Chapter Nine

KNOWLEDGE OR COMMUNICATION: TOWARDS A NEW
ROLE FOR MODERN FOREIGN LANGUAGES IN THE
SCHOOL CURRICULUM

Witold Tulasiewicz

INTRODUCTION

Modern foreign languages is a difficult subject to
accommodate in the school curriculum. Most young people
do not often find themselves in a situation where they have
to send messages in another language, and they are
especially reluctant, if in order to do so, they have to learn
the other language first. They have after all a vehicle of
communication in their own language. In any case, even
after studying a foreign language at school, students are
usually incapable of saying what they really want to say in
that language. Language is so much an integral part of
human personality that we are impatient when our ideas
outrun our limited competencies in the foreign medium, and
we turn to our mother tongue to help ourselves out.

The concern in modern foreign language teaching in
school has been on correct or incorrect language, and on
knowledge of language (grammar), with little notice taken
of the factor of acceptability, the comprehension of the
message alone as a worthwhile objective for the learner to
strive for. Since we can communicate without an absolutely
correct command of a language, the undue emphasis on a
piece of faultless language structure is a cause of student
frustration. Unlike other creative subjects, art for example,
the foreign language has to be taught to students in their
native environment of the classroom; they do not normally
find it for themselves. It relies on a handed-down body of
language and does not lend itself readily to discovery
methods of teaching. Those who invent a private language
can do so within a setting of their own choosing; they do not

have to comply with the classroom constraints of imposed group learning, which is particularly irksome in modern foreign language lessons, when compared with school subjects in which the student can talk more freely. In any case, the individual's primary needs and experience are normally catered for within the confines of the mother tongue; foreign or invented languages which are not so closely linked with them usually meet the individual's secondary needs only.

Social intercourse, therefore, with speakers of another language, which requires a minimum of active and passive knowledge of the other language, must be firmly recognized as a need, a product to possess before it can produce the motivation necessary to learn that language. This motivation is conspicuously absent in modern foreign language teaching in school. Nor has it traditionally been accepted that the modern foreign language learning process can be expedited with the help of the mother tongue, with the latter often banned from foreign language lessons. Creating a foreign corner in the classroom to help student motivation is difficult. The question whether natives or foreign nationals are better qualified to be entrusted with teaching the foreign language has been asked, but the further isolation of modern foreign languages from other subjects in the school curriculum, which may arise from choosing a foreigner as teacher, complicates the issue. In Britain the status of English and American English as world languages adds to the students' low motivational factor. As a legacy of the political and economic past, Anglo-Saxon culture is readily accepted even in parts of the world where Russian language and culture might be expected to provide a popular subject for study, with young people in Poland and Yugoslavia, let alone in the Federal Republic of Germany, showing a strong interest in Anglo-Saxon culture, which cannot be matched by an equally strong interest in German or French in British schools.

More than other subjects of the school curriculum, modern foreign languages splits unequally into purely skill and intellectual content/concepts sides. It can be pursued for the acquisition of mere skills or to provide an education, in other words the way it is usually taught, it is a primary or even nursery school subject taught at the secondary level, or a completely out-of-school pursuit. It has been taught in school through 'drill and skills' methods, when teaching as an intellectual activity was expected, and indeed the opposite, when an academic approach was used to teach it to 8-year-old children. Though this sort of thing may still be accepted in the case of more narrowly conceived 'traditional' school subjects, it is difficult in a living language, which is therefore bound to fit badly in any school setting.

Not surprisingly perhaps, it has been suggested by that educator extraordinary, Harry Rée, that foreign languages be taught entirely outside the school context: a suggestion rarely seriously considered for other school subjects. Small wonder that in many countries teaching modern foreign languages in school, indeed also in those multicultural and multilingual societies where the knowledge of another language would be useful for a variety of practical reasons, has often been opposed by cultural identity preservation enthusiasts who wish to promote their own mother tongue. Many speakers of ethnic languages in Britain would subscribe to this view.

This chapter looks at the situation of modern foreign languages as a school subject in the United Kingdom, with particular reference to their assumed educational and social values, while considering the role the mother tongue can play in the classroom.

TRADITIONAL METHODS OF TEACHING FOREIGN LANGUAGES

Since classical languages were taught for their intellectual and cultural values, the 'simple' linguistic proficiency and communicative skills of modern foreign languages were regarded as rather more marginal to the school's educational objectives. The primacy of conceptual academic learning, particularly at the secondary level was reinforced by the lack of respect for 'skills' which were thought to be easily acquired through the process of mere instruction, picked up in the street or indeed, on the job.

British schools have traditionally aimed to educate students rather than to instruct them. The names of nineteenth-century Abbotsholme and twentieth-century Summerhill or Stantonbury, the open-plan primary school methods, known from before the Plowden Report, stand for hundreds of other schools and innovatory educational practices which have inspired generations of educators. This comment also applies to those schools which have drilled into their students the values of patriotic service and submission to authority. The British contribution to education has been strongest in the non-instrumental area, the extra-curricular, institutional practices, like student involvement in the running of the school, the 'pastoral' duties of the teacher standing in for the parents, or the importance attached to physical, as well as character education through games or sports. The English all-day school, often fee-paying and independent of the local education authority, founded for a specific educational purpose, has long been recognized as a community, its teaching programme going beyond the purely cognitive, technical or vocational development of the student. (1) It is the school which for many students represents 'real' life, a reality often stronger than the home, the church, or the sports club, confirmed by old boys' and old girls' gatherings, which, though most frequent in the independent 'public' schools, have also been encouraged in the LEA-maintained or church-controlled schools. Parents' expectations of their children's school are stronger in Britain, where the practice of entrusting one's child to the school is much stronger than in countries where the home has played a more active part in children's education. If the acquisition of skills has been a problematic task, no doubt students' and staffs' attitudes to the role of modern foreign languages will also have been affected by the school.

The English public school traditionally educated the future administrators, top soldiers, and, in so far as they were accorded a distinctive status, businessmen, through what might appear as a narrow curriculum, represented by the multifaceted complexities of one school discipline, notably classics. However, long before the Leathes Report of 1918, (2) which made out a convincing case for the educational value of modern languages, or what was also known as modern studies, 'every highly developed language affords scope for the exercise of distinguished talents', there had been schools, mostly independent ones, concentrating on modern foreign languages as providing 'a proper education'. This educational concept of a curriculum which includes a full course in modern foreign languages had been gradually extended to LEA-maintained selective secondary schools, and after the Second World War, also to non-selective ('modern') schools. The comprehensive schools have carried it on.

The change in status from an optional to a generally available school subject complicated the problem of accommodating a modern foreign languages course which would be educationally complete (and which for many students was rounded off by a university degree) within compulsory schooling terminating at the age of 15. This was regardless of whether the aims of education emphasized the student's personal or social development. The expansion also had implications for the staffing of the new courses. The dissatisfaction with foreign languages in school was compounded by the exaggerated, vague educational aims and claims for the subject which took scarcely any notice of the learning reality and expectations of the student majority: conflicting aims of education on offer, little guidance on respectable and realistically achievable objectives and teaching styles which were totally unadjusted to the different types of student. Courses would concentrate on the academic or aesthetic pursuits, like teaching French literature rather than communication in French or English, as in the rest of Europe, a content and method which showed no concern with the future employment, in which languages would figure, indeed life-styles of the non-academically motivated early school-leavers. This did nothing to combat the students' ethnocentricity, their suspicion of foreign languages and their speakers. Although students could opt out of modern foreign language courses in school without finishing them, curriculum planning had little regard for the fact that incomplete programmes, which did not fulfil their objectives, further alienated school-leavers who left school without obtaining a complete 'education through the foreign language'. If post-1945 social policies in the United Kingdom, until the early 1980s at least, gave equality of educational opportunity and provision to all students, and this included the introduction of modern foreign languages into the curriculum of all schools, (3) the figures for students actually taking modern language courses were appalling: out of 89 per cent of 11-year-olds starting a language in 1977 (in the 1960s it was 25 per cent) only 35 per cent were still carrying on with the language at the age of 14 and only one out of ten, some 8 per cent of students that is, passed the Ordinary Level GCE examination at 16 or so.

RECENT INITIATIVES

Various initiatives for extending the place of modern

173

languages in the curriculum, like the Annan Report (on the teaching of Russian in schools) and the Schools Council Working Paper on the introduction of French into the primary schools, were abandoned, in the latter case when it was found that no improved academic education resulted after an earlier exposure to a foreign language. (4) Though often a positive attitude, an interest in the other country and its people did result from early teaching, the academic, purely cognitive view of the role of modern foreign languages in school prevailed over the affective and social, leading to their abandonment at various points in students' careers. Aims, methods, and the surrender value in commercial terms were in conflict. The failure of the subject has reflected its class character, with only the independent (with their own methods of selection) and the selection-by-ability grammar schools guaranteeing a 'complete, humanities education' through modern languages, objectives which the LEA-maintained, non-selective schools, thwarted by early leaving and other factors, could not meet. This situation persisted well into the 1970s.

By that time the exaggerated educational claims of modern languages in the curriculum were being questioned. A comparison of two Scottish documents on modern foreign language teaching (1950 and 1972) shows that the latter document had abandoned the rhetoric of the earlier one. (5) The 1977 HM Inspectorate's Report, Modern Languages in the Comprehensive School, notes the 'unsuitable objectives' set. (6) However, in suggesting a sliding scale of syllabus goals, with less expected of the less able students, it proposed a quantitative not a qualitative remedy. It did not consider the fact that less able students may not necessarily wish to communicate less, nor how their different type of language interest could be fostered. A reappraisal of the language learning reality of the majority of students: poor motivation in view of the unsuitable objectives in terms of the foreign language matter studied and little account taken of the realization of objectives likely to affect the average student's future situation had not taken place. Poor allocation of time and other resources remained. Reduced contents courses could provide neither the full conversational skills nor the language education expected. Though identifying the different groups of learners of modern foreign languages, most teachers and advisers still accepted the largely linear view of foreign language learning, requiring a step-by-step acquisition of the language skills as a first hurdle to be taken, before the next one, education through language, could be attempted. This also continued the divisive homogeneous ability groupings and norm-referenced testing of language learners resulting from it. Courses more specifically designed with a view to the needs of the majority, however, were about to arrive.

A re-examination of the educational aims and objectives of the school enabled a fresh look to be taken at various areas of what was known as students' educational experience, achieved at school, and the distinctive contribution made by various school subject syllabuses to their development. This was receiving renewed interest in the 1970s, for example in the Curriculum 11-16 Working Papers. (7) No general agreement on this was possible, of course, because the gap between the students' own perceived language needs, and the normative view of what they should be taught to be able to enjoy the educational benefits of modern languages as a school subject, was greater in language, because of its specific nature, than in other subjects. The problem, therefore, was whether there should be different syllabuses for different learners' individual needs, or whether the same syllabus (a common syllabus available at least at the start of a course) should be taught using different methods and exploiting different strategies. However, the concept of global strategies, with the same contents and identical approaches for all students, was being redefined. Both contents and methods came under scrutiny, albeit with different suggestions emerging. One solution, bypassing the organizational and perceptive skills of the traditional linear teaching of modern foreign languages and a rapid progression to students' thematic-semantic reactions to foreign culture, when learning French car registration numbers for example, a common enough topic in the subject European Studies, being introduced into schools for the weaker students in the 1970s, or as one teacher put it to the author, 'colouring Napoleon's trousers', was regarded as not providing a worthwhile language education. Students were missing the distinctive motor perceptive and cognitive skills associated with language learning, when confined to colouring illustrations. If because of unsuitable teaching methods they had found the former difficult, the latter in the circumstances they were taught were too easy by far.

We will not pursue the question of what academic ability (if any) is required to learn a modern foreign language outside the school. The elitist status of modern foreign languages in schools had assumed that 'real' education would begin after some language skills had been acquired. Clearly the school context tends to emphasize the cognitive area of learning, thus making the subject more difficult for some students.

SPECIFIC CURRICULUM DEVELOPMENTS

The two curriculum developments which have affected modern foreign language teaching of which only the second is language specific, will now be examined in more detail.

The first breakthrough came with the re-emergence of the concept of students' areas of educational experience: linguistic, literary, aesthetic, creative, ethical, social, political, mathematical, scientific, spiritual, and others, acquired in their learning process across different school subjects. A linguistic experience, for example, is not achieved exclusively through learning a language, but can be acquired also in the 'language' of science or mathematics. The argument could be pursued that knowledge of a language or its culture can, if properly learnt and facilitated by sensitive teaching, provide an educational experience in a variety of areas: social (contact with and tolerance of others), aesthetic (appreciation of language structure or its literature) or psycho-motor (pronunciation, rhythm, intonation), for example by diverting language teaching from an exclusive preoccupation with factual, cognitive learning to concerns with attitudes, skills, and aptitudes generated by the subject. This development was strengthened by collaborative learning styles, improved interpersonal relations in class with fellow students as well as the teacher, seen as a moderator or facilitator, with a new way of dealing with the students' mistakes or difficulties. The teacher's role was crucial especially in modern foreign languages, which are difficult to acquire at home without sympathetic help and a skilful provision of resources. This is because they are more difficult to spot at home than cultural, natural, or economic phenomena for example, which can be seen through the student's mother tongue. Adults, of course, may be differently motivated and see things differently.

A small research project conducted in Mainz and Cambridge into students' own views of the popularity of their school subjects (not seen in the usual terms of their appropriateness as a preparation for future employment, but addressing their impact on students' personal and social development) setting up categories like: student-centredness (addressing students' own problems and life in and outside of school), help with social contacts (including peer groups, and parents), flexibility and adaptability of the syllabus to students' needs, revealed some interesting facts. (8) In the Cambridge area two different foreign languages were given a different popularity rating, proof that factors like the timing of the introduction of the subject, the teacher's teaching style, and the learning environment were just as important for the students as the subject content. Not all foreign languages were regarded as equally redundant or alien commodities delivered in an alien medium.

What then was accepted as constituting an educational experience through language? In modern foreign languages student-centredness and relevance, apart from language learning considerations, were adopted and developed in student-chosen topics of study, in the form of European (or French) Studies, exercises considered to be especially appropriate for the less able students. (9) Topics like the home, the family, car travel abroad, taught simple language functions to the majority of students through what was felt to be content areas of interest. These studies on their own, however, were not considered challenging and stimulating enough to provide an educational experience through language in the accepted academic sense for even the least motivated students. Moreover, the opportunity for serious, integrated work focusing on Europe or the European Community theme related to the European languages taught was not seized, not even with the brighter students. Developments with 'European awareness' at the Supporting Level of the Advanced Level (GCE A/S) had to wait until the late 1980s. The thematic European studies approach thus had revealed some serious drawbacks; 'colouring Napoleon's trousers' was indeed a counsel of despair.

The second breakthrough came with the reassessment of the status of the five language skills, acknowledging their possession at any level as a legitimate educational objective, and not just an activity pursued anywhere with little intellectual effort. This was due to the acceptance of the fact that even a little communicative knowledge could help develop the student's personality, which coupled with the increased interest shown in foreign language skills by

177

industry, a recognition of the desirability of social integration, became an extension of the original concept of 'education through language'. The newly defined subject of modern foreign languages could be seen to contribute to developing both linguistic and non-linguistic skills, attitudes as well as knowledge: cultural and linguistic awareness, business and social skills, to name but some. In this approach the minimal functional conversational units, the topics of student interest, like the home, travel, but also the wider European studies, were practised not so much for their non-linguistic content, the students' personal ability and their relevance for them, as in the first development, but precisely for their communicative, their language function. Once again the linear methods of the study of language were discarded in favour of self-contained conversational units, starting at the lowest level of meaningful communication with others, or self-expression, taught through language games, role-play, pattern recognition, and memorization. Also in this development the personal involvement of the student rather than the subject structure was taken as the point of departure. This approach accepted the purpose of the speech act. (10) Students should be able to function as communicators, having their linguistic utterances confirmed and rewarded. Authentic themes were chosen as desired and adapted to different linguistic requirements and potentials, leading to different levels of proficiency and scholastic achievement.

In this approach, with skills being acquired for their immediate realization in communication at a level commensurate with the learner's ability, it was not immediately appreciated that the speech act was severely limited not only by the student's own ability and speed, but also by the school constraints of inadequate resources, especially time at the learner's disposal. With one teacher in charge of some twenty-five students in a lesson in an LEA school, it is obviously difficult to enable all students to say what they want to say. However much choice they have in choosing a topic, students have no ready access to the foreign language source, the repository to activate their topic. Unless they can find and acquire the language they need to communicate, their communication will hardly match their communicative needs. Methods which were dictated by the school situation, the way students were learning their conversation topics by being asked to write out entire dialogues with little concern for the goal of primacy of the spoken language, the total failure to estimate the difficulty of writing, were clearly unsatisfactory.

The constant classroom pattern of repetition and drilling was boring for the students, and the speech act nowhere in sight. In this scenario modern foreign languages once again became an awkward school subject. 'You have to wait so long before you can say anything' was an often-heard complaint, voiced particularly by the academically less well-motivated students, uninterested in things foreign, who, unlike those committed to investing their effort for the future, expected instant returns. It was fortunate therefore that this communicative initiative coincided with the introduction of new electronic hardware and the use of audio-visual and computer-assisted language-learning techniques. They enabled many students to enjoy even the limited communicative success confirmed by passing what became known as Graded Tests in modern foreign languages, receiving certificates of five standards of performance, ranging from the most elementary to the equivalent of the Certificate of Secondary Education (CSE) or Ordinary Level GCE examination. Others were just pleased to be praised for being able to order a cup of coffee or book a hotel room. The opportunity to gain certificates after relatively short bursts of study relieved the all-too-frequent long wait for the disappointment of failure at the end of the traditional course lasting several years, which tested cumulatively, relying on the students' notoriously poor long-term memory rather than testing what they had learnt and remembered recently. Buckby <u>et al.</u> found increased motivation for modern language study as a result of using the Graded Objective Tests in Modern Languages (GOMLs), including a gain in personal confidence. (11) Improved social contacts with foreigners and a greater interest in the foreign countries were also noted, helped by the use of more authentic situational language courses, based in Dieppe or Boulogne, with students paying visits to these cities and carrying on a correspondence and exchanges with their contemporaries in France or in Germany.

The use of GOMLs with their instant rewards was responsible for the increase in the number of students completing their modern foreign language courses, no longer leaving within one or two years of starting them. In seven Cambridgeshire schools between 1982 and 1987 the percentage of students continuing with modern languages up to GOML Grade 5 (CSE equivalent) had gone up from 63 to nearly 90. What was especially encouraging was that this figure included 24 per cent of non-academic students. Although in other schools the corresponding top figure was only 50 per cent, there too an increase in real terms had been recorded. (12) GOMLs are a very thriving enterprise in schools, their novel way of testing one skill at a time (e.g. speaking a short dialogue or following simple instructions) having been incorporated in the new General Certificate of Secondary Education (GCSE) examination. (13)

In the GCSE credit is given for satisfying certain criteria through criterion referenced testing, students being considered for an award according to the number and difficulty level of discrete skills in exercises completed by them, such as elementary writing or advanced (higher) speaking. Also their course work over the years counts in the award of grades. The slower students benefit greatly from this new policy. With GOMLs modern foreign languages has pioneered an approach to testing and teaching now used in the GCSE, and being adapted in teaching and testing other school subjects. This has boosted the standing of the subject.

It is important that the topics are capable of adaptation. Thus the new Technical and Vocational Initiative (TVEI) in schools, intended to bring industry and schools closer together, has spawned 'industrial' GOMLs, with situations located in work and environment, and students taking on the more active role of hotel receptionists or cashiers rather than the inevitable juvenile customers. The dialogues practised discuss employment or production problems rather than the usual 'school pupil' topics.

An element of residence abroad is a highly desirable condition for successful modern foreign language learning. In the time and location constraints of the school, language has to adapt to being taught and tested in little parcels. This inevitably puts a brake on language, whose natural flow is not in little parcels. In such circumstances language becomes just another school subject, with obvious drawbacks. If TVEI work experience can be taken in foreign countries, (14) with school students spending time in enterprises abroad, and if the polytechnical pattern of production and education becomes established in schools, further developments will be possible. These will be discussed in the following section of this chapter.

The second breakthrough, like the first, also took the

student majority's situation as its starting-point. The relative lack of success of both was in the first case due to an overemphasis on the educational experience, inevitably restricted by the limits of the foreign 'knowledge', including language, available. The policy of using this approach mainly with the less able students did not make it any more popular. In the second, it addressed itself to the lowest common denominator of language as a minimal communicative instrument with a limited speech act. Both developments were characterized by being targeted on a 'correct finished product', the usually very small skill or knowledge acquired at the end of the course. The limits were set to offset the too ambitious and unattainable educational aims of modern foreign language teaching of old, however they took little account of the nature of language. This could not entirely satisfy the weak, despite their relative success with GOMLs, nor the bright students, because it left so much of their language potential unfulfilled. To produce an exciting and educationally challenging study of language, it was necessary to go beyond the simple language skills and facts very much earlier in the course. Three things were necessary to prevent the disappointment of learners who could not use their modern foreign languages the way language is intended to be used.

1   The possession of the skills had to be recognized by the learner as a means of discovering the other reality behind the words, encouraging a genuine wish to learn this reality as a value in itself. A wish in other words to get to know the foreign country, its people and way of life in a larger variety of appropriate areas than hitherto, to which knowledge of the language could be one of the keys.

2   The learner had to accept the limits to which modern foreign languages can be learnt in school, without being deprived of a 'language education'. This could only happen, allowing for the constraints of modern foreign language teaching, if the limitations were clearly understood to be located more in the extent of the knowledge made available and less so in the perceived quality of education achieved through language received in the process of acquiring language. The focus on the process emphasized the enquiring role of the students rather than their unthinking effort. (15) It was necessary to get away from the exclusive and prolonged

preoccupation with the elementary aspects of modern foreign languages, especially in the secondary school, which fail to address the more mature student. At the same time, the view that the educational value can arrive only after the language to which it belongs has been learnt, had to be repudiated, otherwise the average student would once again face the problem of having to master the qualifying skills used by the long-term learner to embark on the advanced 'complete education through language', taken to mean its literature, philosophy, and history.

3   If the modern foreign language was to function as a language, a symbolic representation of reality as such, it had to enter into an alliance with the student's mother tongue, with the latter admitted into the modern foreign languages classroom on a much larger scale.

This development requires a new definition of 'education through foreign languages', one that differs from the rather esoteric 'high culture' associated with the elitist view of modern language study in school. This education can be had by activating all faculties involved in the process of using language skills, including the simple, and not just the perfected advanced ones, as well as the social, the artistic (musical, dramatic, painting, or photographic), psycho-motor and others which function fully through and with the help of the learner's more developed mother tongue and its way of looking at the world. Painting would not be confined to colouring Napoleon's trousers by the less able students. An article in Liberal Education in support of the intellectual justification of the study of a modern language for all students, appeals for the release of the wider cultural, educational values to all learners. (16) Because of the restrictions inherent in the foreign language medium, the student's mother tongue must be involved in the process of that part of education designated by modern foreign languages before the acquisition of the foreign language skills has happened. In other words, it has to be accepted that the mother tongue will also focus on the foreign reality.

This is bound to appeal to the reluctant learners of modern foreign languages identified earlier, who in their own environment, already skilled mother-tongue users, are normally curious to find out more about many aspects of the familiar world around them, and will in the course of study be encouraged to use this world to penetrate into the unfamiliar, and this should include the foreign one. (17) This approach requires a new methodology. To educate for the foreign part of reality it is necessary, as suggested above, to make the learning process rather than the finished product, the language skill measured by so many 'successful' acts of minimal communication, the sole centre of concern.

This has two implications. On the one hand modern foreign language learning with its stress on learning would become more like all other school subjects: you accept its limitations, as when trying to speak the foreign language, as you have to learn mathematical computation first. On the other hand, by linking it with the students' mother tongue, it becomes more like a language, which can be used in the acquisition, the perception of reality, ensuring an education at a level more appropriate to the students' degree of maturity and development, in a way that was not possible with the limited foreign language speech acts at their disposal. This approach extends the two new developments discussed earlier on pp. 176-80: it opens up for the students the concrete foreign reality including the symbolic, linguistic quantity of the foreign language. Most importantly it puts modern foreign language learning into a specific language learning context. In a way similar to the one in which students are acquiring reality through their mother tongue, they are made to acquire a significant chunk of foreign reality in the process of learning their foreign language. However, since this is their second language, this approach acknowledges the fact that their mother tongue is actively involved in the process of learning the new reality of the foreign language being studied. In English Second and Foreign Language Teaching (TESL and TEFL) in countries with an official language other than English, because of the world-wide influence of English and American, the British and American realities have always been much 'closer' to the learners of the two languages and much easier to grasp than have the realities behind the words of the other languages taught in school, especially in Britain. In the latter case language has been emphasized almost to the point of exclusion of the reality behind the words with serious repercussions for the learner's attitude to the subject. It is essential that more total foreign contexts, with all that this entails, are also learnt in modern foreign language classes other than English in Britain, and that the mother tongue (usually English in the case of British schools)

Witold Tulasiewicz

is used to expedite the process.

The reality to be discovered behind the words then, is of two kinds. First, there is the purely linguistic quantity; while learning their second language (L2), the students are given the opportunity to observe and consider language facts, which they may compare with those of their mother tongue (L1). However, because L2 is learnt rather than acquired, it gives the students better scope for exploring language awareness than does L1 which in the rapid process of acquisition, much of it outside the formal classroom situation, becomes automatic and unreflected. In the teaching directions of the two recent developments described above, a small segment of the modern foreign language to be learned, an utterance which does not tax the students, and is manageable in terms of comprehension by them, may be used to enable them to perceive language patterns, recognize structures and analogies, and, as observers, to make predictions. For example the text chosen may be: 'ich mache uns eine Tasse Tee - wo ist die Teekanne?', indeed if necessary it may be even simpler. By helping to make the students aware of the use and the power of language, teaching them to manipulate it in a way which contrasts with their mother tongue, modern foreign languages in school can help in the acquisition of an improved mother tongue, so that it becomes a more effective, precise, or persuasive tool of communication. A case can be made out for studying L1 and L2 more closely together for language awareness. (18) Studying L2 in tandem with L1 helps in redefining L1 concepts. In the often haphazard way in which mother tongue concepts are acquired, with overworked parents failing to correct their children, many concepts have become blurred. Modern foreign language learning, which enables a second look to be taken, can help to redefine them. (19)

The exposure to foreign sounds gives the students an enhanced sensitivity to patterns of intonation, stress, and pitch, when they perceive them in an unfamiliar context. Guberina's work with partially hearing children has shown how their hearing became reactivated after exposure to strange sound frequencies, when they began 'to hear long lost language sounds'. (20) This psycho-motor development would not have been possible, if modern foreign languages had been taught exclusively as a vehicle of communication, without becoming an object of observation by the students or used in conjunction with their mother tongue to show up

184

contrasts. Teachers of English mother tongue have given a welcome to an integrated language experience across the curriculum; this could range from an awareness of language as language to a more 'social' language awareness encouraging linguistic tolerance of dialects or non-standard varieties of English. Modern foreign languages can play an important part in this process. All this is of course eminently useful in learning the process of language acquisition and language learning. Though this approach on its own may bear some similarity to the first step of modern foreign language learning suggested by some linguists, the learning of the words, we do not see it as being taken in isolation from the acquisition of foreign language reality.

The second reality is the much larger world behind the symbols of language. There is for instance the personal social enhancement: a better self-concept students can achieve when they realize they are learning an interesting school subject. The non-linguistic benefits can be social and political as well as emotional. There is the phenomenon of breaking down the parochial arrogance of monoglots who see the world in terms of their own language only and ask everyone 'to speak a human language' when addressing them. When exposed to another medium, their horizons are widened, and their sympathy and understanding of others improved. This is a variant of the more narrowly 'linguistic' tolerance mentioned previously. Beattie gives a neat definition of awareness of another's language, not as 'language awareness', but one which makes the speaker and listener 'aware and respectful of each other's values'. (21) The effect of this could be an educationally worthwhile version of European studies, a serious study of European and national institutions, problems faced and shared, differences and similarities and common solutions, which can be taught at different levels of difficulty. The United Kingdom Centre for European Education (UKCEE) has encouraged teaching school students 'European awareness' and sponsored a programme monitoring trainee teachers' European awareness, a dimension which makes sense in view of the fact that the European Community provides the three most widely taught foreign languages in Britain. (22)

Handling a variety of artefacts (in the widest sense of the word) of the other country's civilization and culture leads to 'creating designs of your own based on foreign art', the performance of song and drama, not necessarily in the foreign language, though this is to be encouraged, writing or discussion and role-play of topics of interest to youth. All these are realistic, achievable goals, accessible, depending on the level required, with only a smattering of the foreign language, a few words of lyrics or the name of some dance steps. (23) A class of the author's students recently had much fun trying to interpret, in English, the meaning of different foreign gestures, and learned a number of foreign words in the process. For really fluent speakers, of course, the other language can add a further dimension, endowing them with another personality, the opportunity to lead an alternative existence. A start can be made with declaiming a speech of Cicero's in the original Latin, when students may imagine themselves in the Roman Forum.

Considering further implications of the new approach, we may point out that the endless repetitions of language structures, polishing utterances to perfection, believed to be indispensable when foreign languages are taught as a vehicle of communication, are replaced by teachers and students together examining things brought into the classroom, discussing their findings in the mother tongue but with some modern foreign language activities not ruled out, in which the students supported by a sympathetic teacher can take the initiative.

Acknowledging the difficulty of much of modern foreign languages and the unpopularity of the subject in school, we have de-emphasized rapid communication in modern foreign languages and introduced the student's mother tongue into the foreign language classroom. In bringing the two languages into contact, however, we have shifted what the student is learning of the foreign language into the mainstream of the school curriculum as language. This is because when speaking, learning, or just looking at them, the two languages together educate by opening up reality for the student. The mother tongue reveals areas which for want of the foreign concept would remain hidden. Though the foreign reality may in that moment be somewhat distorted by being seen through the lens of the mother tongue, the truth is revealed as soon as the foreign term arrives, and the students enjoy the pleasure of discovery or rediscovery, as the case may be. Using the mother tongue in the foreign language classroom to help learn about the foreign reality enables modern foreign languages study to contribute a distinctive, additional dimension to students' social, political, aesthetic, affective, psycho-motor, and cognitive development.

Though we may still start with the minimal GOML-type language packages, short structured utterances, single words, and expressions in the language when teaching modern foreign languages, these packages will be exploited more fully in the learning process. In language awareness lessons, for example, students would look at (and discuss in English if necessary) lexical phenomena, when odd words would turn up like the French <u>pied</u> which means more than 'foot' and 'leg' (but where does that leave <u>jambe</u>?) with answers arrived at through language games and other lively exchanges. In a different lesson context students would learn about the different colours and shapes of traffic signs abroad in a way which would whet their curiosity and sharpen their perception by being encouraged to find out the reality (including the foreign terms) for themselves. (24) In still another unit they would ponder, not without humour, German attitudes expressed in polite dinner-table phrases and learn them at the same time. Discovering the foreign reality behind the new foreign language symbols is intended as a challenge to students, because for a long time they are participating in a learning process which is not as automatic as it is in their mother tongue.

In well-planned mother-tongue lessons students have been stretched by being given work which makes demands upon both the more and less average among them. This has been difficult to achieve in the foreign language, where because of its different status in the hierarchy of learning objectives and its problems, especially in the lower secondary classes, only the simplest of dialogues are being practised. It is easier to initiate and keep up a secondary-level discussion (the level at which modern foreign languages are usually introduced into schools) in the student's mother tongue than in a problematic subject like modern foreign languages unless the latter can be made to serve a wider purpose than a mere minute's worth (or less) of communication. By opening up a wider reality the teacher can create a learning situation which is more appropriate to the age and maturity of the learner. Only then can modern foreign languages make a contribution to education through language on a scale similar to that of the much 'bigger' mother tongue. Exploiting the foreign reality present behind modern foreign languages makes it possible to take a step in the direction of a fuller realization of students' language potential. An intelligent use made of the foreign country and its people can contribute to international (or European) understanding. All this should result in a more positive attitude to learning modern foreign languages, thus improving motivation and performance when using them. The logic of this argument is intended to point towards the establishment of faculties of language (or communication, widely interpreted) in schools rather than keeping separate subject departments.

With the use of school trips, especially extended visits, as an accepted integral part of the course of study it should be possible to provide at least some of the modern foreign language tuition in countries where the languages are spoken. Work experience abroad, pioneered by UKCEE, is beginning to make contacts less remote. After 1992 all kinds of visits and exchanges should become more frequent. Lessons abroad in blocks of time measured in weeks rather than in hours will facilitate both learning and the acquisition of language. When modern languages are learnt in their countries of origin the test-tube-experiment effect of the school will be translated into real life. Study and work will come closer together, the student's job in Europe ensuring that the foreign language will be used, or at least learnt. Full speech acts will take care of motivation, while the preparatory stages of the school language learning process will be available to those who are less fluent. Our concept of language awareness is thus a more Vygotskian one: awareness is not confined to the facts of language.

The new methodology and syllabuses can be described as more democratic. In the way suggested, culture can be learnt without the student having to go through the old condition of a language selection process first. A vast array of aspects of culture, language and society, those traditional elitist objectives, can be learnt in mixed ability, thematically linked groups, exploring a particular point, not cumulatively, but as an ongoing process. Integration is achieved by attempting a simultaneity of language progress with other subjects. Study is addressed to students' own problems and becomes personalized, resulting in significant attitudinal change. Moreover, all this can be started in the classroom now, which, because of the greater variety and more advanced character of learning the reality, satisfies the thinking students. They can help to educate themselves by being encouraged to use learning aids, such as posters, pictures, and other reproductions of reality, or for a complete experience to go abroad, the visits leading to new contacts. Exploiting the school as a community (which does include abroad) is an effective method of keeping modern foreign languages alive in school. (25)

NEW CURRICULUM DEVELOPMENTS RESTATED

This discussion has revealed a position in which modern foreign languages study is motivated largely, if not exclusively, by extrinsic considerations, the desire to get to know the people and their country. This is to be expected. Society, employment, and leisure, the emotions, language in the widest sense, impinge on the student, and course priorities should reflect this. Exercises like language awareness in the more narrow sense quoted above, can be expected to make their own contribution to the more traditional modern foreign language specific objectives.

Our main concern in modern foreign languages has been to encourage the student to want to learn the foreign tongue. Once that motivation has been established, the process helped by recent developments in the European Community, of language learning itself will proceed more smoothly and, after the student's exposure to the reality, it will start at a higher level of communication. Like several distinguished linguists therefore we too see a two-phase approach to modern foreign language learning. However, although we accept that in the course of acquiring reality some foreign words and expressions will have been learnt by the student as part of the reality, in a way similar to Krashen's monitoring language, (26) our first phase is less exclusively linguistic, the elements of language being learnt alongside the acquired reality. Also in the second phase learners will make continuing use of the monitors, but at a level which is more sophisticated and fluent than in the first, because of the experience gained during the first phase.

Since modern foreign languages are less popular in the United Kingdom than in most other countries, the reformed language option is particularly urgent here, not least in view of the impending requirements of the 1988 Education Reform Act. Committed and suitably trained teachers for the new approach will be needed if the advent of a single European Market is to make the fullest impact on students' attitudes as well as demand on their skills. Developments affecting employment, workers' increased mobility within the Community after 1992 may come to the rescue. There has already been registered an increase in the number of native foreign speakers taking up teaching posts in British schools, no longer exclusively as teachers of French or German. There will certainly be more such teachers, and they will be able to make a distinctive educational contribution by teaching the foreign reality in their lessons in English, as well as teaching French, Spanish, or German.

This third breakthrough, to keep to the wording used earlier, has not happened yet. Modern language teaching aims in England still give top priority to the practical, active skills, although it is interesting to note that in Scotland GOMLs are less restricted to the simple survival encounters, like ordering a cup of coffee, expecting a more cultural, ethnographic conversation.

Surprisingly all recent relevant, official, and semi-official publications, like Curriculum from 5 to 16, Modern Foreign Languages to 16, and the GCSE National Criteria, (27) list the psycho-social aims of foreign language study: tolerance, a positive (this is left unexplained - surely it cannot mean 'uncritical'?) attitude to foreign culture, international understanding, and the linguistic ones: sensitivity to and awareness of language, the ability to use language in such a way as to be able to 'develop skills for further language study'. Since curriculum guidelines from the DES still have to appear (modern foreign languages seem to have a lower priority than other school subjects) there are no precise details as to what is intended. If L2 does indeed help in language learning, that aim has certainly not been much in evidence in schools. However we note that the Modern Languages Committee of HM Inspectorate have recently completed a sampling of Language Awareness courses in schools, a topic which at first received scant attention from them. (28) In all the above publications the educational aims appear in second place; they follow the communicative ones, which meanwhile indicate in very clear terms the discrete functions in situations students have to master, in GOMLs topics about themselves, their family, friends, and others. The Secondary Examinations Council's GCSE - A Guide for Teachers: French sets out the language skills only. (29) Especially surprising is the marginal treatment of the cultural aims in the Teaching GCSE Modern Languages handbook. (30) The Inspectorate's publications give rather more prominence to them but no specific details.

The national aims for modern foreign languages are still

very much oriented towards foreign language skills, with all the drawbacks that this entails, rather than whole language specific in the sense that has been argued here. Indeed, the National Criteria in GCSE Sociology show more international commitment than those in modern languages. ESL and ELT with their greater emphasis on the background reality and their better resourcing are a good model to adapt for use in French and German courses. A paper by Altman dismisses the view that ELT teaching is authoritarian and teacher directed. (31) Although most modern foreign language classes concentrate on the communicative skills, there are centres which are more adventurously innovatory. The new emphasis on authentic materials helps to bring the reality behind the words nearer to the student.

It must be said, however, that, because the limitations of the curriculum affect attitudes to the foreign language, we should stress the need to make the most of the foreign language as language, and especially to beware of a commitment to narrow practical priorities and background studies for the less able. All students are capable of being stretched through imaginative modern foreign language study.

FOREIGN LANGUAGE TEACHING IN EUROPE

This chapter has concentrated on the situation in the United Kingdom. In several continental countries two modern foreign languages are expected of nearly half the school student population and modern foreign languages has been confidently regarded as part of the provision of worthwhile education. Because the system is rather less elitist, this worthwhile education with at least one foreign language, has been available to all school-students.

Very often English has been that language. For a variety of reasons, therefore, students of modern foreign languages in these countries have been well motivated. This must be emphasized, because, alas, these countries too have experienced an upsurge of nationalism on occasion. Perhaps if they trimmed their long and full course requirements in modern foreign languages, they too, like ourselves, could devote more energy to international understanding and progress through language education.

Chapter Ten

INDUCTING THE HUMANISTIC TEACHER

Doug Holly

INTRODUCTION

I want in this chapter to suggest an approach to the initial training of teachers which problematizes the 'reality' for which they are being prepared. For this purpose I wish to oppose to the currently fashionable notion of a national British curriculum, the alternative concept of a curriculum which is school based and student oriented. In this context, a school-based and student-oriented curriculum is one which seeks to relate the actual individuals in a school to their human context of the physical universe and the ways their fellow beings have appropriated that universe ('technology') and which also, importantly, seeks to relate these individual learners to one another, to their teachers, their families and neighbourhoods and all their fellow beings as forming one vast, interacting series of purposes and responses. The last aspect of the curriculum is the business of humanities and English faculties.

To induct the would-be teacher into any part of this is clearly a complex undertaking: far more complex than if one were content to accept the unexamined conventions of school learning, especially secondary-school learning. In the past, initial teacher-training institutions have, on the whole, taken the line of least resistance and simply accepted the conventional 'subject' approach to training in which 'methods' were central and were taken to mean 'how to teach X'. As long as secondary education was a selective affair with limited goals this was on the whole functional. But as graduates have found themselves, since the 1950s, teaching more and more recalcitrant classes in schools where the goals were potentially unlimited but largely confused or undefined - first secondary moderns, then comprehensives - this approach has become steadily less credible. If these training institutions now find themselves under more-or-less philistine attack from a populist government, they should not be surprised. Calls to 'get back into the classroom' are, however, misplaced: to a considerable extent the staff of such institutions have never been in the classrooms of schools catering for a majority of the population. We have come to a point where the precepts of many teacher-educators have become necessarily abstract, at best.

A positive response is certainly needed to justify criticism of the profession, not to say the half-understood utterances of politicians and the almost complete incomprehension of civil servants drawing on memories of private institutions called 'public'. Since the expectations of student-teachers have, until comparatively recently, reflected a personal history of selective schooling, this response will have to take into account the induction of would-be teachers into a relatively alien environment as well as their initiation into a rapidly developing practice. While this problem can be expected to lessen as more student-teachers come from comprehensive schools, it won't disappear until more comprehensives become largely mixed ability: both because of the students' likely selective experience within their own schooling and because 'less able' classes will continue to present problems which are socio-psychological rather than basically pedagogic.

But I want in this chapter, while by no means ignoring the persistent imperfections of the system, to focus on how we can initiate new entrants to the profession into the best practice, and since my own experience in this field has been in humanities, (1) I will relate the discussion specifically to good practice in core 'integrated' humanities such as is to be found in a growing number of schools in England and Wales. (2) But before doing so there are certain general aspects of training for secondary education that ought to be considered. First, the central focus of training. In the past, as I have said, the central focus of the initial training of graduates, in particular, has been 'how to teach my subject, X'. If we are to attend to the wisdom of civil servants, this must continue to be the central focus. Inside the dreaming spires of Elizabeth House what defines the good teacher is 'the man who loves his subject' (not many of them were taught by women). However, those of us who actually know the common secondary school of the 1980s - may actually have taught, Minister, and in a comprehensive school! - know that what defines the good teacher in reality is not the 'love of subject' but the 'love of teaching'. Nothing but such a love could keep women and men in comprehensive classrooms in spite of dislocation, dwindling capitation, and the all-pervasive misunderstanding of what the job really entails.

To prepare young - or not-so-young - student-teachers for teaching in comprehensive schools entails preparing them to be 'teachers', not 'teachers-of-X'. It necessitates an all-round understanding of how public education has evolved; how they and the students happen to find themselves in the same place at the same time. It also entails giving them some insight into the consciousness of young people in the closing decades of the twentieth century - a consciousness they are at once closer to than most of their tutors, yet further removed from than those who have direct experience of the whole range of adolescents in school. Such a consciousness is formed in the context of the working (or workless) lives of parents, friends, and family, so, whatever the subject-background of student-teachers, they need some awareness of work and unemployment as they affect people in general, outside the normal circle of those who enter higher education, particularly universities. Finally some initial introduction needs to be made into the science of pedagogy, the theoretical underpinning of professional teaching. By this I do not mean 'psychology of education'; I mean a branch of knowledge both more specific to the classroom and more broadly based than psychology. If an English equivalent is sought for an alien-sounding term, then probably 'learning theory' will do, provided that this is understood in an infinitely wider sense than that familiarized by behaviourism. Learning theory (pedagogics) is about the fact that learning always takes place in a given social context, that is between human beings. School learning is clearly a special sort of context and the 'political' relations between those involved is a vital ingredient. The majority of students in comprehensive schools - as in all the institutions of mass education which preceded them - are not there by choice, but by Act of Parliament. Teachers mostly attended school because they or their parents wanted schooling; they have chosen to teach (though they may not before training to be teachers have fully appreciated what that choice now implies). What student-teachers have to discover is what the grounds are on which they can expect to enter into a fruitful learning encounter in classrooms - something much more subtle and complex than behaviourist carrot-and-stick 'motivation'. What, in fact, they have to acquire is the skill of 'getting through' to young people: winning confidence and respect as people who really believe in learning and who have themselves experienced it, at some time in their lives, as personally rewarding. If they have not, they had better not attempt to train as teachers.

All of these things should form the central focus of teacher-training: the 'method' of teaching chemistry or modern languages is really tributory to it. Before you can teach French in a comprehensive school you need to understand the point of it being a subject on offer in such circumstances and the varying policy of schools in relation to the general curriculum and its constituent parts. Very few, as a matter of fact, have yet arrived at a consistent languages policy. Some consideration will need to be given by the would-be languages teacher as to why this should be so in the context of what she or he has gathered from the focal study of schools. Precisely the same applies, mutatis mutandis, to the would-be teacher of chemistry, music, geography, or any specialism of the curriculum.

Before leaving the general question of how subject specialism articulates with 'learning to be a comprehensive-school teacher' it is worth reflecting that secondary-school teachers - and, at the behest of government, primary-school teachers increasingly, too - need often to prepare for a dual role. A minority of students in schools require an academic preparation which is really semi-vocational. For this minority some detailed acquaintance with the conventional subjects of higher education is still required at age 16 by many employers and by some of the higher educational institutions themselves, so the 'teaching of subject X' as an end in itself is still an activity which secondary teachers are involved in. But (unless they teach in tertiary post-18 colleges) it is not their main activity. Subject specialism is, in their dealings with most students, the vehicle of educational encounter rather than an end in itself. This is in my experience the most difficult thing to get across, to young graduates particularly. Their expectations in entering teaching tend to be wrapped up in their experience from sixth form onwards - the positive feelings they have about

Doug Holly

'their subject' and the comparative success they have achieved in it - and in academic education generally. These expectations are only too often buoyed up further by 'method' tutors living vicariously in the classrooms of their past via the totally different world their students now find themselves inserted into.

This is fortunately not the whole picture. There are university departments of education where a general policy of 'school-centredness' has been followed for many years and individual tutors in all training institutions are quite alive to the profundity of the change which comprehensivization has brought about, and, like me, actively approve of that change. As time goes by, a larger proportion of tutors will have taught the whole range of ability in secondary schools, will have experienced the tutorial-pastoral system, will have worked alongside colleagues of varied academic and non-academic background. We are gradually (sometimes painfully) evolving a 'comprehensive' teacher-training system, though there remains the obstacle of the 'binary divide' in higher education itself. And, I will argue, the defining characteristic of this evolving system is a new centrality for the very activity of learning - both as experienced in schools and as experienced in the business of preparing to be a teacher. The movement now must certainly be towards unifying the conventional duality of teacher-training courses, synthesizing a concern for 'method', shorn of its preoccupation with subject content, and a concern for general theory, shorn of its tendency to take refuge in the academic respectability of philosophy, history, and the social sciences. The curriculum of the training institutions must, in short, be evolving in the same direction as that of the secondary schools: a general educative 'core' with specialist options. The teaching of language, mathematics, literature, geography, economics, and the rest all demand special consideration and this they should have for a suitable proportion of the time available. Some, like language teaching, would seem to require more, or more intensive, attention than others. Also there will be a need, for the next few years at least, to train specialists in integration. During most of what follows I will outline what I believe such 'specialist generalism' requires by way of an induction course. Much of what I have to say, however, will be true of any general induction of women and men into teaching in comprehensive schools.

Recently direct involvement by the government in

teacher-training has been greatly accentuated and much of this attention has been concentrated on the question of 'on-the-job' learning, for university tutors as well as student-teachers. The implication seems to be that teaching is about classrooms and, therefore, all concerned with the initial induction of teachers should spend a large proportion of their time in classrooms. The rhetoric here, it is true, seems to conflict with another rhetoric which implies that many teachers are not really doing their jobs properly while in those same classrooms. The preferred resolution of this contradiction may be to select only those schools for training where the model of 'successful' teaching and learning is closest to that advocated - or, rather, hinted at - by those who write the current 'discussion documents' on the curriculum. (3) While much of the writing in these documents is bland enough and avoids too great a degree of prescription, there is nevertheless a definite air of conservatism, even complacency, about them. The world of Mr Chipps appears to continue undisturbed in the minds of these anonymous pundits, despite occasional dutiful references to 'a multi-cultural society' or the 'needs of the less academic'. We must hope that teacher-trainers will not be expected to take too seriously this highly culture-specific (1930s public school) view of the practice of education but be allowed, instead, to draw upon their own rather more 'recent and relevant' experience. (4)

And in terms of the classroom experience most relevant to comprehensive schools there is no doubt where the focus ought to be: on work with the widest available range of students in learning groups not segregated by ability. Such groupings are most likely to be found in music, drama, PE, design education, combined science, English, and integrated humanities. Since my own experience as a teacher and a trainer of teachers has been with the last two it is upon this area of the curriculum that I shall now concentrate.

TEACHING INTEGRATED HUMANITIES

But first a word of explanation about the term 'integrated humanities'. In response, particularly, to the demographic factors which have produced the 'falling rolls' phenomenon, secondary schools throughout England and Wales are beginning to adopt a 'core' of study in at least the first two years which subsumes such traditional subjects as history, geography, religious education and, not infrequently, English. Where there is a strong element of social sciences in the school this has tended to give a flavour to the 'integrated humanities' of the early years, and sometimes supports its extension as a 'core' study right up to the new GCSE level. In this latter respect two of the five regional examining groups (Midland Examining Group and Northern Examinations Association) now have duly accredited GCSE syllabuses in integrated humanities. The MEG syllabus, for example, calls for centres to submit 'content exemplars' in relation to five 'organizing ideas' (an example being 'Prejudice and Empathy') with the invitation to contribute an additional organizing idea of their own. These integrated humanities syllabuses are proving to be of growing interest, though a full-scale adoption of them may have to await the clarification of rules relating to multiple certification, that is whether students can gain as many certificates in different aspects of an integrated core as they have previously done in the separate 'humanities' subjects. Certainly the time required to develop a properly thematic integrated humanities core, in terms of timetable allocation, would seem to call for more than one GCSE grade for the student involved. This relates, however, to 'qualification pressures' rather than the intrinsic needs of course assessment. The tendency has been, over recent years, for higher education establishments and prospective employers to accept a 'core' of strategic certification in key subject areas at age 16 rather than the 'blunderbuss' effect of earlier years.

In any case 'integrated humanities', taught to mixed-ability groups as a central part of their learning experience, is becoming more common each year - if for no better reason than to conserve the energies of a dwindling supply of non-replaceable specialists in history, geography, and the rest. Once firmly established in the 'lower school' it has tended to spread upwards to the traditional 'examination years', especially with attractive and highly flexible school-based, continuously assessed GCSE syllabuses now available. This reflects the enthusiasm of teachers who have hitherto seen themselves more narrowly as 'subject-specialists' who, having tasted the possibilities of thematic work and team-planning, now tend to consign their 'specialism' more and more to post-16 work. All of which is as it should be if we are to address the needs of the comprehensive school students of today and tomorrow rather than dwell nostalgically on the days of the grammar school of yesterday.

Properly speaking, integrated humanities is really about 'relationality'. At the beginning of the present chapter I further defined this term as having to do with relating learners to one another and their fellow beings in general, including their teachers. For there is good sense in Freire's precept that learning is 'dialogical': as between teachers and learners and between learners and one another. (5) It is only in formalistic schooling that learning has been seen as proceeding from the directives of teachers. The 'didactic' model which ignores the involvement of learners in their own learning has always been a nonsense, and always condemned as such by those who, throughout the ages, have given any thought to what actually happens when people really 'learn' anything. In particular, those who have set themselves to the task of educating the children of the masses - rather than simply 'schooling' them - have pointed to the necessity for teachers to have respect for their students and really know them as people. Lev Tolstoy was only one of the more illustrious of these. (6) What this involves is the discovery by would-be teachers that while they may learn to be effective controllers of classes by the exercise of will alone, they will never bring about any learning by this means. I will return to the vexed question of class control, but for the moment I want to concentrate on learning, and how it is inspired.

In the best practice of integrated humanities the pedagogic style is deliberately indirect: exposition, while not absent, is relatively rare. Information is, from time to time, presented to the students in as inspirational and stimulating a form as possible; the organization of a learning game, say. This demands considerable resourcefulness from teachers; as resources get scarcer, resourcefulness is in ever greater demand. The first set of requisite skills that a teacher of integrated humanities must acquire is organizational: operational knowledge of machinery, the ability to adapt and devise learning activities like games and simulations, critical appreciation of the possibilities and limitations of film and video-tape. Anyone who aspires to respect as a teacher in today's schools, particularly in humanities and English, needs to be completely relaxed about the snags to be encountered with a video-player or projector, for instance. An affected disdain for mechanics is an indication of pedagogical incompetence, not of humanism. Machines go wrong anyway, but never faster than in the hands of someone who sees machinery as at best uninteresting and at worst 'the enemy'. As with much else, we are dealing here with basic social, educational, and personal philosophy. At the risk of dogmatism I will assert that no one who believes that humanism involves the rejection of technology irrespective of its use is likely to make a good teacher of integrated humanities, or anything else in the mainstream curriculum. After all the blackboard and chalk is simply a piece of primitive - and highly flexible - technology; books are the result of ever more sophisticated technology.

'Class management' means, first and foremost, the management of a learning environment. The way students are invited to seat themselves (or move around, if required) is intimately connected with the success of each particular activity. Pair work or small-group discussion needs a different disposition of furniture from work on a resource pack. Since relatively few desks are now actually screwed to the floor it seems worth encouraging student-teachers to follow the example of the best practitioners in this and cause the furniture to be moved as the occasion demands. And since the needs of cleaners differ from those of learners, whichever class is in a room at the end of the day needs to bear that in mind also - an important piece of integrated humanities learning according to the goals proposed earlier, and by no means a joke.

Class management also means the management of materials, making sure that they are in the right place at the right time for the right people: colleagues or students. And class management means the disposition of rooms and their facilities; it also means being as near certain as possible that such machinery or equipment as is necessary (from video machines to scissors and paste) is available and in working order. It means all these things and more. What it never means is the management of people: such a rendering is a polite variant of 'manipulation', and quite out of place in education of any sort. People-management in humanities is a contradiction in terms. One of the first pieces of learning available in a humanities classroom, as in any other, is an inevitable one: it is the 'relationality' between people and their professions. If the teachers profess to be involved in something called 'humanities' and then treat one another and their students in a way that demeans humanity, the students have learned something important. While it probably takes a pedagogical academician to articulate that lesson elegantly the simplest, least 'academic' student intuits it immediately, if less elegantly: 'This humanities is crap'. And so it is, because it is unprincipled and probably unwanted. Those who know clearly what their goals are in integrated humanities, and are really serious about wanting to achieve them, use ways of organizing learning that treat learners with respect and invite respect in return.

At this point there will no doubt be many who object: 'But that is to romanticize the average adolescent; what the average adolescent respects is firmness and authority'. I have a great deal of sympathy with this point of view, having spent a decade teaching adolescents and longer being a parent to adolescents. If firmness means a lack of vacillation and indecision and a determination to fulfil a professional role in the face of seriously anti-social actions no one is likely to disagree. Nor would many wish to deny the admiration due to a job visibly well done: 'authority' in the non-oligarchic sense. It is likely that students will learn better from contact with people whom they admire and unlikely that they will learn much in the company of those they despise. So much is truism. What is disputable and what can be demonstrated, in fact, to be untrue in the daily experience of people in schools is that exerted authority achieves anything other than policing. No one ever learned anything from being shouted at, sneered at, or dressed down, other than the fact that social inequality can start with school. How much a country allows its teachers to act tyrannically or even brutally is a measure of how seriously it takes democracy.

The nub of the problem that faces every student-teacher is, indeed, 'discipline', another word liable to a wide range of construction. The early Soviet educator Makarenko showed long ago that even the most apparently regimented system is fully compatible with the most sensitive humanism. (7) But those who praise Makarenko's military style expedient with delinquent waifs must also attend to his concomitant demand – that the colonists should love him. How many of today's admirers of 'discipline' also talk of love as part of the relationship? What strikes me in reading Makarenko now is the extent to which he was prepared to argue with his charges, even the youngest: not shout at, not sneer at, not even coldly remonstrate with, but argue. And there have been many strict teachers, sticklers for a set order, who have won affection. But it has not been because they bullied or wielded the cane triumphantly; it has been because they talked to young people as though they mattered. 'Discipline' in an educative context is like 'authority': it works only where it is not imposed.

In the humanities classroom, as anywhere else in a school where the students are there initially by legal compulsion, the good of the collective will occasionally have to be upheld, and even more occasionally that 'good' will be unambiguous. A humane learning situation cannot accommodate the oppression and insult of one student by another; racial and sexual harassment, for instance, are clearly unacceptable as are physical violence or intimidation. Far more common are instances of 'disruptive behaviour' which don't involve any of these things: incidents directed at the teacher, rather than at fellow students. Since the teacher is a member of adult society and in loco parentis, in a position to invoke sanctions, such a challenge is often directed indiscriminately at the whole system of which the teacher is at the moment seen to be a representative. If the challenger is a boy and the teacher a woman (unfortunately a not unlikely situation) there may well be elements of sexism, or of racism if the miscreant is white and the teacher black or brown. Clearly, again, such challenges cannot be evaded: they are part of humanities learning, albeit unplanned. In general such behaviour exhibits yet another malady of our society - 'ageism'. What the disruptive student has not learnt and what it is the business of the teacher to bring forward - though not necessarily by confrontation - is that to treat an individual as the mere representative of some evil attributed to an abstract category: 'adults-in-general', 'teachers-in-general' is wrong not because it 'challenges authority' but because it is prejudiced behaviour. Teacher-baiting is no more tolerable in a humanities classroom than student-baiting. Learning is a work activity. In a civilized work situation people treat one another with respect whatever their various statuses. Schools can hardly be called on to prepare students for an uncivilized work situation, common though these may be. 'Preparation for the world of work' (another favourite slogan of governments) certainly entails humanities education. (8)

When 'incidents' occur in the classroom, trainee humanities teachers need to be encouraged to deal with them in a principled way. Of course such incidents are very threatening to student-teachers and inexperienced teachers, and one essential in the practical training of all teachers - and the supervision of probationers too - is that they are never in 'sole charge', in the sense that the student-teacher feels isolated. In a moment I will turn to the preparation of teachers for team work as an essential element in humanities training. The 'team' approach entails a collectivity of teachers and students. 'Discipline'-type problems are a challenge to this collectivity. 'Us - them' relationships such as are implied by a challenge to a teacher and disruptive behaviour indicate, if they occur frequently, that that collectivity is not a reality. So does the isolation of a student-teacher or an inexperienced teacher. In a really effective humanities situation student-teachers feel supported, at least tacitly, by the majority of school-students, and therefore less threatened by aberrant behaviour which they can see as a fairly mundane failure of communication, akin to the misinterpretation of a work task, and discussable with the student, with other students, and with colleagues in an unembarrassed way, since it is not the student-teacher's failure. Sometimes, of course, the student-teacher as an inexperienced practitioner will make a mistake in class management - inadequate work instructions for instance - which lead to disruption due to frustration or amusement. Again in a good humanities setting such mistakes are accepted by all, school-students as much as colleagues: there is no mystery made of the fact that the trainee is a trainee, albeit with much to contribute to the learning and, above all, valuable as a fallible human being.

Fallibility, in fact, ought to be a part of all learning. It is, for instance, one of the necessary conditions of science. In the humanities area of the curriculum, while wilful negligence is as inadmissible as anywhere else, human fallibility is one of the things to be appreciated. The good humanities teacher is never afraid to admit being less than omniscient and quite prepared to admit mistakes - even to be corrected by a school-student without affront to her or his self-respect. School-students are not assumed to be incapable of teaching one another or even their teachers, though another part of humanities learning is the danger of too-rapid conclusions on incomplete evidence. If a teacher stands corrected it is likely to be because the students are in possession of information which the teacher lacks at that moment. One of the things a student-teacher has to come to terms with is that, by the nature of things, students will

203

often 'know better'. It is important for the tyro to see that there is no shame in this: it is quite natural.

Herein lies one of the chief worries of student-teachers - not being able to show superior knowledge and wisdom at all times. It is one of the most deep-rooted of expectations among those entering teaching that they will be called on to act the part of an omniscient infallible being. This is the model they will have admired most in their own traditional schooling. It is quite misplaced in the relationships of a good humanities department, where the message is about curiosity and perseverance not infallibility. Quite a different set of relationships obtain, involving mutual respect, not awe. In my experience it is those who have had an unproblematic experience of their own education who find the greatest difficulty with teaching in a comprehensive school in general and teaching core humanities in particular. I sometimes think that good educationists almost need to have experienced academic failure at some point in their lives. Certainly my own initial failure of the 'scholarship' exam (forerunner of the eleven plus) served to cause me to reflect about my teaching aims very early in my career, and the same seems to have applied to many teachers I have encountered. Those, in particular, who have actively chosen to train for integrated humanities over the years in my own 'method group' have quite frequently been what a colleague once termed 'alienated specialists'. people whose own experience has caused them to challenge the established verities. Perhaps we ought, in selecting people for training as teachers, to privilege those who have had ambivalent relationships with learning themselves - and still want to teach. 'One should love learning unconditionally but one's subject critically' should perhaps be the motto.

But I would not wish to suggest that a troubled or underprivileged background is either a sufficient or a necessary predictor of good teaching: after all Tolstoy had neither. Much more fundamental is a liking for people, young and old. Without this, teaching success is quite impossible, if by this we understand the ability to inspire others to learn. No doubt a bully or a sardonic but cold-blooded genius can terrorize people into memorization and regurgitation. Such a person can never produce self-sufficient, self-motivated learners. Nor will any amount of love for childhood and the young unformed mind suffice of itself to produce good humanities teachers: such teachers actually like grown-ups as well and are as at home among colleagues as among students. This is necessary, because integrated humanities is a team activity.

It is important to be clear about the concept of 'team' as understood in good humanities practice. As I indicated earlier, this is not a matter of 'team teaching' in the manner of the earlier US exponents, but of 'team learning'. The 'song-and-dance-act' aspect of team work is certainly employed from time to time, with a stimulus session involving several teachers in argument perhaps. It is important to underline that humanities is not about some 'party-line' on truth, quite the reverse. It is most unlikely that any group of humanities teachers will have come to the same conclusions about how to view the world: and if they had they would probably not enjoy too much success with their students. Instead they share a common pedagogical conviction: that what matters is for students to learn the relationships between things in the world of people and their own significance in those relationships. A common social, academic, or political perspective is not necessary for this, and indeed gives quite the wrong messages. The world is complex, and while people have to make up their minds on some consistent political approach as part of being participant democrats, this should never be represented as a simple uncomplicated matter: therein lies the death of democracy anywhere. And, as a matter of fact, ordinary people intuitively know this, including ordinary adolescents. They distrust the cut-and-dried explanation, the unproblematic programme of action. Therefore such are quite out of place in humanities learning.

And the focus in schools should be on this - learning. This is a form of work, liable at times to be quite hard and at other times rather routine and unexciting. In this sense humanities, like other school activities, is a 'preparation for the world of work' in the phrase so beloved by politicians. It is this atmosphere of individual involvement in a collective enterprise which team learning at its best produces. In such circumstances students and teachers work alongside one another on a shared task and the collectivity defines the mores. The 'difficult' students in such circumstances are not just a nuisance to teachers; they are an embarrassment to all, not least to themselves. And, it must be said, the 'difficult' teacher is an equal embarrassment. Integrated humanities has a place for 'characters', never for egotists. It is this aspect which is the most difficult for student-teachers to come to terms with. Their expectations may have been of something they are still most likely to have experienced themselves (passive reception of wisdom from some guru 'up-front' with the door closed). Sometimes they complain of 'not finding a role', of rejection by their own students used to their familiar group of teachers. It is interesting, however, that many never experience this as a problem, simply because they are not afraid to 'get in among' the groups working on whatever project, not afraid to admit ignorance cheerfully or unfamiliarity with the theme or the materials, interested above all to find out about their students. These are the student-teachers with the most 'open' approach to teaching in new and unfamiliar circumstances, those with the least concern to 'prove themselves' as experts, the greatest desire to make the acquaintance of the unfamiliar. The worst disadvantage for a humanities teacher is a distaste for the 'non-academic' adolescent. Such people had, quite frankly, better not contemplate teaching integrated humanities, or indeed in a comprehensive school at all.

INTEGRATED HUMANITIES IN LEICESTER

So what sort of people have shown themselves, over the past fifteen to twenty years, to be the most suited to an integral approach to teaching humanities in the context of the comprehensive school? In my experience success in becoming an integrated humanities specialist has related to the person rather than to formal qualification. I have had student-teachers with backgrounds as far apart as doctoral research in chemistry and study of religion, though the recruitment for humanities of graduates in science and mathematics would not now be tolerated by those who control teacher-training! A large number have had 'combined' degrees which give them no guaranteed place on the school timetable. On the other hand, there has been a steady proportion of those with 'single honours' degrees in English, history, the various social sciences, and philosophy. What has united people with such diverse backgrounds has been an interest in the concept of integration, and a concern with the 'humanistic' education of people rather than their training. Quite often, entrants to the course have been interested in wider aspects of education, aspects external to 'school'.

In this sense the decision of the Leicestershire LEA to promote 'community' education via community colleges has been a very fortunate coincidence. Soo, too, has the institution and development by Leicestershire of senior schools with a more open approach to learning and to public examination - typically involving the so-called 'Mode 3', school-assessed approach to the CSE and O Level GCE examinations - and now to the GCSE. A fairly recent instance of this interaction between the practice of local humanities departments and my own approach has been the development, largely by a committee of senior humanities teachers, of the Midlands Examining Group's GCSE syllabus in integrated humanities. Although not the only integrated humanities syllabus on offer for GCSE, its 100 per cent coursework (school-assessed) structure and its imaginative system of 'organizing ideas' rather than set themes is proving very attractive to schools throughout the country. A few of the main architects of this syllabus have been ex-students of the 'humanities' course at Leicester, themselves very successful and imaginative teachers.

An important aspect of integrated humanities, and one which has always been emphasized by the course at Leicester, is the question of the needs and development of school students who are identified as 'remedial', usually in relation to reading and writing ability. The new emphasis in Britain on 'special needs' following the Warnock Report has therefore coincided with this concern, and with the wider concern that the learners rather than the content of learning are the focus. (9) Warnock's effect has been to cause many schools to 'integrate' youngsters who would previously have been taught separately in special schools for the sight-impaired, hearing-impaired, physically handicapped, or educationally sub-normal. Such integration is not likely to be too successful where the prevailing learning mode is didactic and the focus of attention is on some body of knowledge to be ingested and later regurgitated. In this situation those interested in humanistic learning in the sense described in this article are obviously quite at home: 'integrating' the individual learner, appreciated as an individual, has always been the goal of 'integrating' the subject-matter. It is not surprising that many of those trained in integrated humanities have later become involved in what was once described as 'remedial' work, now better and more comprehensively designated 'special needs'.

It is an enduring worry that 'special needs' is seen as a

specialism, something to preoccupy the tender-hearted while the rest get on with the unsentimental day-to-day business of teaching history, geography, chemistry, mathematics, and the rest. Whether espoused by men or women, such an attitude - and it is still probably the dominant one among those attracted to secondary-school teaching - is quite certainly sexist-patriarchal. It is clearly at variance with the aims of humanities education as here understood. Teachers in any part of the general secondary-school curriculum should see their job as helping young people to develop, irrespective of ability or disability. Concern for the learner as a person is no side-issue for the soft-hearted: it is central to the entire project of education. The prevailing notion that 'caring' is some sort of specialism probably best undertaken by women is the direct result of our society's elitist and patriarchal values, with the emphasis on competitive achievement in fields inevitably defined by usually elite and nearly always male preoccupations. In this context knowledge itself is seen as valued property: whether it be of the 'great figures' of history or the abstract formulae of science and mathematics. The whole field of humanities is thereby disvalued and, within it, 'hard' subjects such as mathematical or morphological geography or accountancy economics accorded disproportionate worth. Many of the gifted teachers whom the Leicester Humanities Course has been privileged to introduce to the classroom have been in a unique position to contest this dominant ideology, since they have often combined impeccable academic antecedents with a sensitive awareness - women and men equally - of the skills and concerns of pedagogy.

But not all the alumni of the course have been 'academically impeccable': quite a number of the most successful have been people whose strength has been derived from the school of life experience rather than any school of philosophy or political science. The tendency over the years has been to recruit an ever larger proportion of 'mature' students, quite a number of them women whose formal education has been neglected until relatively late in life, often graduates of the Open University. The presence of such people in the method group has tended to strengthen a critical approach to conventional learning and underline the importance of education outside the school context.

But a course which has trained no more than a dozen people a year, while it has obviously contributed some initiatives to the integrated humanities movement, clearly accounts for only a minority of the committed and successful 'integrationists'. And it would be silly to pretend that all those who have undertaken this particular training have been outstandingly successful. Indeed it is always a potential problem that recruitment criteria which sometimes favour the 'marginal' in terms of a conventional approach to becoming a teacher occasionally recruit those whose marginality turns out to be permanent - though some of these have gone on to become very useful practitioners of social work and community work. On the other hand a number of ex-humanities student-teachers are now senior teachers, some with headships. They would be the first to acknowledge the influence on their careers of integrated humanities teachers who, while gifted practitioners, had themselves never received a specialist integrated humanities training. Indeed whatever success the specialist course may have achieved has always rested heavily on the work of 'teacher-tutors' or 'co-teachers' working in the Leicestershire schools. In fact the course should properly be seen as a co-operative venture involving practising teachers, student-teachers and the school of education based subject 'method' work.

In all this my own role has sometimes seemed almost accidental: I was originally asked to develop a rationale for a group whose previous designation had been 'general arts'. That rationale, which has since emerged as integrated humanities, is still being developed, and much of that development stems from what its tutor learns from the work of 'principled practitioners'. In recent years, through the growing network of the Integrated Humanities Association, the practice being 'fed back' into the course is country-wide. (10) But some of the development is the result of my own reflection, as a former teacher of English, on the tension which exists within humanities between the investigative, evidence-based preoccupation of history and the social sciences and the 'experiential' approach of the socially aware English teacher. I am now more than ever convinced that a 'pure' integration within humanities will demand a close association of those two streams, the 'literary-personal' and the 'sociological-historical' which have combined in the intellectual formation of many of us.

CONCLUSION

To summarize, therefore, the argument of this chapter: the expectations of the majority of those intending to enter teaching are likely to be at variance with the reality of what they will find in schools, because those expectations tend to be founded on a selective, non-typical experience of schooling. To a certain extent, especially for primary-school teachers, this has always been so. Lawrence's portrayal in The Rainbow of Ursula Brangwen's encounter with elementary education at the turn of the century vividly reminds us of this. But until recently many were sheltered from such knowledge by the continued existence of institutions where they could safely repeat their own childhood in the vicious circle 'school-university-school'. For those who will teach in the private sector this remains so. But we cannot organize the preparation of teachers in the public education service for the benefit of this minority. Maybe they ought to have their own seminaries, presided over by those pundits from Elizabeth House. Governments do well to remind us that even universities are publicly funded institutions and must be responsive to the needs of society at large; the concern of teacher-training is the public (in the proper sense) secondary school: the comprehensive school. And the comprehensive school, in these straitened times, cannot afford a proliferation of selective groupings for the more able and motivated; still less can it afford teachers only prepared, temperamentally and professionally, to teach such groups. The main focus of attention must be on the learning of adolescents unsegregated by presumed ability, grouped for the most part in classes where general education, rather than specialist knowledge, is the aim. Among such groupings that of core humanities is becoming more important. All entrants to secondary teaching with a background and interest in the humanities and social sciences need, therefore, a preparation where the focus is on the learning process itself, duly contextualized, rather than on a particular area of 'subject' content. The appropriate 'method' therefore is one which stresses 'how to encourage a humanistic learning', rather than 'how to teach my subject, X'. Teaching 'subject X' will have its place and its due emphasis but for some will be very much subordinate to expertise in organizing learning in the humanities team. In the status hierarchy of the schools their career aim could be Head of Humanities rather than Head of X, Y, or Z traditional subject, though they may well spend some of their time teaching aspects of X, Y, or Z in separate option studies and enjoying that experience too. What we need is people who have experienced learning as a challenging and stimulating activity, problematic or not, who may have a love of literature, history, or topography but who are mainly interested in people: true humanities specialists.

Chapter Eleven

RESEARCH-ORIENTED TEACHER-TRAINING: THE CASE OF MATHEMATICS

Hermann Maier

The main objective in teacher-training is to enable prospective teachers to plan and to prepare lessons in particular subject areas. School-teaching should therefore no longer be regarded as a craft or an artistic skill, nor should teachers be seen as obedient servants of well-elaborated centralized curricula, which diminish their educational responsibility in their particular situation. Planning and presenting lessons rather is to be seen as individual, professional, and creative work based on academic knowledge in different fields, on the analysis of a number of important conditional factors, leading, in consequence, to autonomous decision-making upon mature reflection.

It is by no means sufficient to provide student-teachers with only the technical knowledge of the contents which they will have to teach their pupils later on. Neither is it at all sufficient to equip them in addition with a repertoire of methodological advice or tricks of the trade, however admirable they may seem to be. In Bavaria teachers of mathematics, in whose education I myself am professionally engaged, are educated not only in mathematics itself, but also in such subjects as psychology, pedagogy (science of education) and subject method, philosophy and sociology or political science. That seems to me to accord with the above objective. But what nevertheless has always disturbed me was the observation that the students seemed to store isolated bits of knowledge which did not have any real effect on lesson planning and lesson presentation. Indeed they were left totally alone in their attempts to relate their knowledge to their teaching activities.

I decided, therefore, to regard my subject, namely 'mathematics method', which is compulsory for primary student-teachers in Germany, as an area of integrated comprehensive teacher-training. Indeed my research in the field of mathematics education depends a good deal on subject-integrated work. It may be concerned with classroom language and its relation to the process of conveying knowledge, building up concepts or solving problems; it may also refer to pupils' mistakes and their interpretation as an indicator of disturbances in the learning process itself. There is no alternative to taking into consideration psychological, linguistical, pedagogical, and sociological aspects, besides mathematical ones, in this context.

Nothing can better illustrate the interrelation and interaction of knowledge from different disciplines than research work itself. If I were to restrict my contribution to the education of mathematics teachers to lectures reporting and commenting upon results of research and analysis, I would be adding more isolated fragments of knowledge to existing ones. Furthermore, I would run the risk of giving no more to the students than simplified technical knowledge and rigid methodological prescriptions. Why separate research from teaching? Why not involve the student teacher in the research work itself? Such an involvement could become most effective for the task of lesson planning and presentation, if it took the form of action-research. (1)

These considerations were the determining principle for establishing periodical 'research-courses', as I called them, in which the participants were given guidance by me to plan and carry out a small project of action-research in the field of teaching or learning of mathematics at school. Their character and their effects as a medium of teacher education may possibly best be illustrated by an example, which I wish to present in the form of the following report. It concerns a particular course given in one winter semester and taken by about thirty students. The topic of the research project was school pupils' ability in carrying out the division algorithm.

The course started with a discussion about the well-known fact, also confirmed by research, that pupils' achievement in long division is among the worst in all arithmetical notation. My students were mainly asked for appropriate reasons to explain their pupils' difficulties in bringing about the algorithm and the great number of

213

mistakes usually made by them. The question arose, whether this might be due to too little reflectiveness, too little understanding of the structure of the algorithm and the real meaning of its individual steps and their sequencing. In this context the course participants were to become especially involved in finding solutions to two problems: Is there any relation between pupils' ability to describe and explain the particular steps of the algorithm? If so, then what sort of relation is it found to be?

In order to find solutions, the student-teachers were confronted with the task of providing a design for an empirical investigation into the above problem and of carrying it out. In this way the course proceeded to the following seven activities.

First, compiling a test on long division. This test was administered to a randomly selected group of thirty seventh-graders of the 'Hauptschule St. Wolfgang' in Regensburg, in order to establish their mistakes with regard to number and category. The test items were nothing other than well-chosen division tasks of different degrees and kinds of difficulties.

Second, interviewing the testees. The course participants had to design a dialogue, by means of which each of the testees could be made to give descriptions and explanations of as detailed a kind as possible of the individual steps of the algorithm.

Third, analysing and representing the test results. To accomplish this the students received a hand-out including a description and definition of different kinds of mistakes usually made by school pupils in long division. (This paper was the product of a previous course.) Thus they were able to classify their pupils' mistakes in accordance with the following five categories:

1   mistakes in establishing quotient figures
2   mistakes in reminder evaluating
3   mistakes in bringing down further figures
4   mistakes concerning the figure 0 in the dividend and in the divisor
5   mistakes in handling the remainder at the end of a division.

The fourth activity was to carry out an analysis of the interviews on the basis of the tape recording made and the observer's notes. For this purpose the students were given a second hand-out pertaining to the study of children's linguistic performance in describing and explaining mathematical facts and actions. It advised them to analyse the interviews mainly in regard to the following questions:

1 What and how many technical terms were used by the pupil?
2 Is the meaning in which technical terms were used in accordance with the conventional definition?
3 Were the pupils' descriptions correct, complete, and clear?
4 What sorts of explanations were given? Were they correct, complete, and clear?

(The definitions of these categories were laid down in the hand-out. They too were the result of a previous investigation.)

The fifth activity consisted in planning a sequence of three lessons, with the aim of improving the testees' ability to describe and explain division (not their skill in carrying out the algorithm). The lessons were planned and taught by an experienced serving teacher.

The sixth activity was to repeat the above test with analogue items and the interviews, in both cases including their subsequent analysis.

The seventh activity compared the individual pupils' results both in test and interview. Thus the student-teacher could try to find out whether corrections with regard to the mistakes are an outcome of the testees' change in verbal, communicative performance. They could also try to judge the relations between mistakes and explanations of the individual steps taken and the structure of their sequencing in long division.

In the framework of this chapter it does not seem important to me to give more details on the research project itself. On the contrary, that would take too much attention from my main message on teacher-training. (2) I would much prefer instead to emphasize the benefits student-teachers have gained from their participation in it. It is expected to show in several fields of study and in the promotion of different abilities.

In the research project the students themselves were led to a very detailed analysis and a very elaborated understanding of the division algorithm. This was a necessary condition for the construction and analysis of the tests themselves, but even more so for designing, carrying out, and analysing the interviews undertaken. Most of the students confessed their feeling of having understood, for the first time in their lives, what 'is really going on in long division'. They realized what the meaning of the individual steps is and how their sequencing is structured. Lastly many of them seemed to have realized that in general a profound understanding of mathematical concepts and actions is an indispensable precondition for a successful teaching of these matters. The example of division may also have been a valuable experience of ways of arriving at this understanding.

As the next step the student-teachers came into close contact with pupils in the learning process. They had the chance to observe their mistakes and difficulties, their ways of (mis)understanding and of bridging gaps in knowledge and insight, their problems of explicating mathematical facts and ideas (even if understood). They at least obtained an impression of pupils' mental and emotional attitudes towards mathematics and learning of mathematics, such as their cognitive styles of using information, their attitude to work, and their motivation for doing mathematics. They could experience the tension which can arise between objectives of the syllabus, binding for the teacher, and the pupils' readiness and ability to achieve them, following which they may draw consequences for the necessary attempt to assign objectives best suited to the capacity of the individual learner. Last, but not least, they will have realized what deficiencies and omissions may be caused by questionable teaching strategies.

In the research project, besides mathematical and psychological problems, the course participants became acquainted with aspects of communication theory and linguistics. For not only had they to plan a dialogue according to an adequate communicational strategy, but also new possibilities of language analysis had to be learnt. They had to apply their new knowledge about the properties of language in the attempt to fit their own use of language to their pupils' skill of perceptive understanding within the interview. The students were also encouraged to study the relevant literature in the fields of psycholinguistics and classroom language. (3)

This one example of professional lesson-planning described above familiarized the course participants with the urgency of considering a number of closely interwoven factors: referring to the mathematical content, pupils' learning, the demands of the syllabus, methodological ideas and traditions, and the social conditions of learning. As different ways of proceeding were taken into consideration the students had to decide between alternative teaching strategies. Thus they could learn that, at least in this case, there is no teaching programme which a priori can be evaluated as 'the best one'.

One must add that by designing and carrying out an investigation, even on this modest scale, the student-teachers obtained much important experience of research in the educational field. They became acquainted with such research techniques as working out a test, planning and implementing an interview, analysing materials, formulating observations, and presenting results. This one example demonstrated in a convincing way the great effort needed if valid results are to be achieved. It also showed the mutual interdependence of research and professional practice, while indicating its complexity and intricacy as well.

It must be conceded that the research work possible in the framework of a one-term academic course cannot be more than a small field study or a trial run for a larger study. In my situation in general it makes little sense to continue the work in the next research-based course, since it will be attended by only a few of the original students, but by many others as a result of an individual study plan. The project has to be relatively self-contained which does not exclude bringing in results of earlier ones. Other topics for research-based courses already administered or planned by me include:

1   The understanding of work in mathematics by pupils.
2   Communicational disturbances within the classroom in the context of 'question-answer-teaching'.
3   Ways of concept-forming in pupils' minds.

My experience with such research has been very positive and I would like to recommend the approach to colleagues engaged in the education of mathematics teachers. It can be effective as a powerful motivation of student-teachers. Besides its effect of comprehending knowledge of different areas, it can be used to solve educational problems in the field of mathematics. It is not within my competence to decide whether the idea is capable of transfer to the training of teachers of other subjects.

Chapter Twelve

HUMAN HANDICAP AS A PROFESSIONAL EXPERIENCE FOR TEACHERS OF NATURAL SCIENCES

Günther Vogel

BEHAVIOUR TOWARDS HANDICAPPED PEOPLE

Relations between those not themselves handicapped and their handicapped fellows are marked by a high degree of ambivalence. Thus Jansen (quoted here after Klee) (1) could show after conducting his extensive research tests series in Germany that 90 per cent of those tested did not know how to behave towards a handicapped person, 63 per cent believed that handicapped people should be kept in special homes, 56 per cent said they did not wish to share a house with a handicapped person, and 70 per cent admitted to feelings of aversion when confronting such persons. (The total adds up to more than 100 per cent because the tests allowed several answers to be given.) If 90 per cent of 'normal' people confess their feelings of 'uncertainty' about how to relate to handicapped persons, it is not surprising that in two recent Frankfurt court cases, judgment was given which allowed a woman 'the right not to have to see handicapped people during her holiday' and in the second case the court ruled that a Tenants' Housing Co-operative 'could stop the construction of a home for handicapped people near their premises'. Other examples are not difficult to find, and what they all have in common is normal people objecting to the presence of those who differ from the norm because of their physical or mental handicaps, such as severe disfiguration. Indeed even small deviations can induce a clear defensive reaction on the part of many: physical features such as green hair, dwarfism, protruding ears, even more frequently the use of unusual dialect or expressions of speech, or just awkward behaviour. This kind of disapproval followed by avoidance of the handicapped is a deeply engrained human behaviour pattern. Bilz uses the term 'biological radicals' and applies it to inborn hereditary phenomena, that is those propensities found in human beings, indeed also in animals, and triggered off by virtue of an experience which brings about an action and reaction in our body structure. (2)

The ethical reforming of this 'biological radical', a sublimation or overcoming of feelings of revulsion, that is, must clearly be a basic task of education in schools. This task however has been either totally ignored or at least widely neglected. Its school curriculum potential remains hardly realized and therefore highly problematic. To what extent the subject of human handicap can be utilized in school lessons will be shown at the end of this chapter in a discussion of a number of appropriate curriculum applications.

HUMAN HANDICAP AS A CURRICULUM COMPONENT

The demands that have been made recently for intensive teaching about the problems of the disabled person as well as the associated question of integrating the disabled into society are certainly justified. The lack of such provision in many syllabuses, particularly for the subject of biology, has been treated comprehensively elsewhere. (3)

Judging by our experience, conventional teaching is most unlikely to be able to change this situation, especially since biology syllabuses are very much oriented along cognitive content structures. The subject area of 'the disabled person' can be grasped only imperfectly through the mere acquisition of information, even if action objectives in keeping with the requirements of society are discussed conscientiously and implemented according to plan. This kind of treatment remains confined to the level of the acquisition of knowledge only and is not capable of conveying real information about sickness and disabilities. Such teaching does not tell the student anything about the sick and disabled person as a person, about his or her demands and needs; about the person's means of discerning, experiencing, and comprehending the environment. These aspects of human experience, which we regard to be the central aim of the subject biology, are passed over.

To show to what extent the simulation of the state of

disablement can initiate this emotional process is the intention of this chapter. A number of experiences with students of different age groups, in different school types, as well as those actually studying the 'Special education for the physically handicapped' option are the subject of this study. When simulating the phenomenon of being disabled as a means of imitating a state of deficiency, the experience, that is the subjective state, usually dominates. It is determined by the encounter with an environment, by the state of simulation as well as by moods, emotions, and affective reactions.

'SIMULATION' IN A LEARNING CONTEXT

Simulation is an equivocal term, as can be seen from the Latin origins of the word. Simulation (simulatio, Latin pretence, hypocrisy) means on the one hand the deliberate pretence of symptoms (illness or inadequate performance), and on the other, the imitation of circumstances which cannot be investigated directly owing to the need for costly or dangerous procedures. The latter aspect is a major part of the flight-training programme carried out by pilots and astronauts. (4)

In the context of education, simulation may refer to such imitations or reconstructions of particular situations. Simulation has gained importance for classroom teaching over the last few years. In educational literature the term is often used in connection with the word 'game'. We encounter simulation games mainly in the form of acting out a given situation or role-playing. Out of a great number of publications, some major basic ones should be named, those by Abt, Boocock and Schild, Lehmann, and Lehmann and Portele, where further bibliographical information can be found. (5)

In educational management, simulation games play an increasingly important role, so that companies have been established which concentrate solely on designing such games - ABT Associates Inc., 'Project Simile', and others; magazines dealing with this subject are published in the USA and UK. Game is to be understood as an action subject to rules and not in the sense of playing without rules. Simulation games have the characteristics of both games and simulations; they overlap, as shown in Figure 2.

Lehmann and Portele identify three basic properties for such games. (6)

Figure 2 Overlap of game and simulation

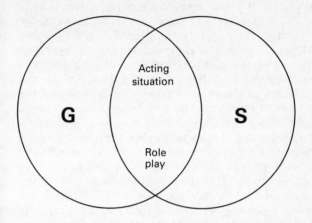

1   They are autotelic, thus they display the essential character of a game. The activity itself is carried out for the pleasure and functional joy it brings, coupled with the pleasure found in its objective content and end result. Such games are also played by higher vertebrate animals, albeit only during a brief growing-up phase. A retention of this juvenile characteristic is typical of human beings.
2   They are subject to rules. All the players submit voluntarily to a fixed code of rules which they have drawn up themselves or taken over after old tradition. The participants are in a competitive relationship to each other. In the process of such purposeful activity there are both winners and losers.
3   They simulate reality. In the pretended 'as if' situation participants assume a new, clearly delimited individuality and thereby agree to understand and respond to the role of the other players. The assumed situation thus forms the basis for resolving conflicts which may arise according to one's free personal decision, albeit without the fear of adverse consequences that any wrong decision or action taken in reality would bring with it. Any assessment and critical analysis of such an exercise must consult the simulation game itself as to its own agreed reality.

In the light of the above we might ask whether a simulation of being disabled can be seen as a game. For the simulation of 'disability' the action is autotelic, but it is in no manner subject to rules and only in part is it an 'as if' situation. It is also clear that simulation games are based only on activities which are in progress: such as solutions to conflicts in the economic and political sector and changes in the living environment. The simulation of a disability on the other hand imitates in the main a state, a deficiency of the faculty and senses of mobility. The simulation game requires the person performing the 'as if' action to become deeply involved in the role: a girl who is playing the director of a bank and a boy who takes the role of a mother must have fundamental insights into the activity in order to act out these roles accordingly. This is a reflection of the living circumstances, and the actor acquires new insights and expands old ones 'by doing'. However, the case is completely different when a disability is being simulated. An 'as if' situation is also present but it does not presuppose any basic knowledge about the condition itself; neither is the effort of doing justice to the condition a part of the role as in the simulation game. The 'driver of a wheelchair' would be indeed immobile without his chair at all times; the 'blind person' really cannot see. The person simulating these conditions does not have to play the role: the external circumstances are forced upon him and are fully accepted by his environment. The important aspect for him is, on the one hand, to adjust to the new situation and, on the other, to experience, understand, and interpret the reactions of the people he encounters. It is therefore totally inappropriate to place the simulation of disability in the intersecting or overlapping area of game and situation, as presented in Figure 2.

Simulation of a disability can be seen as an experiment in learning 'by doing': confrontation with the outside environment and the reflection of one's own condition in the simulated situation are the two dominating points occurring while simulating the state of disability. In this process of experience the act of simulating itself remains in the background, as mentioned earlier. It serves only to provide the new environment with which the simulating person is confronted as someone who is learning and experiencing. It is therefore appropriate to call this situation a test condition and thus to refer to it as an experiment in experience and learning by doing. It is also feasible to

Figure 3 Overlap of simulation and experiment

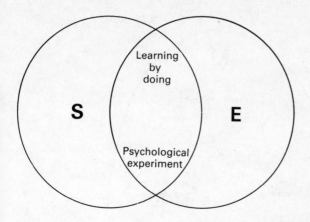

regard the simulation of 'being disabled' as an overlap of simulation and experiment that has first of all to be set up from scratch.

Figure 3 shows exactly the two basic concerns: on the one hand there is the simulative aspect in the sense of imitating or pretending a certain condition, and on the other hand there is the experimental one in the sense of

> controllable research situations in which conditions ... can be recognized and determined according to their elements of influence. (7)

In the following pages the term 'simulation of disability' is used in the same sense as an 'experiment in learning by doing', that is experiencing the condition of disability. The preceding definition demonstrates the processes and the dynamics involved in the interrelations affected better than the term 'simulation' alone. If we follow Raser's definition, (8) then simulation already describes the basics of a process in the sense of an operative model, that is simulation is the attempt to reflect a living circumstance in a frequently simplified model and also involves trying to cope with it actively. (9) When entering simulation into the previous model, we obtain the overall diagram of the simulation term and its intersecting areas as shown in Figure 4. In the surrounding areas, the non-simulative parts of the model - experiment and game - are represented as a

Figure 4 Simulation and its interrelations with model/ game/experiment

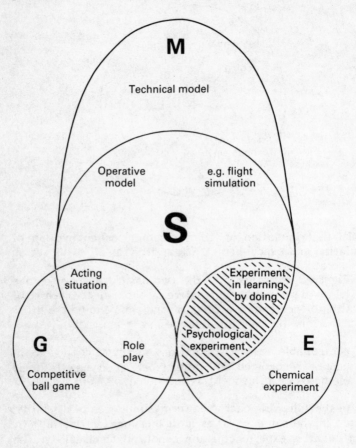

technical model, scientific experiment, and competitive ball game. The fields in the centre define simulation as an operative model and show the specific forms described here as overlapping with game and experiment.

IMPLEMENTATION OF THE EXPERIMENT IN 'LEARNING BY DOING'

There are important questions arising from the experiences available. First of all, we must ask to what extent such a simulation of 'disability' truly reflects reality. Does the simplification not lead to a gross reduction and misrepresentation of reality? Can the acting out of such conditions as paralysis be justified? Are children and young adults - indeed adults too - really capable of taking the simulated action seriously; are they able to draw appropriate conclusions for future behaviour? Or is it in fact that they tend rather to see this activity as fun and games and practice in the use of a wheelchair or how to cope with being blindfold? These questions must be taken seriously, if a decision is to be made whether the simulation of 'disability' should be incorporated into the sphere of curriculum development and teaching programmes. The necessary comprehensive field studies and research concerning the effect of such simulations in teaching are still lacking. Apart from my own experiences with wheelchair experiments in classroom teaching, (10) and in the further education of teachers, (11) as well as with the phenomenon of simulating blindness with students and teachers, I only know of a workshop conducted by Eva Preuss, who is also concerned with learning about being disabled 'by doing'. (12) Furthermore, for higher education colleges which offer training in the field of social sciences there exist some implementation machinery and concepts. There are also reports by Ernst Klee about learning by doing with students and careers advisers. (13)

It becomes apparent that the basic questions concerning such a curriculum cannot be answered off-hand. Three matters must first be clarified:

1   Which experiences can we draw on?
2   What theoretical base does the simulation approach have?
3   How important a role does the simulation technique play in the classroom situation?

SIMULATION IN THE CLASSROOM

As there is so far no educational experience of this phenomenon generally available, no objective discussion of facts does exist which could provide the basis for a theoretical evaluation. It is therefore inevitable that we concentrate on the third point: the importance accorded to simulation in practical teaching.

Learning by doing enables the students better to render reality than is the case with earlier teaching methods. The 'simulator' engages with their environment actively: this allows them to practise the situation, to experience their own role and the reactions of other people which thus results in a higher level of willingness to co-operate. It can be assumed that apart from these general socialization effects (due to the apparently greater understanding), critical thinking and significant changes in attitude are achieved. This does, however, have to be expected, if - in keeping with a greater readiness to exchange experiences and to become involved in group discussions - a guided internalization is included. For the classroom situation, it must be noted that the teacher must not interfere too much with the action, because the action in particular is a major advantage of learning by doing: the students may acquire experiences in a relaxed atmosphere; they are able to move freely without the usual confrontation between teacher and student. The gap between the classroom and the 'real world' is bridged practically completely in the 'learning by doing' approach. Two classroom experiments may illustrate this.

Simulation in a wheelchair

Some bibliographical references concerning the 'learning by doing' approach are given in Klee, Preuss, Rasper and Vogel. (14) It is important for classroom teaching that a sufficient number of technical details are taught, practising certain movements with the wheelchair, overcoming small obstacles when riding, and also that tasks to be accomplished are clearly defined (for example certain routes to be taken, asking for information, shopping) and finally that precise objectives to be achieved are specified: to find out how people react to you, how does it 'feel' to be in a wheelchair? The person in the wheelchair has someone accompanying him. Taken as a whole, this experiment in learning by doing requires extensive preparation and just as extensive follow-up. 'Real' wheelchair-confined people should be asked to participate in the discussion, and the same goes for other disability situations being simulated.

Blindness as an experiment

We have found that the acquisition of basic experiences in the highly individual living conditions of a disabled person can be achieved without a great deal of time involved, while providing at the same time a very intense simulation of what it is like to be blind. We have chosen to implement the simulation experiment 'blindness', to illustrate our classroom situation. In order to depict this 'deficiency' of non-optical perception of space as exactly as possible, it is important first to look at some of the conditions of the procedure.

Procedure: a 'blind person' is given the task of trying to perceive an unknown room as well as possible. A 'guide' ensures that the 'blind person' can move around the room freely and without hazards. During the experiment (approximately 10 minutes), no verbal communication is permitted between the 'guide' and the 'blind person', because through acoustic stimuli alone exact spatial patterns can be assembled. Immediately following the experiment the formerly 'blind person' makes a sketch of the room under supervision that is as close as possible to the room he or she has experienced and the objects in it. Verbal communication is to be avoided throughout. In the next step the 'guide' and the 'blind person' exchange roles. Another room is investigated. At the end of the second round, the sketch and the room are compared.

In order to make the experiment as effective as possible, it is advisable to discuss the following seven questions concerning the observation with the students:

1   What role does the tactile sense play in the experiment (touching with hands and feet)?
2   What role does the acoustic sense play (paying attention to noises, knocking on objects)?
3   Do other sensory perceptions play a role?
4   How do I try to remember an impression of the room?
5   How do I make a sketch?
6   What feelings do I experience during a perception deficiency?
7   How do I perceive the presence of the 'guide'?

In the ensuing discussion of the results between teachers and students the depiction of the emotional aspect of the experience must receive special attention.

The total phenomenon of being blind is impossible to

grasp, because as people who normally see, we have an almost exclusively optical orientation and cannot adequately assess the tactile and acoustic impressions which are the focal perceptions of this short test situation. If real access to the situation of being blind since birth (primary blindness) is therefore impossible, acquired (secondary) blindness can be experienced in some of its dimensions through simulation. Particularly the blind person's confinement to the immediate surroundings, the feeling of extreme isolation and a certain embodiment of the self on the one hand as well as the heightened sensitivity of the 'remaining' senses on the other can be conveyed by means of a well-planned and implemented simulation experiment.

In distinguishing between the optical and non-optical perceptions, optical perception is often compared to the process of photography. However, the comparison of the visual organ with a camera is only partly correct. Already on the retina the visual stimuli are processed according to their size, colour, contrasting movement, and other parameters. Corresponding stimulations enter separately several areas of the cerebral cortex, finally to combine into a coherent image, an integrated perception of space.

Spatial perception achieved by tactile stimulation is based on an entirely different principle. In the case of tactile orientation the environment to be perceived can be apprehended only for a brief period of time, the moment of touch itself, in a narrow segment of space. This is because space is palpated in successive moves and therefore, a topographical image can be rendered correctly only while the successive tactile simulation models are still stored in the brain. Since an optical orientation does not require such a successive storage effort to apprehend space (it is simultaneous), tactile perception will always be deficient when compared with optical perception.

EDUCATIONAL IMPLICATIONS

The educational situation described above has shown a way to sensitize students to the topic of human handicap by means of simulation via a learning process which is not their everyday experience. What value such an education can have will be demonstrated, using both curriculum development and teacher preparation as examples.

Handicap and the curriculum

The possibilities of simulating handicap experience in order to provide students with a real and comprehensive understanding of the problems of human handicap which we have described run counter to the traditional inflexible teacher-led interpretation of the school curriculum. Experiencing a situation, which though simulated can nevertheless assume the character of a real happening for the student and the environment reacting to it, largely eludes any deliberate teacher activity. This is because rigid preparations and intended syllabus plans cannot be maintained. Ben-Peretz refers to the teacher in such a situation as a partner in curriculum development. (15) A space on the school timetable free from subject constraints which teachers can plan for themselves and for which they alone are accountable is a necessary condition for success. Very important for this particular function is the teacher's ability to interpret the curriculum on offer. (16) We agree with Ben-Peretz that syllabus materials may be altered and supplemented by teachers in a given teaching situation according to their own creativity and their own concept of curriculum interpretation. Only this role can give teachers the chance to realize their educational task in school. However, this requires that teachers are given the duty and the opportunity, while still in training, to inform themselves about human handicap and especially about the repercussions of handicap on the people afflicted by it, as well as their dependants and their immediate environment.

The situation in the Federal Republic

An appropriate framework for realizing this educational task has existed in the Federal Republic since early 1973. In that year the Bildungsrat, following the recommendations of the Education Commission (Bildungskommission), published a short compendium of syllabuses on the topic of human handicap for use in all institutions concerned with teacher education. (17) It suggested that one-tenth of the total professional course study time for future teachers of infant, junior, and senior (Hauptschule) primary-school pupils, as well as an unspecified 'some time' of the study period required of all other student teachers, be devoted to matters of special education and relevant preparation. The

229

document names three areas:

1   The infant teachers must have the knowledge of the common, as well as those likely to surface, handicaps in learning and behaviour in speech and the psychomotor areas, including the necessary psychological and sociological procedures.
2   Their course must include a survey of educational measures for dealing with handicaps, including the ability to apply differential and individual preventive measures, such as in the case of epilepsy.
3   The student-teacher must be given a survey of facilities available in special education establishments at pre-school level.

In the transition period in which tertiary education cannot fully take these on board, all establishments for the further and in-service training of teachers should assume these duties.

The recommendations go on, stressing that information is to be available in professional meetings, conferences, courses, during school visits, and secondment periods for teachers.

Meanwhile, more than a decade has passed since the publication of the recommendations. Unfortunately hardly any changes have occurred in the training of teachers in this respect. It seems therefore particularly important that this educational task be accomplished through the teachers' non-subject specific contact time referred to above. For example, in the Land of the Rhineland-Palatinate the so-called teachers' 'unassigned time' (18) is allocated at least 20 per cent of teachers' regular contact time on the school timetable, (19) which in more recent circulars of the minister of education has been increased to 30 per cent of time. (20) Now this means that teachers have about one-third of teaching time at their disposal, which they themselves can decide how to use, as to method and content. We can expect even more requests for help and advice from teachers on how to use their newly found free time. It is likely that simulation games of the kind described here have therefore a good chance of being allocated the space they deserve on the timetable. The British experience of integrated special needs and 'support teaching' pupils is a development worth watching, although we are not aware of the use of simulation techniques with this group of pupils.

OUTLOOK

Work with teachers and student-teachers and practical work in schools has shown that the concern with the topic of human handicap can be effective only if it is linked with personal physical experience and social encounter of handicap. This is bound to have consequences for all practising teachers. Teachers who have themselves seen how avoidance, reluctance, revulsion, shyness, and other 'biological radicals' can be overcome or diffused, have at the same time made a significant contribution towards understanding the many 'lesser evils' of their students. They will be better prepared to handle successfully the shy, awkward student or the student with speech difficulties. By helping their students to overcome prejudice teachers will have contributed to making our schools more 'human' once again.

Chapter Thirteen

COMPUTER-ASSISTED LEARNERS: AUTOMATONS OR THINKING INDIVIDUALS?

Brent Robinson

> The computer is the Proteus of machines. Its essence is
> its universality ... Because it can take on a thousand
> forms and can serve a thousand functions, it can appeal
> to a thousand tastes. (1)

The information technology imperative is currently felt by
educationalists in all spheres of pedagogy. It is only likely to
increase in urgency and in breadth in coming years.
Internationally there are state initiatives to increase the
level of electronic provision and usage in schools. Locally
parents and employers wish to see children using the
technology. So teachers, teacher-educators, and advisory
staff respond to the prompting, urged on by their own
colleagues and by academics keen to exploit the potential of
the new technology for enhancing the educational processes
to which we subject our children. But what is the reality?
Are computers really going to change these educational
processes? Are they indeed capable of enhancing learning
and, if they are, will teachers let them?

The computer is an exceedingly flexible and adaptable
tool in education. That is both its strength and its weakness.
It can provide a multiplicity of learning activities and
learning rates suited to the needs of individual learners. But
it can also mean, and in practice has meant, that the
machine can be hijacked: its uses predicated upon
traditional patterns of teaching and learning styles which
pay little attention to the needs of individuals and to
personal growth. Too often, teachers have visions of serried
rows of students seated at terminals to undertake
mechanized learning processes which curb curiosity, which

stultify creativity and which reduce individuals to automata. And yet our use of computers in classrooms today only reflects what designers and teachers have decided to do with the machines. Critics who castigate the new technology for the style of learning it presents often do so only on the basis of what they have seen. They base their comments upon observation of such limited software as we have produced to date and upon the unimaginative ways in which we have chosen to deploy both hardware and software in the classroom. Many critics are not aware of the intrinsic attributes of the new technology, far less are they aware of the potential which has yet to be realized.

It should not be denied that the technology itself does impose some constraints upon the ways in which we may use it. Of course there will be some educational activities for which a computer will be totally inappropriate. And even if a computer does seem appropriate, it would still be foolish to assume that the technology imposed no constraints or influences of its own within the classroom. The technology probably is not totally neutral despite its apparent flexibility. MacLuhan alerted us, for instance, to the fact that the new technology has a certain logic, a certain social form through which it must operate. (2) It is easy to see how software promotes certain educational values at the expense of others both in its content and in its style of function. Less obviously, even content-free 'utility' software might involve constraining influences. The way in which a database is designed will say something about the way in which knowledge is viewed by the designer: what type of knowledge is considered important, how human beings do, or should, process and organize that knowledge. Similarly a word processor makes assumptions about the way(s) in which we write, why we write, and whom we are writing for. Indeed it is a not uncommon remark among computer users that electronic databases and word processors have extensively altered the ways in which users process information and sometimes even the purposes for which they process it.

What we have seen to date has been a very limited subset of what computers can do. Early software designers were not educators but programmers. They knew more about machine architecture than about learning and the operation of the human brain. It is quite probable that they were attracted to borrow from the disciplines of education and from psychology only that which was immediately perceived

233

to be programmable. At the same time, however, their understanding of the potential of computer technology was influenced by what we may now regard as the unhelpful models of mental processes and of learning which were then prevalent. Mechanized models of the workings of the human brain are not new. Freud thought of the mind as a steam engine with dreams as its safety valves. With the advent of computers, various analogies were noted between human learning and the processes of computing. Green and Laxon observed that our grasp of number could be seen in computing terms: input, feedback, processing, store, and output. (3) Behaviourist theories of operant conditioning also provided an essentially mechanical model of human learning. It is within this context that much early software was designed and its legacy is still with us. So much tutorial software today is still of a drill and skill approach little different from that implemented by Skinner's primitive feedback machines in the 1950s and 1960s.

Behaviourist theories of learning also had a significant effect on the classroom practice which early software designers drew upon in the teaching styles they embodied in software. This was especially so in the USA where computer technology was first fully developed and its educational potential explored. Even beyond the USA however, where the behaviourist influence was less widely felt, formal classroom teaching styles still tended to depend upon tightly structured learning patterns which lent themselves easily to software design. In terms of hardware, the homogeneous style of whole class teaching also favoured the adoption of multi-user computer networks rather than stand-alone work stations necessitating more individualized, or at least, group working contexts. (4)

There was no really strong technological reason why networks and computer laboratories should have been promoted. Historically student access to computers was first limited to large mainframe and (later) mini-computers, since the microcomputer had not been invented. Obviously the sheer size and expense of such large computer systems precluded widescale access. The direct experience of using the computer ('hands-on experience') was therefore restricted to individuals or very small groups. Interestingly however, this individual use was not sustained as the technology developed. When more than one terminal to a computer became possible, it was considered desirable for students to be provided with one-to-one access, the terminals normally grouped together within the same room. Today networking has become a widely accepted norm. The French '10,000 computers' plan is a typical example. It was initially designed to provide an average of eight microcomputers per secondary school on the basis that 'by pairing the students, half a normal sized class could work together at the keyboards'. (5)

Why should simultaneous large group or whole class access be demanded? There is no technological reason why multiple terminals have to be sited together. Doing so facilitates supervision and support by experienced technical and teaching personnel. If the computers are networked so that they share some of the same facilities (like printers and file servers) then this is also more economic. Perhaps, however, there are more telling causes than these.

There has certainly been expressed a fundamental belief that using the hardware is about hardware familiarization and not about the enrichment of educational processes. Government agencies, in particular, have become very concerned with the economic and social implications of a technologically ignorant society. In both France and Britain part of the funding for technological innovation has been provided by government departments concerned with industry rather than with education. The innovation is thus concerned with computer familiarization and vocational skills rather than with the enrichment of learning in a wider sense.

In Britain the initiative to put a computer into each school was taken not by the DES but by the Department of Trade and Industry (DTI). It was an attempt to provide the necessary 'high tech' skills enabling the country to regain, or at least to retain, its former leading economic and political position within rapidly developing advanced societies in which the technology of information was expected to play a fundamental role in the maintenance of the social, economic, and political infrastructure.

There is no doubt indeed that society is rapidly becoming transformed into one which is both information rich and information dependent. Nor is it disputable that familiarization with information technology should play a vital role in the education of our children. The term 'computer literacy' emphasizes the importance of the skills involved and familiarization with the new technology must be placed alongside reading and writing as basic skills vital to our functioning within society. This initiative, however, in its present state, is unlikely to succeed. The last great technological revolution changed the nature of the educational system. The present technological revolution has so far failed to modify schools to meet its needs. It was the demand for a skilled and disciplined work-force that led to the establishment in Britain of a state education system. It was not merely the content of the curriculum which was determined by the technological needs of society. Alvin Toffler draws some interesting direct parallels between the factory system, the structure of the school day, and methods of teaching. (6)

Much of what Toffler identified as symptomatic of that first technological revolution is still in evidence today. Indeed, recent political interventions in British education seem likely to result in a curriculum and methods of teaching and of assessment which retain nineteenth-century values and expectations rather than a progression to meet the demands of the final years of this century. It is within such a context that the new technology is being introduced. And it is a context which is singularly inappropriate.

The new technology demands skills of a quite different nature from those traditionally taught in schools. Computer usage requires not only familiarity with the mechanics of operation, but also higher order cognitive reasoning. Word processing is a liberating activity in the formulation and transmission of ideas. Another typical use of the computer in the adult world is for the storage of large quantities of information which can be quickly interrogated, sorted, and retrieved. Here, too, sophisticated skills are required of the users. Moreover electronic communications are accentuating the demands being made. One of the latest British government initiatives, again from the DTI has been to offer to each school the ability to link at least one computer to the telephone network for the transfer of information between remotely sited computers. It is now possible for schools to use a computer to communicate with computers in other schools, or with large computers in other institutions and countries hosting databases and other forms of information provision. The government's educational initiative reflects what is happening in society. Cheap, fast, and large amounts of information are now being stored and communicated in a myriad of ways around the world. Information-seekers are no longer confined to the information sources available locally, but have global sources available to them. They need to know how to enter this vast storage labyrinth and how to get the information out. Moreover, the user needs to be aware of the transitory nature of such knowledge. Electronic storage means that the information provider as well as the seeker can quickly and economically manipulate that information. Electronic information is not permanent. It can be quickly revised and updated. This raises affective as well as cognitive issues. Individuals in a 'high-tech' information-rich society must have confidence as well as proven ability to seek out information as and when they need it. They must be able to evaluate what they retrieve and to be critically appreciative of the fact that electronic information, like any other information, is socially constructed and humanly mediated. Perhaps more than anything else, students will need to be willing and able to gather enough information about the reality of any situation to be able to change and adapt to it.

Students will not gain the vital requisite skills without radical changes in the way in which many teachers currently use computers in schools. The computer is a very flexible tool but this entails both advantages and disadvantages. Outside school, society has been quick to activate the potential of the technology, putting it to new uses which make new demands upon its users. But it is a naive assumption that the introduction of computers into classrooms will make similar demands which will then affect the teaching or learning patterns within schools. The machine is still too often predicated upon existing patterns of education. The computer classroom is, for example, indicative of a formal class-based style of teaching which is a legacy dictated by the needs of an earlier technological society. It does nothing to develop the confident independence, enquiring mind, and masterful adaptability demanded by our technological future.

Our current use of computers is little different from that of any other new technological device, perhaps any other resource - technological or otherwise. In all these cases, the possibilities for altered styles of learning have rarely been developed. Audio tape recording is a typical example. Magnetic tape recording gave the opportunity for a new type of resource to be made available for students. While it would be true to say that it has promoted listening activities within the classroom, its use as a genuinely alternative resource to suit the needs of individual learners has not been fully exploited. The invention of the compact audio cassette made tape storage, cataloguing, and playback very simple even for young children to manage. Some schools have made notable advances in the provision of audio cassette resources, making them available for individual and group use in resource centres and class or school libraries. For the most part, however, the audio cassette is used for whole class activities. It has been assimilated within the traditional learning patterns of the school and has not in itself led towards the development of any student-oriented or resource-based learning.

The computer might appear to be a very different medium. Its dynamic and interactive mode of presentation implies, indeed necessitates, an underlying pedagogy and because it is an active rather than a passive medium, it would seem to be difficult for teachers to repress the manifestation of that pedagogy. Of course, since much of the software has been designed with traditional pedagogic models in mind, there is no immediate mismatch between the resource and its context. It simply reinforces what already exists in the classroom. Yet even innovative software which has not been founded upon formal, traditional styles of learning can very often be constrained by its context. A word processor can be used simply as a copying device, an 'electronic typewriter', for the production of a final draft of a student's work. The initial drafting can all take place away from the computer. Other excellent software designed for collaborative group work can also be used by isolated individuals sitting at a multi-user network. Teachers will choose software which supports a pedagogy familiar to them. Failing that, they will deploy both hardware and software in ways which support the existing infrastructure and explicit teaching/learning styles of their classrooms. In this the computer may be no different from any other resource. As with any resource, the uses to which it is put depend very considerably upon the classroom context, the way in which the teacher is prepared to use that resource.

To a very large extent, what the technology can do depends upon what we make it do. It is as flexible as the software we design to run on it and the context within which we choose to deploy it in the classroom. We should thus ask ourselves what it is that we want the computer (and education) to do and whether that can in fact be done.

Most learning theorists, whatever their background, would agree with Sperry that learning is a very individualized process:

> The more we learn, the more we recognise the unique complexity of any one individual intellect and the stronger the conclusion comes that the individuality inherent in our brain networks makes that of fingerprints or facial features grossly simple by comparison. (7)

Students have different backgrounds, different abilities, and different ways of learning. The problem is therefore how to reach each individual student effectively. The issue is seldom addressed adequately in our educational systems. In a typical classroom everyone receives the same material in the same way at the same rate. The time available for individualized attention is very small indeed. This is not to say that our current institutional structures cannot achieve individualization in some circumstances. Interaction between the teacher and students on a one-to-one basis is one possible example of how teaching can be individualized. But this can be only a small part of a student's total learning experience. Given typical student-teacher ratios, the dearth of resource provision and the constraints of our organizational systems, most teachers abandon any thoughts of individual attention.

Typically our standard learning procedures treat all students in the same way. If a student at a particular point in a particular course lacks some important background information, that student is carried along with everyone else in class. Missing information is hard to acquire. The rational procedure would be to allow any student needing special help to stop the major flow of learning at that point and to go back and pick up any necessary background information.

On a one-to-one basis, the computer has distinct advantages in this respect. With good material available, computers can allow individualized learning responsive to student needs. Student input is analysed and appropriate action taken. With a computer, each student can move at a pace best suited to him or her. Each student will be responding frequently to questions so the computer can determine what the learner understands or does not understand at any particular point. Remedial aid can be given where appropriate simply as part of the flow of the material with no break from the learner's point of view. Indeed, a very definite advantage is that there need be no impression that any special treatment is being provided.

The way in which the computer can respond to

individual development is becoming potentially more sophisticated as the technology advances. It is not only the rate of delivery which the computer can vary but also the type of delivery. Information can be provided in a variety of ways. Some students progress well through literate modes of learning. Others function better in graphic modes. It is quite possible for a computer to respond by presenting information in a variety of modes (depending of course on the nature of the information). Microcomputers can already store, present, and manipulate considerable quantities of text and produce high quality graphics. Laser technology has increased both attributes. Videodiscs can hold over 50,000 frames of text together with a vast library of still and moving captions and real life images.

It is not only the display which can be diversely presented in this way. The type of interaction can also vary. Keyboard input allows a variety of interactions to take place. These might be literate or numeric. The keyboard also contains keys which allow for cursors to be moved around the screen to identify particular textual or graphic options to be followed. Other types of input device are becoming common. Touch sensitive screens, joysticks, light pens, tracker balls, mice, and touch pads are all found in varying applications. There is no reason why their use might not be further extended to suit individual needs.

Beyond the mode of delivery and response, the degree of interaction and its type are also important variables. A problem in education, particularly education which must deal with very large numbers of students, is the fact that the possibility of having learners who are always playing an active as well as an individual role in the learning process has been lost. In a Socratic approach to learning, two or three students worked closely with the teacher, answering questions individually directed at them.

> The acquisition of knowledge, be it the recognition of a pattern, the attainment of a concept, the solution of a problem, or the development of a scientific theory, is an active process. The individual ... should be regarded as an active participant in the knowledge-getting process. (8)

Logistically we cannot afford to model our educational systems in this way. However it is precisely one of the computer's main advantages in learning that it is able to provide an interactive learning experience. Any technology which creates individualized learning and makes the student more active is bound to be attractive. When the student appears to be in control of the speed and difficulty level of the program and when a one-to-one rather than a thirty-to-one situation is possible, a student is likely to be more mentally active and learn more.

However, using a computer is no guarantee against passive learning or minimal active learning, especially where the user has only to press a key to turn the page or perhaps choose one key from three to indicate an answer in a multiple-choice program. Paradoxically it also appears to be the case that students can be made more passive by computer-assisted learning. The student is often responding rather than inaugurating. Any technology which prescribes what is to be learnt, controls speed and difficulty level, and judges correctness of student answers, may contain a hidden curriculum. When working with such technology, the student learns to accept authority and to accept an authoritative view of knowledge. The computer can appear to be legitimizing what is taught, what is correct and incorrect, with the consequential effect that students become passive recipients of authoritative knowledge. This is obviously very true of drill and practice software but it is also true of more imaginative computer-assisted learning packages. It is to its credit that one Piagetian-based piece of software, LOGO, reverses the situation; that is it places the children in control to program the computer to explore their ideas rather than programming them via the computer. Even here, however, as with word processors, databases, and other content-free software, the students are still completing a task specified by the teacher.

It is not just software which militates against autonomy of learning: there is also the factor of the hardware and the way it is organized. The linking together of computers into networks and the use of computer laboratories are now the norm in many countries. These also ramify the hidden curriculum replicating the authority structure of the classroom, promoting acceptance and passivity at the expense of self-enquiry. As a result, students may become less likely to develop confidence in personal knowledge, less likely to develop the ability to seek out knowledge from diverse sources. Computers will not suit every student's optimal way of learning and yet no alternative activities may be provided and no alternative resources to achieve the same learning goals. If computers are networked, the problem is compounded because the variety of programs is restricted to what is available on the network at any one time: the limit of software available on disk or what can be accessed simultaneously. The only differentiated activities might become simply alternative levels and paces provided within any one programmed activity.

In all this, students learn to accept authority and an authoritative view of knowledge. They become dependent upon the program, being programmed by the microcomputer rather than developing multi-experiential routes through a curriculum area. Their own individual learning styles fail to become exploited. They are not encouraged to develop independent and enquiring minds nor the confidence to use them.

In Britain in primary schools at least, it is possible to detect a growing desire to place the child at the centre, not the machine. With only one or two computers available to them, teachers are being forced to adopt new ways of structuring classroom activity. To enable all children to gain access to the computer a much more fluid learning environment has to be created. The class is often broken down into groups or even individuals working on a variety of activities in succession. In this way all children get access to the computer in turn. At other times, children may be allowed to work at their own rate so that demand for the computer can be staged. Students may even be allowed to work on activities of their own choosing which may or may not involve the computer, thus also alleviating the demand made upon it.

The computer is becoming simply an enabling device through the use of a range of content-free software. In the humanities students are beginning to use databases as alternative information sources. They are also constructing databases as alternative ways of recording the information they gather and of their reworking of it. Distanced electronic networking is opening up channels of communication to new and extended audiences for work in English and modern foreign languages. Powerful modelling packages help students understand scientific processes while computer calculation and word processing are being taken up as useful adjuncts to study throughout the curriculum.

In all this, the eventual aim must be to enable and develop learners as autonomous individuals capable of choosing when, where, for what purpose, and with what effect they will turn to the technology which will surround them in future life. Teachers must therefore give students a much freer hand in how they use the technology, or indeed, whether they use it at all. A range of software should be available for student choice. We think here of both computer-assisted learning packages and of the more open flexible content-free packages like spreadsheets, word processors, and databases. The computer is one resource among many. Sometimes a student will want to turn to the teacher for information or advice, sometimes to a book, sometimes to a database (on disk or on line), sometimes to a computer-assisted learning package or simulation. In an ideal world, the student should have a range of software available for each particular task. After all, the computer is as flexible as the software we design to run on it. One word processor can make the machine behave in a very different way from another word processor. Children should be able to decide when to use a pen, when to use a word processor and, if the latter, which word processor best suits the needs of the moment or their own preferred way of writing.

The need for personal autonomy in tools for the task as well as in choice of task creates an imperative need to foster individual awareness of each task in hand and for individual awareness of his or her own nature. As a number of authorities are now urging, we should stop thinking about technology in education, that is thinking chiefly concerned with equipment, the elaboration of ad hoc messages and the incorporation of technology into traditional teacher-centred activities. Instead, we should think about the technology of education, that is the systematic application of the resources of scientific knowledge to the process that each individual has to go through in order to acquire and use knowledge.

In itself, the computer will not change the curriculum. Unless the curriculum changes, it will not equip children to use computers fully. In order to achieve this, we must recognize the importance of skills rather than factual content, of individual needs rather than common impositions. Teachers too must change their role. For some time now the teacher as the sole provider of information has been challenged. The new technology is accelerating the amount of information generated and its rate of change. No one can keep up with this. No one has to. It is far more important that students learn with confidence how and where to access information when they want it and only what they want without information overload. It is not for the teacher to provide the data but for the teacher to provide students with the means of obtaining that data wherever in the world it might be.

It is easy to see why so many teachers are wary of the new technology. Even though computers are becoming more robust and 'user friendly', computer usage still requires a degree of expertise. There is further the insecurity induced by reliance upon resources which may at times be unreliable. Such insecurity is fuelled in this case by the fact that the resource is totally unlike any other in the classroom. It is one which the students are likely to know far more about than the teacher. It is a dynamic and interactive resource. Indeed it is one which can be seen to rival or replace the teacher, generating its own teaching and learning styles (according to the software running upon it) and becoming the focus of classroom attention. This last claim should not be overstated. As was argued above, teachers are very good at dynamic conservatism. It is all too easy to confine the pervasion of new technology to an isolated subject within the curriculum. Failing that, it is normally possible for teachers to find software which does not threaten their existing roles and styles of classroom teaching. But if the technology fails to threaten, it is because we have so far failed to take up the real challenge of the new technology. This is true not only of teachers but also of society at large. The threat of the new technology is symptomatic of the very real need for change in the way we organize our education. Until we move from an industrial to a post-industrial curriculum which is student centred with students' real needs at its heart, we cannot possibly educate our children for their future.

Part III

THE SCHOOL REALITY

Chapter Fourteen

THE POLITICS OF TEACHER EDUCATION

Denis Lawton

INTRODUCTION

It may be helpful to begin by defining both terms in the chapter title. I am taking the word 'politics' to be concerned with power and control rather than party politics; teacher education covers initial training as well as the in-service or continuing education of teachers. I will try to write about teacher education in a way which will permit as much generalization as possible, but the examples will tend to be drawn from a limited number of countries, especially the UK.

WHY CONTROL?

Sooner or later in most countries attempts are made to exercise greater central control over the teacher education system. There are at least three reasons for this: first, if education is regarded as politically important then it will be just as necessary to control teacher education as to have, for example, a centrally planned curriculum; second, politicians will wish to ensure that the politics of education do not stray too far from the politics of the controlling party - teacher education is clearly an important element in this; third, education, including teacher education, is expensive - politicians and civil servants have an interest in limiting expenditure and obtaining what they perceive as value for money. A prior political issue to questions of control is, therefore, the need to establish whether teacher education should exist at all: is it really an advantage to have school-teachers who are professionally trained?

Denis Lawton

DOES TEACHER-TRAINING MAKE A DIFFERENCE?

Is there a clear case for establishing or retaining a national system of teacher education and for making teacher-training compulsory? The World Bank, for example, was sceptical about the benefits of teacher education in 1974, and commissioned no fewer than thirty-two studies to investigate the relationship between the quality and training of teachers and student achievement; by 1978 they were convinced of the value of teacher-training and moved on to more detailed investigations. (1) In general, research demonstrates that the quality of teachers is important, and that a significant variable is initial teacher-training. If this appears to be a statement of the obvious, it should be remembered that much of the US research of the 1970s suggested that home background and other factors were much more significant than the influence of the school and the quality of the teachers. (2)

One of the reactions to those studies was a series of attempts to demonstrate that schools could be made more effective by identifying, and changing, isolated factors which were considered to be significant in effective schools such as class size, quality of school buildings, or curriculum materials. These studies were generally unsuccessful in finding the answer to improving quality. The next wave of studies concentrated on 'holistic' approaches: identifying high-scoring and low-scoring schools and relating them to features of the school as a whole, such as school climate.

Purkey and Smith carried out a very interesting review of the 'effective schools' studies. (3) From a re-analysis of the results, they derived a theory of school improvement based on the idea of the importance of school culture. They concluded that the characteristics of effective schools were as follows:

1 autonomy for school staff to tackle problems of achievement
2 good 'leadership'
3 staff stability
4 curriculum planning
5 staff development
6 parental involvement and support
7 recognizing the importance of academic success
8 maximizing learning time (time spent on task)
9 support from local authority.

248

In addition to the above structural factors, Purkey and Smith identified four process variables connected with school climate:

1   collaborative planning and collegial relationships
2   sense of community
3   clear goals and high expectations commonly shared
4   order and discipline.

It would therefore appear that effective schools need teachers who are not only well trained but who are committed to certain educational values as well as possessing a number of personal qualities. It would follow from this that far more attention should be paid to problems of recruitment and selection of appropriate personality types for teaching.

THE QUALITY OF RECRUITS

To some extent it must be true that the quality of the teaching profession is related to the quality of the recruits: initial training may be an important factor, but irrespective of course quality, the calibre of the entrants will also be an important determining factor. The recruitment of good quality candidates to the teaching profession is partly a question of the status of the profession compared with other opportunities which may be available. Any administration which allows the attractiveness of the profession to fall below a certain (undefinable) level runs the risk of causing damage to the system which may be irreparable.

Part of the problem for the teaching profession is the number of teachers involved: there are usually so many teachers that it is difficult for them to be regarded in the same way as small elite groups such as doctors and lawyers; it is equally difficult for most countries to afford to pay teachers salaries comparable with other professionals. Not only is the teaching profession a large one, but also it has expanded very rapidly in the recent past: from approximately 16 million in 1966 to about 35 million in 1984, according to world figures from an ILO/UNESCO study in 1984. When such large numbers are involved, it is probably illusory for teachers to seek parity with the 'learned' professions, and it may be tactically more sensible to develop different arguments for improved conditions of service.

Many countries experienced a dramatic fall in numbers of pupils in primary and secondary schools in the 1970s and 1980s, and consequently a decline in the demand for teachers. The new situation of a surplus of teachers often carried with it unfortunate side-effects: the declining job prospects in teaching deterred some from applying and there were fewer candidates to choose from. Moreover the intellectual calibre of students opting for teacher-training tended to decline: in 1981 the Dean of Stanford University's School of Education reported that the aptitude scores for college entrants of those enrolled for teacher-training were second from the bottom of the list. (4) In the UK difficulties of recruitment and problems of quality were reported in 1985 and 1986.

In those countries with a high age participation rate in higher education as a whole it is more likely that the supply of teachers will be adequate: the more educated young people there are available the more likely it is that selection will be necessary. Some countries such as the UK are particularly vulnerable if they retain a policy of keeping the age participation rate low. Where there is an overall shortage of graduates the teaching profession is unlikely to attract the best and most qualified.

SELECTION

Where selection is possible, those responsible for selecting candidates for teaching are usually more confident about specifying academic qualifications than assessing desirable attitudes or personality traits which are notoriously difficult to identify and measure.

In recent years it has been suggested that practising teachers should be involved in interviewing candidates for places on initial training courses. It has also been suggested that if preliminary interviews could take place in a school setting, involving the applicant in some kind of contact with children, then this might give better predictive results. Properly controlled studies are needed to put these ideas to the test. Meanwhile, uncertainty about the effectiveness of such selection procedures has not prevented some governments from introducing them as official policy. Initial training establishments have also been urged to weed out candidates with personalities incompatible with school-teaching, but no guidance has been given about how this might be achieved. (5)

In Scotland there has been greater recognition of the existence of a selection problem and more efforts made to solve it. From 1982 to 1985 the Scottish Education Department (SED) financed a project on 'Criteria of Selection' at Moray House, directed by Dr John Wilson. As part of the survey of existing practices the researchers examined selection procedures in other European Community countries:

> Evidence on practice in EEC countries was patchy and ambiguous. Nevertheless it indicated that all countries were facing a supply problem, and that almost the sole means of selection for teacher training was on the basis of formal criteria, especially academic qualifications. Only in England and Wales is collection of face-to-face evidence (at interview: editor's note) the norm. (6)

Wilson, having examined the selection procedures in Scotland, found them to be often 'invalid, undeveloped and unfair'; his attempts to devise improved selection procedures seemed to be successful, but the SED unfortunately refused funding for the longer-term evaluation study. There is no reason to believe that selection in England and Wales is any better than in Scotland, and it will be politically prudent to take steps to improve selection procedures as soon as possible. A number of other interesting factors emerged from the Wilson studies: for example that centrally determined quotas or targets militate against achieving quality by means of selection. Wilson showed that some applicants who were classified as 'not immediately suitable' were later admitted when successful applicants withdrew; filling places took priority over selection criteria.

INITIAL TRAINING COURSES

Initial teacher education has often been subject to criticism, ranging from allegations about low academic standards to lack of relevance. Specific examples of this kind of controversy include the following:

1   Should initial training be concurrrent or consecutive?
2   What is the correct balance between theory and

practice?

3   How should practising teachers be involved?

Concurrent or consecutive models

With the concurrent model, the personal academic development of the future teacher is fostered at the same time as he or she is exposed to educational theory, professional training and practice in schools. The alternative, consecutive model preferred in the James Report requires a future teacher to complete general education at an appropriate level and then to concentrate on a period of professional training, usually for about one year. (7) The claims of each approach have often been stated and compared: the advantage of the longer period of exposure to educational theory and practice in the case of the concurrent model; the greater maturity of student teachers and the advantage of concentrated effort in the case of the consecutive model. In some countries distinctions are made between teachers preparing for different age groups: the consecutive model being preferred for secondary teachers; the concurrent model for teachers of younger pupils. But even that simple distinction has been challenged, and the current tendency in England and Wales is to prefer the consecutive model even for future primary teachers, although this trend has been criticized by those who see it as an example of political and administrative convenience triumphing over educational priorities.

The balance between theory and practice

Rhoades suggests that the basic problem of teacher education is that it finds itself between the two very different worlds of higher education and the school. (8) On one side teacher education is pulled in the direction of being more academic; on the other side, teacher-educators are urged to get closer to the world of reality in the classrooms. Sometimes this problem of opposing claims is seen in a different way; should the initial training course prepare the student for an entire career in teaching, or is it simply a survival kit for the first few months? In the UK in recent years the balance of opinion has been to concentrate on the immediate future and to stress the need for post-initial in-service education for all teachers.

Recent studies also stress that it is misleading to consider the relation between theory and practice as a process of learning the theory and then putting it into practice. There is an increasing tendency to regard the relation between theory and practice as extremely complex, and to see genuine educational theory as something which is generated out of practice, relying to some extent on theoretical insights developed in other disciplines such as philosophy, sociology, or psychology. The theory which emerges is, however, experience-based educational theory rather than a simple amalgam of extracts from other disciplines. (9) In England the Universities Council for the Education of Teachers (UCET) has recommended the rethinking of initial training on these lines; in the USA Lortie and others had earlier criticized the 'Foundation Studies' approach to professional training and urged the adoption of alternative models. (10) Similarly in England many criticisms have been made of the BEd degree on the grounds that it is an education degree for teachers, not a degree for teaching. (11)

The involvement of practising teachers

In some countries, especially the USA, the notion of 'master teachers' who take on partial responsibility for the training of student-teachers is well established. The master teacher idea forms a useful bridge between the world of the school and the academic world of the university or college; it also provides an additional career route for good teachers who would prefer to remain practitioners rather than become administrators. Other countries have also developed similar roles for supervising teachers, without using the term 'master teacher'. 'Teacher-tutors' are becoming very important in several countries such as Australia, England, and Holland; (12) typically teacher-tutors spend the majority of their time in schools but a significant amount of time in the training institutions. This development has had implications for the location of teacher education establishments, with some of the sessions concerned with educational 'theory' actually taking place in schools rather than in the teacher-education institution.

CONTINUING PROFESSIONAL EDUCATION

The problem of teacher quality needs to be seen as a sequential process: recruiting potentially good teachers; providing good quality initial courses; and finally retraining good teachers in the profession and making the best use of them by continuing professional education and development. This post-initial aspect of teacher education is probably the most important as well as the most neglected; it will be helpful to consider the three phases separately: induction, in-service education, and professional development.

Induction

In most countries passing an initial training course is followed by a period of induction or probation (often one year) before full qualified teacher status is achieved. During that year induction into the profession is an important stage of professional development which is taken more seriously in some countries than in others.

In the UK the Plowden Report suggested that

> It is doubtful if the majority of young teachers are given the conditions and guidance in their first posts which will reinforce their training and lead to rising standards in the profession as a whole. (13)

With that deficiency in mind the James Report recommended that during the first year of service, the newly qualified teacher should be given a lighter teaching load so that the equivalent of one day each week could be spent on further training, guided by a professional tutor. This has not been applied as national policy in the UK but some local education authorities (LEAs) have made efforts to use the first year in the profession as a mixture of useful teaching experience and further professional education. Bolam and Baker reviewed the success of these experiments, but politicians and administrators evidently accorded them low priority and many were among the first victims of the financial cuts in the 1970s. (14)

In-service education

In many countries annual intakes of new teachers are now small compared with the number of experienced teachers already working in the schools. If changes and improvements in quality are desired then the resources devoted to in-service education and training (INSET) will be much more important than money spent on initial training. In 1970 a DES survey indicated that over a three-year period about one-third of teachers had not attended any courses, and the average was less than four days a year. (15) There was also considerable regional variation. The James Report in 1972 put forward a set of recommendations, including a proposal that 5 per cent of all teachers should at any one time be on study leave, but by 1980 the figure was only slightly more than 1 per cent. From 1987 there has been a change in funding arrangements for INSET giving precedence to specific national priorities, and encouraging all LEAs and schools to develop INSET programmes, but there is still no national plan or coherent national programme.

Professional development and teacher appraisal

It has been suggested that one of the characteristics of the teaching profession is that it is more concerned with recruitment than with retention. (16) Some of the most able teachers leave the profession after very few years' service, never to return. (17) Politicians and administrators should give more consideration to the need to make the teaching profession more attractive as a life-long career by building in a progressive career structure, closely associated with the kind of professional development recommended above as desirable in-service education.

Schemes of teacher appraisal which are properly devised and administered may assist in the process of professional development. But in recent years politicians and administrators have advocated the appraisal of teachers as a means of weeding out the ineffective or for promoting the excellent. It is essential, however, that the appraisal of teaching quality should be regarded as part of a process of professional development rather than as bureaucratic control. If appraisal is seen positively as an aspect of staff development rather than negatively as a means of dismissing the incompetent, then the whole process of professional development is much more likely to be both effective and acceptable. Where such appraisal schemes are introduced it is essential that adequate resources are provided for the implementation of any professional needs that are diagnosed.

THE ROLE OF THE TEACHER AND CONCEPTIONS OF TEACHING WORK

In order to improve the quality of teaching it will be necessary to specify more clearly what is expected of teachers in their various schools. At present the teacher's role is extremely diffuse and there is a lack of agreement about the kind of work teachers are expected to do.

An extensive review of the literature on teacher evaluation in 1983 examined the role of the teacher from the point of view of 'conceptions of teaching work': (18) teachers have been compared to craftspersons and professionals, bureaucrats, managers, labourers, and artists. Darling-Hammond et al. conflated these comparisons into four views of teaching work: labour, craft, profession, or art. They suggested that those four conceptions of teaching provide a useful theoretical framework for analysing teacher effectiveness, because they reveal the political or ideological assumptions that lie behind different techniques for evaluating teachers.

Teaching as labour

According to this conception of teaching, the activities of the teacher should be 'rationally planned by administrators: programmatically organised and routinised in the form of standard operating procedures'. (19) The teacher is merely responsible for carrying out the instructional programme as prescribed. Evaluation involves direct inspection, and monitoring by a supervisor. It is assumed that effective practices can be determined and specified, and that the desired results will be produced simply by following instructions. The teacher is a labourer or routine worker who does as he or she is told.

Teaching as craft

Teaching is seen as requiring a repertoire of specialized techniques. As well as mastering the techniques the teacher must acquire general rules for their application. Within this conception of teaching, once the teaching assignment has been given, the teacher will be expected to carry it out without detailed instructions or close supervision. Evaluation is indirect; the school administrator is seen as a manager keeping teachers up to standard.

Teaching as profession

When teaching is regarded as a profession, the teacher needs not only a repertoire of specialized techniques but also the ability to exercise judgement about the application of those techniques. In order to exercise professional judgement, the teacher must acquire a body of theoretical knowledge as well as a range of practical techniques. Standards for evaluating professionals should be developed by peers, and evaluation will focus on the degree to which teachers are competent at professional problem-solving. The school administrator's task will be to ensure that teachers have the resources necessary to carry out their work. This conception of teaching work assumes that standards of professional knowledge and practice can be developed and assessed, and that their enforcement will ensure competent teaching.

Teaching as art

Within this view of teaching, techniques and their application may be novel, unconventional, or unpredictable. Techniques and standards of practice are personalized. Gage suggests that the teaching art involves

> a process that calls for intuition, creativity, improvisation, and expressiveness - a process that leaves room for departures from what is implied by rules, formulae and algorithms. (20)

Gage argues that teaching uses science but cannot itself be a science because the teaching environment is not predictable. According to this view, the teacher must rely

257

not only on a body of professional knowledge and skills, but also on a set of personal resources that are uniquely defined and expressed by the personality of the teacher.

The teacher as artist will be expected to exercise considerable autonomy. Evaluation will involve self-assessment as well as critical assessment by others. Such evaluation will entail

> the study of holistic qualities rather than analytically derived qualities; the use of 'inside' rather than externally objective points of view. (21)

It would rely on high-inference rather than low-inference variables, on observation of patterns of events rather than counts of specific discrete behaviours. (22) According to this view the school administrator will be seen as a leader encouraging the teachers' efforts. Teaching patterns (that is holistic qualities that pervade a teacher's approach) can be recognized and assessed by using internal and external referents of validity.

The four conceptions of teaching work are ideal types, not to be found in a pure form in the real world. But the way that politicians, administrators, and others regard teaching, and the way that they want teachers to be appraised, may be closely related to one or other of those four categories. Moreover, in any discussion of the role of the teacher, it is essential to clarify and make explicit the underlying assumptions about 'teacher work'. Underlying many open disputes about teachers' salaries and conditions of service there are covert disagreements between employers who regard teaching as 'labour' or 'craft' and teachers who want to be treated as 'professionals' or 'artists'.

SUMMARY AND CONCLUSIONS

1 Education is inevitably a political activity. Teacher education is a crucial part of the education system and will often be exposed to pressures and criticisms of various kinds from politicians and administrators who will wish to control the activities of teacher-educators and limit the costs involved.
2 There is ample evidence to show that initial teacher-training is desirable and necessary; nevertheless, attacks will continue to occur.

3   The education of teachers should be seen as a
     continuing process: recruitment, selection, initial
     training, in-service education, and professional
     development. It is an expensive process and evidence
     should be provided to show that resources are being
     well used.
4   The role of the teacher may be defined differently
     according to prevailing political and administrative
     ideologies. It is important for teacher-educators to
     resist pressures to treat teachers as routine workers
     rather than as professionals.

EDITORS' NOTE: THE SITUATION IN THE UK

Teacher education and conditions of service in Britain
provide a good illustration of the problems raised.
Recruitment has been low and to the long-standing
shortages of specialist mathematics and science teachers,
new shortage areas in English, foreign languages, and craft,
design and technology have been added in the run-up to the
proposed national curriculum.

Salaries and conditions of service are widely reported
to have deteriorated; the salary gap between the most
highly paid teachers and the rank-and-file has widened. As
against that, the highest paid teachers have become more
and more divorced from actual classroom work, having
become involved in an increasing variety of committees and
working groups. It used to be said that in Britain every
teacher, including the headteacher, was a classroom
teacher; this is no longer the case with the top scale
personnel being labelled as 'executives', with headteachers,
in particular, being expected to operate as 'managers',
taking on full responsibility for 'local financial management'
of their schools. The classroom teacher's work-load has
grown with extra re-training days such as those for the
GCSE examination, while the marking of GCSE scripts, a job
which used to be done outside the schools and paid for
separately, has now been added as an extra unpaid duty. The
teachers remain the only public sector employees without
the right to negotiate their own salaries.

Teacher preparation itself has been brought under the
control of the DES with teacher-education courses having to
meet centrally laid down criteria, established by the Council
for the Accreditation of Teacher Education (CATE). The

courses themselves have been extended in length which brings them more into line with practice in a number of other countries, and which, for the first time, takes note of the greatly changed conditions in schools: multi-ethnic and mainstreamed special needs classes for example. The teacher-educators concerned with pedagogy ('methods') will be expected to have had 'recent and relevant' teaching experience in schools. Again some of these innovations have been regular practice in several European community countries and elsewhere for years. However, they have been introduced in England and Wales without adequate consultation and with no thought to the provision of the extra resources needed by both schools and teacher-education institutions.

All this has been done in the name of Better Schools and Teaching Quality. (23) This concern for an increased 'professionalism' in the area of teacher education contrasts strongly with the current proposals for the establishment of 'licensed teachers', who will be accredited by their LEAs after a period of 'on-the-job' training and whose qualifications will be, at best, various, and, in some cases, barely minimal. (24)

Chapter Fifteen

THE NATURE AND LIMITATIONS OF TEACHERS' PROFESSIONAL AUTONOMY

Friedrich W. Kron

The writer of a theoretical account of the nature and limitations of the teacher's autonomy in the classroom must take account of the social and political factors which can impair, or prevent, this activity. The present chapter is mainly concerned with the following issues.

First, it will examine the social and political developments in one state (Land) of the Federal Republic of Germany, in which, on the one hand, teachers are expected to enjoy full pedagogical freedom and where, at the same time, their freedom to act is restricted by a number of constraining factors. Next, the social and political backgrounds to the foregoing will be examined so that it may be seen how these contradictory demands arise.

After this, five theoretical concepts will be introduced through which these issues may be explored further. Then a theoretical explanation of the nature of socialization will be presented which may contribute to a better understanding of the problem. This is followed by a discussion of some steps which may lead to the enhancement of the teacher's autonomy in the classroom.

TEACHERS' AUTONOMY WITHIN THE CONSTRAINTS IMPOSED BY THE INSTITUTION

In the British tradition of full day schooling, the pedagogical autonomy and responsibility of the teacher (that is the role of in loco parentis) has, until very recently, been taken for granted. The concepts of pastoral responsibility in Britain, and the more recently introduced idea of Active Tutorial

Friedrich W. Kron

Work, have been of major importance. (1) In all schools and school systems influenced by the Anglo-Saxon view of society, teachers have been accepted as pedagogical experts and thus granted a substantial amount of freedom for their own planning and decision-making. In continental Europe, on the other hand, especially in France, Italy, and the Federal Republic, it is only in recent years that discussion has begun about allowing such freedom to the teacher.

In the case of the Federal Republic it is significant to note that the social and political innovations that have taken place in the 1960s and 1970s took account of Anglo-American models. These have principally affected the democratization of the school system and, in particular, the introduction of the comprehensive school (Gesamtschule), and the transformation of the traditional dual (academic/vocational) curriculum into a more modern integrated one. Following the first wide-ranging phase of reform, primarily relating to changes in the structure of the school system, a second more subtle, but at the same time more profound, reform affecting the participating partners in the system - the pupils, the teachers, and the parents - is now taking place.

In particular with regard to teachers, the type of autonomy which should be accorded to them is the subject of animated debate. (2) The implementation of this innovation, however, has led to rather mixed results. On the one hand, a positive development can be seen. The interest which is now being shown in the teacher's role has engaged public attention and must be welcomed because for some decades past only questions concerning the aims of education, the curriculum, and school organization, the achievement of pupils, including their psychological reactions to schooling and their social relationships within the classroom, have stood in the foreground of debate.

It is this fact, amongst others, which in 1984 encouraged the Minister of Education and Culture of the State of the Rhineland-Palatinate to decree a 30 per cent reduction in the quantity of centrally prescribed subject-matter in the curriculum. This has effectively reduced the compulsory curriculum content taught from forty weeks per annum to just twenty-five weeks, leaving fifteen weeks of the total school timetable per annum at the disposal of the teacher's own planning. In addition 10 per cent of the week's lessons, some three hours per week, are to be used for social activities, such as special interest groups on topics chosen by the pupils themselves. The explicit aim of these ministerial measures was to grant teachers more freedom for their own pedagogical activities. These innovations are reminiscent of English practice such as the non-timetabled 'Day Ten' at Stantonbury Campus School, Milton Keynes (or 'floating' days of the week in other schools) with the important difference that, in the Federal Republic, these suggestions emanate from the ministry and are couched in more prescriptive terms, although they are not linked to any specific assessment requirement.

This tendency can be seen in the further development of centrally designed syllabuses (Lehrpläne) in the Rhineland-Palatinate. The new 1984 syllabuses for the subject 'sociology' for the final three years, Grades 7-9, of the Hauptschule (senior primary/secondary modern school) mention fewer prescribed topics for work in the classroom compared with the 1978 syllabuses (see over). The number of compulsory topics for classroom discussion has been reduced so as to be accommodated within twenty-five instead of forty weeks. The topics themselves are clearer and more pupil oriented compared with the previous ones.

In the Federal Republic, however, alongside these liberating measures some disturbing opposing trends can also be observed. In the 1985 Letter to Parents from the Rhineland-Palatinate Ministry of Education, the minister writes concerning the purpose of pedagogical autonomy as follows:

> With the beginning of the 1984-85 school year new curricula have been determined for the primary (Grundschule), the secondary modern school (Hauptschule), the professional technical secondary (Realschule), and the grammar school (Gymnasium), and a number of courses provided by the vocational (Berufsbildende Schule) offering training for specific jobs. Characteristic of these new curricula is an emphasis on 'what is really essential and necessary', only those learning goals and contents being included which can be achieved with 25 lessons per week per school year under normal conditions. A significant amount of professional autonomy is thus given to the teacher, which is 'available for revision, practical exercises and further specialist studies'. (4)

Friedrich W. Kron

Sociology Syllabus 1978
Themes and Learning Aims

Class 7 - Topic 1
Theme: The form seen as a group

Class 7 - Topic 2
Theme: The community as an area of political activity

Class 7 - Topic 3
Theme: The family as a socializing agent

Class 8 - Topic 1
Theme: Understanding the mass media

Class 8 - Topic 2
Theme: Functions of social and political groupings

Class 8 - Topic 3
Theme: The law and legislation

Class 9 - Topic 1
Theme: The political organization of the Federal Republic

Class 9 - Topic 2
Theme: Socialism in the GDR

Class 9 - Topic 3
Theme: Problems of international politics

Sociology Syllabus 1984
Themes and Learning Aims

Class 7 - Topic 1
Theme: This is our classroom (7 hours)

Class 7 - Topic 2
Theme: Education and social learning in the family (8 hours)

Class 7 - Topic 3
Theme: How can I participate in the political life of the community? (10 hours)

Class 8 - Topic 1
Theme: What are the tasks of the mass media? (6 hours)

Class 8 - Topic 2
Theme: The political organization of the Federal Republic:
the Federal Land of Rhineland-Palatinate (14 hours)

Class 8 - Topic 3
Theme: Law and legislation (5 hours)

Class 9 - Topic 1
Theme: Socialism in the GDR (7 hours)

Class 9 - Topic 2
Theme: Securing peace as the aim of international policies
(15 hours)

(3)

The disturbing thing is that there is not one word in the minister's letter about the teachers being given the pedagogical responsibility and freedom in decision-making which is the basis of their professional competence. On the one hand, teachers are supposed to be introduced to and given full professional responsibility for determining their pedagogical role in the classroom based solely upon the context in which they find themselves. At the same time teachers, parents, social agencies, including the churches, echo the minister's emphasis in concentrating on what is seen as the essential part of the curriculum, interpreted as knowledge of subject content, while totally ignoring its wider dimensions.

It is regrettable that the minister himself has encouraged and perpetuated this notion of the primacy of subject content in his parental letter, since he clearly sees pedagogical autonomy, that is the use of 'unscheduled time', solely in terms of defined curriculum subject areas, to be used for 'revision, practical exercises and further specialist studies'. Such a formulation not only gives rise to possible misconceptions but also is, pedagogically viewed, one-sided. The misconception comes about through advocating the use of the available time solely for purposes related to revision and practice within the defined curriculum subject areas. The expression 'specialist studies', without the addition 'educational', can be interpreted only as relating to extra components in subject matter. Moreover the pedagogical one-sidedness of the formulation lies in the explicit reference to subject matter within which the use of unscheduled time is placed, without mentioning the pupils' social and personal development. Indeed, the link of the two factors, social and personal development with instruction, is not an invention of educational theoreticians but a condition of educational aims imposed by the Federal Constitution itself. (5) This is also supported by educational research which has been documented by Schnitzer. (6)

This train of thought stands in opposition to obviously differing conclusions made by the public and politicians which seemingly derive from an appraisal of the same situation. To enable individual children to have a worthwhile future in present circumstances they must be provided with a curriculum even more confined to specified subject areas, thereby increasing their formal qualifications, rather than one with a social dimension - so the argument goes. This is the familiar argument for a concentration on the numeracy and literacy basics rather than a consideration of what is truly essential in terms of educational purposes. The professional role of teachers and their autonomous use of unassigned lesson time, as guaranteed to them by ministerial decree, is thus misdirected into a further concern with content and this is done with the full approbation of society using arguments emphasizing the personal well-being of pupils in their future role in society.

THE SOCIAL AND POLITICAL BACKGROUNDS

The reason why, in popular politics, it is the teacher's general educational activity which has become the topic of debate lies in the wide-ranging social transformation in the Federal Republic. In the grip of an economic recession, not always fully understood abroad, the functional relationship between society and schooling has become problematical. Concepts have been discovered within academic circles which were completely overlooked at a time when the school was seen exclusively as a training institution and as a function of the production machine and thus a contributory factor to social and economic prosperity. This exclusively economic approach to schooling is now questionable. It has been discovered that pupils were being steered towards predominantly cognitive and subject-oriented goals at the expense of their affective, social, and psycho-motor development; that the teaching process itself, as well as the conception of schooling, was founded upon economic thinking in which lessons became a process of presenting facts and accumulating knowledge confining teachers to communicating and assessing while restraining them in their roles as educators, advisers, and innovators. (7)

These phenomena are seen to have a causal relationship with the fact that many pupils are dropping out of school, that they reject the concept of achievement and turn to drugs, showing anxiety and aggressive behaviour to the extent of attacking their own schools, classrooms, and clubs. A growing incidence of mental and psychosomatic illnesses has been observed amongst both pupils and teachers. (8)

These problems must be set against the specific institutional and organizational backgrounds of the schools. Schooling which is based upon the concept of the so-called 'continental day' (that is half-day school attendance) predominates; curricula and study goals are clearly defined and teachers take care to ensure that pupils' progress is as constant and consistent as possible. Also the selection procedures for different types of school, and the proliferation of achievement testing in some types of school as well as the legal constraints of compulsory education, evidenced by the different curricula prescribed for different types of school, are facts of history and are a large part of the cause of the present malaise.

As a result of this, teachers themselves have become confused in their professional role. In the past decade they have been increasingly subjected to a multiplicity of external pressures through greater demands for academic achievement on the part of the pupils (so-called 'standards'), through governmental regulations and the legal codification of criterion-based assessment of pupil achievement, through the demands of parents and their official representatives (parent-teacher associations and governors) insisting on tangible results redeemable in terms of economic and social success, through the expectations of the pupils themselves, and, last but not least, through the expectations of the public at large.

On the one hand, then, teachers are seen by the system to be constrained by the need for accountability; on the other hand, as dynamic and rational individuals they are urged by their pupils and their pupils' negative attitudes to society to reflect on their pedagogical role. Thus they find

Friedrich W. Kron

themselves in a dilemma, a situation they share with those concerned with other social and educational agencies.

FIVE THEORETICAL CONSIDERATIONS

In the light of the foregoing what does the call for subject-free unassigned teacher-autonomous time mean in practice? The answer can be explored in five different ways.

The 'realistic' appraisal of the teacher's day

According to a realistic appraisal of their work-place, one might say that teachers can be constantly creating non-subject-assigned education periods within the context of much of their teaching activity as soon as they have closed the classroom door behind them. A professional and social competence is ascribed to them which allows them to create space for freedom of action for both themselves and their pupils during organized lesson time. Experience has shown that that much cannot be denied. (9) The question remains, however, how and whether such individual action can be made general, institutionalized and organized in such a way as to bring a more widely based reform into being.

The 'idealistic' perception of German tradition

The case for an idealistic evaluation can be argued as follows: in principle teachers are accorded full freedom to exercise professional autonomy by the relevant paragraphs of the Federal Constitution and miscellaneous educational legislation. It is, however, clear that they can only realize this freedom when it can be reconciled fully with their pedagogical responsibility, the latter being understood as deriving from the aims and tasks set by the school, that is in terms of the school legislation, the curriculum, and its accompanying study guides, such as syllabuses. Furthermore they need to adjust their teaching to the wider needs imposed on the pupil by society, in reality as well as in theory. (10) Teachers must, therefore, be continuously combining all these factors, a process which forms the essential prerequisite for their understanding of their freedom to negotiate the content and style of their teaching.

This, too, can be accepted in so far as it concerns the educational consciousness of teachers, and thus lies at the very core of the confusion over their professional and personal identity which is plainly causing teachers much distress at present. Its application to the personal development of the pupils can be regarded in a positive light, though this is not often the case in practice. (11)

The 'sociological' dimension

Viewed from the sociological dimension, schooling is conceived as a function of society which pursues its goal of the reproduction of its accepted notions of values and standards. All those active in the institutional area of schooling are subject to this aim. Roles are, therefore, accepted as static, with the entire social structure fixed. Teachers have no freedom of movement of any kind, regardless of their own view of their pedagogical responsibility, or their wish to pursue aims set by themselves or their pupils. Their teaching activity serves only to accommodate the pupil to the system. Should they wish to put more emphasis, or, indeed, any emphasis at all, upon the individuality of their pupils, then this would destroy the system once and for all. (12)

Thus, 'pedagogical freedom of movement', or 'autonomy', for the teacher is incompatible with this assumption. More exactly teachers are confined to prescribed roles which, given a democratic ideal of society and schooling, degrade them; the result being what Groothoff called 'déformation professionnelle'. (13) A solution is apparently only possible by 'revolution', that is by breaking out of the state-imposed curricular strait-jackets.

The 'critical-phenomenological' view

In the critical-phenomenological view actual and structural conditions for positive action, including any impediments, are taken account of as well as the anticipation of successful pedagogical activity. (14) If, in this dialectical amalgamation, one wishes to see the interaction of teacher and pupils in a concrete context, then this activity must be seen in the first place as located in the school as an institution. This means that schooling can also be seen as a developmental process, a 'way', or 'sphere of life', which the pupils negotiate. (15)

Schooling, therefore, constitutes a part of the lives of both pupils and their teacher, for it is in the school that the professional and, to some extent, the personal existence of the teacher is established. The teacher's activity in school is thus constantly linked to the activities of the pupil and vice versa; it is, however, also dependent upon the objective and subjective conditions imposed by the school and upon the anticipation of a successful outcome.

The 'empirical' approach

The first available results of a preliminary survey within the framework of an Israeli-German research project, concerned with what teachers in both countries understood as their 'professional autonomy', are given below. (16) Without prejudice to the final results of this longitudinal survey, they are given here since they show very interesting cross-cultural implications and differences. For the investigation a concept of 'pedagogical autonomy' was chosen which could be understood by teachers of both countries. Agreement was reached on the definition: professional autonomy being understood as the freedom for teachers to plan, conduct, and evaluate their own lessons as well as carry out their professional tasks in the wider, pastoral sense, compatible with their academic qualifications and personal style of action. (17)

The research results present the following picture:

Distribution of perceived pressures on autonomous processes in percentages for each teacher population

Perceived pressures from concerns with: Israeli teachers (N = 80) German teachers (N = 40)

	German	Israeli
Curriculum: contents and materials	76	70.6
Teaching methods	63	5.0
Classroom management constraints	33	-

Parental intervention	18	-
Societal values	10	2.0
Assessment and evaluation	8	20.0
Time at teachers' disposal	3	60.0

We can see that, taking account of the different teaching conditions in the schools of the two countries, both Israeli and German teachers see their concept of pedagogic freedom as being constrained by the curriculum in the first instance. Clearly both groups wish to have more freedom with regard to the teaching syllabus. This is confirmed by the fact that of the German teachers questioned 60 per cent mentioned the time factor as a second cause for concern after the curriculum. The strong didactic orientation of lessons in the Federal Republic, as well as the rigid timetable, which in mosts cases confines the total teaching of classes and their teachers' timetables to the mornings only, shows the great interest which German teachers have in a freer, less constrained planning of their teaching in terms of their choice of lesson topic and activity. As against that, in contrast to their Israeli colleagues, German teachers seem much less worried about the methodological aspect (imposed and prescribed teaching styles) of their lessons (5 per cent). One can thus assume, according to the preliminary results, that German teachers suffer greatly under the strong central imposition of the curriculum and time pressure and thus experience a lack of professional autonomy due to those two factors. They thus seek full autonomy in matters of subject matter and time. Israeli teachers suffer from imposed classroom management styles, while German teachers are more bothered by the rigid grading system of pupils in operation in the classroom.

Results from the USA point in the same direction. Already in 1973 Schwab demanded that curricula should be constructed not only according to specific subject matter but also according to the competencies of the teachers as well as taking account of the needs and interests of the pupils and society. (18) He argued that the narrow-mindedness in curriculum development be abolished through 'an orientation according to structure of subject matter' and the 'self-discovery of scientific concepts' which was introduced, and still is being practised, following Bruner also in the Federal Republic. (19)

The Federal Republic has also supplied research results that support Schwab's ideas. Sacher writes:

> A decisive presupposition for the influence that central curriculum may have on lesson planning, and thus on teaching, is the cognitive, pragmatic and affective curriculum competence of the teacher, that is his knowledge and understanding of the curriculum, his ability to plan a lesson according to the syllabus and his readiness to put it into practice. (20)

Significant in this explication is the reference to the formal and many-sided competencies of the teacher. The content of this pedagogical competence must not, however, be determined not only by the requirements of subject matter itself, but also by the other factors mentioned by Schwab: pupils, society, and teacher. Only through the coming together of all four factors can the curriculum achieve educational significance. Only then can the raw material of the syllabuses be transformed by teachers' planning ability and their recourse to their conceptual understanding of the aims and objectives of teaching. (21) Teachers are thus seen as active agents, as interpreters, (22) and transformers of their curriculum. (23)

These explications are supplemented by an inquiry by Stephan. He finds that the realization of the curriculum is not determined primarily by its overt or covert intentions ('open' or 'hidden' curriculum), but rather it is influenced mainly by the implicit 'theories' (24) which experienced teachers have internalized and applied throughout their teaching. (25) The conclusion may, therefore, be drawn that regardless of their location teachers desire not only more professional autonomy - in this case with regard to the curriculum - but that this wish is to be seen as a basic expression of their personal life and teaching activity, that is of their roles both as teachers and adult human-beings.

IMPLICATIONS OF SOCIALIZATION THEORY FOR THE TOPIC

If we pursue these ideas briefly from the point of view of socialization theory then it is clear that the institution of schooling comes under the category of secondary socialization. (26) From the subjective view of the person involved, particularly in the case of adolescents, schooling is experienced as an objectively existing, firmly established, and often alien world. Schooling thus appears as a detached and authoritarian institution, whose objective meaning can be apprehended not at all, only partially or, at best, with the help of superstructures which teachers attempt to construct by means of their professional activity.

Thus any positive acclimatization to the institution of school becomes difficult. Its significant purport to exert a relaxing and, at the same time, liberating influence, can no longer be experienced directly. Instead this idea is forcibly taught or explained through symbolic means such as admonishment and exhortation or reference to the rules of behaviour and appeals to its beneficial outcomes. This reduction of meaning in the process of acclimatization to the reality of schooling, which affects the personality of every individual involved, makes them either frail and impotent, or aggressive towards the representatives of the education system, while allowing the representatives themselves, as the champions of the system, to argue for the necessary continued existence of the system to the extent of enforcing it.

Teachers find themselves in this dilemma which must be seen as a crisis not merely of roles, but of their very existence, every single day. They must always be assuring their pupils that what they are learning is meaningful and useful for life although they can no longer trust to useful and meaningful forms of socialization such as acclimatization. In the general social context, socialization by school has been destroyed and this destruction affects the teacher particularly. It becomes clear from the foregoing analysis that the significance of the teacher for the pupil as the 'trusted adult', as both subject specialist and older fellow-being, has been supplanted. This is because they no longer have an opportunity for freedom of movement (in 'unassigned teaching periods') and experimentation in activities which grow out of the developing demands of the situation thus providing an opportunity for genuine education which depends not only upon sympathetic circumstances but also upon active participation by the pupils. The institutional constraints of schooling and outside social conditions, therefore, combine to hinder teachers in the realization of their subject-free educational activity.

The opportunity to make any sense of all this and meaningfully to participate pose particular problems for the pupils. In the past twenty years secondary socialization has been characterized by a growing complexity which particularly affects schooling. For example, there are the varieties of language with its accents and dialects, different registers and codes, which daily confront pupil and teacher alike or the range of foreign languages which are offered to the pupil. In addition there are the multiplicity of roles which pupils may be called upon to assume in the most diverse areas of life, including the opportunity to contribute to, and participate in, self-discovery and the expression of their opinions. Pupils have to learn to cope also with the plurality of acceptable codes of behaviour and morals on offer through the church and state, the media, public and private opinion, and to perceive reality as presented to them through history, current affairs, and future projections. All these opportunities for the development of the individual through the realization of the idea of democracy, including the impact of cultural diversity, make for a complexity of the institution of the school in society. It can no longer be seen clearly, particularly if the processes of learning are prestructured for pupils and teachers through rigid organizational patterns, laws, imposed curricula and syllabuses, and the application of out-moded teaching approaches.

If the resulting helplessness of the individual in the case of both pupil and teacher and the related depersonalization of humanity are to be prevented from leading to social stagnation, new forms of teaching and learning must be found which in the words of the Club of Rome

> will stimulate and sustain the active individual to meaningful institutional activity through innovative processes. (27)

The need and interest of pupils and teachers alike for direct experience can be understood as the deepest expression of the sensibility of modern humans for a living link between themselves, society and a moral universe to which the individual wishes to belong. The complexity of experience should not be seen as a menacing phenomenon but as a challenge to society to seek new forms of learning and understanding overcoming mechanical functionalism and ideological control. Here lies the point of departure for a positive reshaping of reality which our current topic explores.

NEW DEPARTURES AND POSITIVE PERSPECTIVES

Departures towards a positive reshaping of reality can already be observed as parents, pupils, and teachers display an increasing desire for a new commitment to transform school into a new way of life. This can be seen in several examples.

The derivation of daily rhythm: the example of the primary school

In this context Schleiermacher's idea of a school as an area of 'social intercourse' springs to the fore, (28) together with some pedagogical thoughts of the 1920s such as when, for example, Klatt brought forward his 'creative recess'. (29) In his concept school was seen as an aspect of life with its own rhythm. Meyer also formulated the outstanding principle from the residual thinking of the 1920s that the non-subject specific (unassigned) teaching periods of the primary school should be used to allow pupils to find a daily rhythm of their own between the change from different forms of play and work or between exertion and recovery. He claimed that,

> in the primary school, the first unassigned lesson at the beginning of the day should leave the children free to arrive when they want to at their place in school within the first half of their morning lesson to enable them to find their own way through village traffic without the fear of arriving late. The institution of flexible school periods according to the change of season serves this end and corresponds to the child's daily rhythm. (30)

The daily rhythm of human beings is thus elevated to being a foundation of educational activity and thence derives the demand for an unassigned, subject-free teaching period for pupils, on the one hand, and for teachers' autonomy on the other. For the pupil such a period offers the possibility of

> freeing himself from hostile restraints, from haste and stress, giving him a greater chance for purposeful undertaking, allowing for a time of peaceful reflection even in a big school and so creating the impression that there is time. The individual classroom, which is at once a secure base in which to live and work, spacious

> enough for 20-25 children, therefore, provides the greatest measure of plurality within an all-encompassing unity. Such an environment is essential. The provision of a multiplicity of play and work materials changes with the child's activity every day; however, the child finds his working area and materials just as he had left it the previous day. (31)

Derived from this, 'unassigned lesson time' may now mean that, mindful of the daily rhythm of children, teachers can organize their tuition with prepared materials, orientate themselves with rethought and non-prescriptive syllabuses, and adapt the organizational structures to the needs of the children as well as to their own teaching ideas. This recognition of the importance of building the classroom programme around the natural rhythm of the child's day may, however, involve the danger of being too individualistic. It is possible to regard the 'day boarding school' and the 'whole day school', which go beyond the common British practice, as the result of these scholastic organizational measures which are based on a structured autonomy of teaching and learning. Examples from primary schools in England employing the integrated day come to mind although the original German experiments went more in the direction of individual tuition. (32)

Organizational developments

Opportunities for change present themselves even within the existing framework of secondary school organization. Over and above the traditional pupil participation in school government and the already established spare time socio-political activities in schools, the trends towards democratization and participation in the school as an institution must be generally reinforced. (33) At the same time it is necessary to consider how to enable educators not to be afraid to demonstrate differences of opinion and how to make dialogue with pupils possible. In the school sector this may mean loosening the ties of compulsory curricula, administering school rules in a more open fashion in order to strengthen the possibility of learning according to individually negotiated patterns, but also to see that communities and institutions outside the field of education are able to open up for the adolescents a wide scope of further opportunities for activities alongside schools. If as, according to Gehlen, (34) institutions are intended to provide a release then surely it is necessary to allow play and festivity to take their place alongside learning as a means for self-realization and for a successful social experience of community. Here the overall criterion should be the general preservation of the institution. However, individual questioning should be encouraged, as only then does the vitality and significance of the institution itself become plausible. This procedure can be designated as fully democratic and encouraging partnership. It is based on the socially and historically endorsed insight that institutions must be seen to be alive, as in the case of the growing number of community schools.

Tuition as a 'field of experience': the development of roles

Even within the realm of lesson planning and preparation, it is important to act in such a way as to develop professional freedom of action, the autonomy of the teacher, in both the organization and the selection of subject matter. This is understood that, first and foremost, it is not the knowledge of subject matter alone, or even the teacher's attitude which should determine lesson planning. Lessons should derive from the pupils' own situation, their reaction to the work in progress, their personal development, and what Velthaus has called 'his fields of experience', (35) which should be integrated in the lesson so that the pupils can experience the subject matter in relation to themselves and to their social environment. The essence of lively lessons lies neither in so-called objective subject-matter, such as the school subject 'biology', which confronts the individuals who are learning it, nor in allowing the individuals to confront the objective reality of their environment, but in a dynamic and reciprocal relationship between the two so that the students learn their biology while exploring their environment, for example on mutually agreed and organized field-trips.

In the critical phenomenological view of school, the teachers are not expected to bring together the objective world and the individual pupils through their teaching skills alone. Teachers can begin in a much more business-like, indirect, and lively fashion to forge relationships between the pupils and the objective world, that is they can build on their pupils' interpretation of phenomena, or, alternatively, they can link up with their pupils' own experiences and preconceptions such as their views on race for example. Lessons must be considered from these two perspectives and, in this case, one may legitimately speak of pupils' 'fields of experience'. It is precisely a 'field of experience' which makes 'an unassigned free period' educationally worthwhile for both pupils and teachers. With the introduction of 'fields of experience' into the lesson, teachers are placed in a completely new role. They are no longer merely communicators of information, instructors, controllers of behaviour, or instruments for the selection and the imposition of attainment goals. Their understanding of their role has been expanded. Teachers no longer simply teach and assess their pupils but also educate and advise them and open up new perspectives for them. Moreover they enter their new role by way of engaging in a dialogue with their pupils and thus, through the medium of social intercourse, become their companion and friend.

Curricular innovation

In the area of the curriculum, too, the teacher will assume a different role. It matters little if the syllabus is quantitatively reduced by 10 or 30 per cent, or more, if it continues to be designed wholly by outside agencies. The decisive factor is that teachers must develop their own curriculum. (36) The prescribed 'formal' curriculum would, however, not become totally invalidated thereby; but the 'situative' curriculum, which the teachers have themselves designed, would become much more crucial. In this way, teachers will discover that they are no longer 'slave' but 'master' of their syllabus and can organize their subject specialist, and social competencies into a comprehensive range of tasks for their pupils. This could be legally introduced even in a country like the Federal Republic with its Länder-prescribed syllabuses and curricula.

In such a scenario there is the model of the teachers who by their initial and continuing professional development are entrusted with the task of social, as well as subject, education. Recent researches show that, in this sense, several types of teachers' role can be found which are linked with specific forms of curriculum interpretation. Connelly and Ben-Peretz present three basic types of teachers' role concerning the curriculum. (37)

In the first role, syllabuses are laid down by educational legislation in the design of which teachers have no control and which may not be altered even in the classroom. Such a model allows only for a small variation of teaching styles. It causes problems since the teachers are limited to the specific interpretation of content, that is, it is impossible for them to introduce in the classroom any innovation of a thematic or social nature. Syllabuses of this kind can be recognized by their predetermined hierarchy of learning objectives which force teachers to organize their lessons along their lines and to control and assess their pupils' achievements in the same way. The teachers lack the creativity of negotiating their syllabus, in terms of the interplay amongst the teaching context, the pupils, societal values, and their own inclinations, alongside the prescribed subject matter. They learn to interpret the curriculum as an 'external' instrument imposed on their activity. Their own role is essentially passive, that of mediators between often unknown curriculum designers and their pupils. (38) Their own pedagogical and professional skills are not called into action, as when they are reduced to teaching biology without any reference to their pupils' environment. (39) The danger of teachers becoming mere functionaries within the system is inevitable since their pedagogical autonomy is reduced to zero.

In the second role there are syllabuses in the development and progression of which (but not in the design) teachers - be it only through representatives elected by themselves - are involved. In this case the teacher's role presents itself as that of a 'transformer' of the curriculum. The changes made by the teacher in the classroom must remain within the framework of the prescribed subject matter. This is why it is thought to be expedient in this scenario to structure the syllabus according to various categories, such as learning goals, learning contents, methods, and teaching materials. Often these syllabuses are confined to the prescription of content to be learned. Syllabuses of this kind impose on the teacher the adherence to a narrow subject matter and thus bear a close resemblance to the first category above. The end products of such syllabuses are standardized tests which, however, allow preparation for them through different methods and approaches.

In the third role there are syllabuses which involve the

teacher as a partner and, in that capacity, as an equal to the curriculum designers. This type of curriculum contains rich and varied materials of all kinds which serve the teacher as a resource. Such syllabuses can be directed not only towards subject matter but also to the pupils' own needs and interests, and adjusted to their various stages of psychological and social development. They also take account of the teachers' own individuality, their preferred methodology, and the resources at their disposal. Teachers can exploit and interpret all this rich potential. Such a curriculum enables them to exceed the limitations and learning outcomes of the syllabus and to set their own goals. For the realization of such a syllabus, autonomy is a necessary pre-condition. Only in a school which practises an institution-generated curriculum is the teacher able to play the role of 'master' of the curriculum. A particular significance of this role expectation is that the teacher is challenged to develop and interpret the material on offer and so to engage with the four dimensions of teaching defined by Schwab, that is subject matter, pupil, society, and teacher. (40) Regrettably this kind of curriculum and role expectation of pupil and teacher respectively have not found their way into the prescribed courses within the Federal Republic, where the overall social and educational reality still points firmly towards a passive curriculum with a teacherless prescribed interpretation of society.

CONCLUSION

The perspective of a critical phenomenological evaluation demonstrates that not only do obstacles to this new definition of the teacher's role still exist but that, moreover, this new role is still in the process of being defined and reinterpreted. Perhaps one of the greatest obstacles to a proper revaluation of the teacher's role is the fact that many teachers have not learned (or, perhaps, have forgotten) how to interpret their professional activity. Not a few teachers will be made uneasy by the ministerial proposals for educational freedom of action, including the provision of the teacher's unassigned periods and will begin to call for new guidelines, as was the case after the Haby reforms in France.

This dilemma will be resolved only if teachers are encouraged to co-operate with others in the design of unassigned lessons so as to safeguard their autonomy. Within the context of those values offered by a humanistic and pluralistic democracy, which should be promoting a fuller understanding of the values of human existence, especially within the institution of school, all attempts by teachers to plan non-subject-specific unassigned lessons should be encouraged. Only then will the discussion of the teacher's free, unassigned time become more than empty rhetoric, and only then will teachers' professional autonomy become a reality.

Chapter Sixteen

RECONCILING THE TEACHER'S PROFESSIONAL TASK AND SOCIAL INFLUENCE

Ulrich Aselmeier (Translated by the editors)

'This is a subject method seminar, we haven't the time for such details'. When shown a lesson plan and an account of how the lesson was to be developed the student-teacher's methods tutor, in a teacher-training college in south-western Germany, reminded him that the group had no time for such socio-psychological details as the student had deliberately emphasized in his lesson planning: these included consideration of the importance of this particular lesson in the development of his pupils' personalities and their social and communicative competencies. The tutor's remarks referred to what he saw as the neglect of subject-specific aspects by the student which he felt impaired the development of the pupils' subject knowledge. (1) A number of questions spring to mind: what sort of teacher is it who has such a restricted view of the teaching task? How clear are student-teachers in their own minds about the full implications of their future professional task? Indeed what sort of ideas about it do they receive during their initial teacher education years? Even without going into a more detailed analysis of these questions, what can be said is that many teachers are still largely, or indeed exclusively, preoccupied with subject-specific instructional objectives - the academic side of teaching - with a corresponding neglect of the teacher's wider educational role with respect to his pupils in the classroom.

This chapter attempts to establish and develop a contrapuntal perspective on the professional and educational role of teachers in relation to their pupils in actual teaching situations by examining the dual aspects of how it is expected they will carry out their professional task as instructors and their human influence as educators on their pupils as illustrated in the above paragraph. The counterpoint is established by considering the implications of a pupil and classroom teaching centred approach.

Such an approach may be characterized by describing the factors involved in classroom teaching and classroom events from the point of view of their total impact on the pupils' personal development. In this the teacher is crucial and we shall examine, in some detail, the teacher's function and role in the classroom. We shall concentrate on three cumulatively linked aspects of the topic and conclude with some remarks on the kind of teacher education which accepts the view of the function and role of the teacher as presented in this chapter.

THE TWO LEVELS OF TEACHER ACTIVITY IN THE CLASSROOM

The pupil and classroom teaching centred approach assumes that teaching a subject lesson not only affects the pupils' acquisition of subject knowledge and related skills and attitudes, but, at the same time, educates their entire personality. The subject-specific concerns of a lesson are found embedded in a total educational context which affects the development of the pupils' personalities to a considerable degree in two respects: the individual and the social. (2) It follows that the teachers as the planners and executors of their lessons, must become involved at both levels, and, through their teaching, exert a twofold influence on their pupils. The reasons for this twofold way in which teaching affects pupils are to be found in the first instance in three inborn characteristics which are entirely pupil-specific:

1 The pupils are endowed with a comprehensive need to find out about things which concern not only the cognitive but also the affective together with the social and somatic sides of their lives.
2 The pupils' personalities possess a dynamic structure, that is their existing characters and their outward manifestations are subject to influence by outside factors and, thus, are capable of change, transforming themselves under the impact of the pupils' own grapplings with their environmental experiences.
3 Pupils are characterized by a fundamental capacity for

Figure 5 Learning outcomes of teaching

	Personality domains of the student affected by learning			
Learning outcomes of teaching	Cognitive	Emotional	Social	Psychosomatic
Subject specific				
Social personality specific				
Individual personality specific				

reflection. By this we mean both the conscious and unconscious referral back upon themselves of their experiences, in the sense that they have an effect on the developing structure of their personalities and their outward manifestations.

In the second instance, these characteristics of the pupil just described come into contact with specific structural realities found in teaching which also have to be considered in this context. For example, the subject-specific instructional aims of lessons can be introduced into teaching only by means of definite forms of mutual social interaction on the part of the individuals involved, both teachers and pupils. In addition there will be particular ways in which pupils handle their subject-specific contents in the process of recognizing, acquiring, and applying them. Thus the essential reality of teaching involves tackling the social-human interactional aspects alongside the acquisition of subject knowledge and skills.

The combination of pupil-specific characteristics and subject-lesson-specific features in the classroom means that the pupils by virtue of their reflective capacity, process all aspects of their lessons, the subject-specific and the social ones, as well as those arising out of the pupils' own way of tackling the instructional aims of the lesson they attend by referring them back to themselves, in all of which learning takes place. The pupils' ability to do so depends on the degree to which they are open to such things - that is they are themselves involved in the formation and development (understood in a dynamic sense) of their personality. The form of human interaction and their manner of tackling the subject in hand, are thus, because of the pupils' specific characteristics, functional not merely in respect of the acquisition of subject knowledge but also possess their own learning outcomes, which concern the development of the individual and social personalities of the pupils. This wider influence of the teaching act on the pupils, therefore, in terms of its outcomes can be illustrated by reference to Figure 5.

This can be illustrated by an example. When practising certain calculating skills, such as mental arithmetic, many teachers use the technique of competitive computation, by getting the entire class to stand and allowing those pupils who are first to supply the correct answer to sit down or allowing them to go home early if it happens to be the last lesson of the day. Here the conscious teaching objective is to 'grind' this skill into the pupil. Using the competitive method is intended to make the grinding process more effective, notes Klafki. (3) Examples from other school subjects abound. Klafki himself drew attention to the fact that such teaching does not just affect subject matter acquisition, that is it is not directed to improving the pupil's calculating abilities alone. He uncovered the underlying deeper level below the surface concern with subject matter:

> Much more happens here than a more or less effective calculation practice. In reality, consciously or unconsciously, the competitive attitude as a form of social interaction is induced: because attempts at helping individual pupils are forbidden, feelings of anxiety, fears of exposure of inability, and states of frustration arise. (4)

Such acts of competition and refusal of help have an effect on the social behaviour of pupils exposed to them. This kind of teaching fosters in pupils a particular type of social orientation, an implicit learning outcome, by diverting their social personalities in a particular direction. The anxieties, fears, and frustrations referred to by Klafki have repercussions on the pupils' emotional balance. By disturbing their own self-concept they affect their individual personalities.

Further 'learning' outcomes, beyond those mentioned by Klafki, can be uncovered in a more thorough analysis of the lesson:

1 The rise of negative feelings towards mental arithmetic, or indeed school mathematics in general, in those pupils who had to remain standing and were thus exposed in front of their peers in lessons such as the mathematics one described above. (5) Teaching here produces a learning outcome which is related to the subject and affects the emotional dimension of the pupil's personality.

2 The nature of the social context in which a subject-specific content was learned will affect the erstwhile learners prompting them in future encounters with subject matter cognate with that originally learned, to assume the same social attitude experienced previously, or to interpret the social context in the same way, in

our example, interpreting the social context by conceiving mathematics in terms of competition. (6) Here teaching produces a learning outcome which is related to the subject matter which affects the pupil's personality in its social dimension.

3   The recognition of fellow learners as competitors on account of having been rejected in the lessons with a consequent rise of feelings of envy and hatred towards them in subsequent lesson situations of this kind or ranking them as inferior to oneself because of feelings of pride and superiority toward them on account of experiencing dominance over them in school. (7) Here teaching produces a learning outcome related to the social personalities of the pupils affecting them emotionally as well as intellectually.

4   The perception of the self as inferior and worthless with the development of symptoms of withdrawal into oneself, on account of learning experiences such as were already mentioned, or, on the other hand, the recognition of oneself as being 'clever', coupled with the growth of arrogance. (8) Such teaching produces a learning outcome related to the individual personality, affecting the pupil both intellectually and emotionally.

5   The onset of psychosomatic conditions of various kinds arising as a result of protracted negative and stressful experiences, especially in the case of weak mathematicians, because of their poor performance in lessons with a consequent inferior ranking in order of prestige within the learning group. (9) Such teaching produces a learning outcome related to the school subject within the curriculum and to both the pupils' individual and social personalities which can affect their physical well-being.

Even now, the analysis is not complete; other repercussions can be found, but it suffices to show how extensively and comprehensively classroom teaching and learning can affect the pupil as a person, going beyond purely subject matter concerns. We can now enter our preliminary findings into the empty spaces of the matrix presented earlier and conclude by producing a wide-ranging picture of the learning outcomes of the mathematics lesson described above (see Figure 6).

The question whether teaching can in fact have such far-reaching repercussions on the pupil, as has been

Figure 6 Total learning outcomes of the mathematics lesson example

Learning outcomes of teaching	Personality domains of the student affected by learning				
		Cognitive	Emotional	Social	Psychosomatic
Subject specific		Improvement of mental arithmetic skills	Attitudes towards mental arithmetic and to mathematics in general	Interpreting new subject matter in ways cognate with previous experience	Specific somatic symptoms when confronted with this subject matter
Social personality specific		Seeing others as competitors, or as inferior to oneself	Feelings of hatred, envy and superiority to others Pride	Competitive attitudes to others Unwillingness to help others	Specific somatic symptoms when confronted by others
Individual personality specific		Seeing oneself as worthless Seeing oneself as very able	Weak self concept Anxiety	Withdrawal into oneself Growth of arrogance	Specific somatic symptoms when confronted with demands made upon oneself

suggested in this analysis, is, of course, fully justified. Klafki concluded his mental arithmetic example with the following important remark:

> The effect may be unimportant in one individual case. When, however, such, or similar, situations are repeated, for the sake of allegedly efficient teaching methods, such frustrations can lead to serious negative social and personal consequences for pupils. (10)

Klafki here refers to the proverbial drop which falls on a stone. Although the immediate, direct effect may be difficult to perceive, this is not so in the case of prolonged exposure. Thomae says that personality changes produced by teaching occur only gradually and as a long-term effect. (11) They are, therefore, not easy to see. This is different in the case of subject-specific, cognitive learning outcomes produced in teaching which can be achieved in a short time and which can be readily seen, because measured by tests. However, personality changes do also happen and are no less important than the others, simply because they are hidden.

Although the teachers have been little considered so far in the above analysis, their task and role in the classroom and their influence on the pupil have implicitly been acknowledged. We can now give a brief account of this in the light of our remarks above. Clearly the teacher is an integral factor in the teaching context we have described. The teacher does not have a reactive role in this process, but on the contrary in a major way is the orchestrator of the entire happening.

It is the teachers who introduce the particular subject-specific objectives into teaching and who acquaint the pupil with them. This they can do, as has been shown, only in a particular way and in a particular form: in fact 'How does he do it?' is the crucial question. In the way in which teachers introduce their subject-specific objectives into the lessons, they set up an unalterable structure, to the extent, of course, that it is capable of being structured, of the social interaction of those taking part in the lesson, that is between their pupils and themselves and between all of their pupils, collectively and individually. They also set up just as unalterably a particular way of tackling the subject in hand, encouraging particular attitudes in pupils meeting it for the first time, elaborating, acquiring, and applying both the subject content and the related skills. As a consequence of

Figure 7 Teachers' impact on their pupils

	Subject matter related teacher activity:	Personality related teacher activity:
Conscious teacher's role (professional activity)	e.g. explanation of a point of grammar in language lessons	e.g. praising a weaker pupil in the course of a lesson in order to encourage him in his efforts
Unconscious teacher activity ('implicit' effects)	e.g. causing negative attitudes to develop in pupils towards a subject, as a result of poor link between subject matter taught and pupil activity	e.g. influencing the self-concept formation of pupils through the form of interaction used between the teacher and his pupils

the importance which the manner of introducing subject objectives into teaching has for the development of pupils' personalities, teachers also find themselves in the role of orchestrator of the pupils' personalities in those areas affected by their teaching. They are bound to assume that role, whether they want to or not, whether deliberately or accidentally, directly or indirectly because of their function, qua teacher.

In our example, therefore, the mathematics teacher is, at the same time that he is teaching mathematics, orchestrating the learning processes of his pupils, their personalities being affected by his teaching. This applies to all teachers, regardless of what subject they teach, or what type of pupil they work with, and where and when they teach. The indissoluble link between their function as purveyors of subject matter and skills and their function of affecting personality is the hallmark of every teacher as they fulfil their teaching tasks and play their prescribed teaching roles in the classroom. The pupil and classroom centred approach thus yields the following two basic considerations for understanding the teachers' role as people who operate upon the characteristics of their pupils and upon the subject-specific features of their lessons.

1 Teacher activity in the classroom is constantly taking place on two levels, Janus-like; on the one level, serving subject-specific demands and, on the other level, concerned with the personality of the pupils.
2 Such activity consists not only of deliberate actions, since, while the teachers are fulfilling those in their professional role, qua teacher, they are at the same time carrying out other indirect activities and functions on which they have not yet been able to reflect consciously, as shown in Figure 7.

The teacher's impact cannot be interpreted purely mechanistically; such an interpretation would reduce the pupils to malleable objects with no powers of their own which could be made into what the teacher wanted them to be by the simple manipulation of skilful techniques. On the contrary, the effect of the teacher's pedagogical activity on the pupils can be understood only in the sense that certain techniques trigger off the pupils' own responses who, as active, participant and autonomous individuals, undergo changes as a result of reacting to the teacher's techniques on a variety of levels, cognitive, affective, social, and somatic. (12)

THE TEACHER'S PROFESSIONAL TASKS AND THEIR TWOFOLD REALIZATION

The teacher's professional task in the classroom is not limited to teaching in the narrow sense of the word, that of instructing and transmitting knowledge and skills to the pupil. It is accepted that it includes a number of other tasks which teachers have a duty to fulfil, generally specified nowadays in descriptions of their professional duties. We may refer here to the detailed schedule published by the Deutsche Bildungsrat for a comprehensive catalogue of teachers' duties as expected of them as civil servants. (13)

According to that document these comprise the following five areas: instructing, educating, evaluating, counselling their pupils, as well as pursuing their own and their pupils' professional development. These five areas can be characterized briefly as follows:

1 'Instructing' is taken to mean the transmission of knowledge and related skills and helping the pupils to integrate these into their own individual levels of intellectual development.
2 'Educating' refers to the use of measures taken to stabilize or modify the pupils' personality traits and dispositions in a direction desired by themselves and helpful for their role in society.
3 'Evaluating' means monitoring the pupils' educational achievements as well as their social behaviour.
4 'Counselling' includes, in particular, informing and advising pupils, and their parents, about the opportunities offered by the school and the educational service, and helping in cases of learning and behavioural difficulties.
5 'Professional development' includes especially the adaptation and preparation for use of new teaching and pupil-relevant approaches to enable teachers to cope adequately with the new challenges facing them in the four preceding professional areas.

This statement, however, detailed though it is, does not suffice to indicate fully the teachers' functions and roles in the carrying out of their professional tasks. This is because the conventional 'official' description of teachers' five areas of duty is too simple and undifferentiated as can be seen from the short characterizations given above. The details of teachers' pedagogical activities are confined to the level of immediate, direct and deliberate actions, which they have to perform in the execution of their professional tasks. As against that, the analysis presented earlier in this chapter of teachers' functions and roles revealed the essentially two-levelled nature of their pedagogical activities. We showed that below the visible surface of teachers' overt and direct classroom activities there lies a second, deeper level of activity which is on the level of a more indirect, teacher-inherent influence which they exert on the pupil unconsciously in the normal course of their work qua teacher. If we now apply this concept to the detailed, differentiated catalogue of the teacher's activity just given - and this must be done if we are to take account of the global nature of teaching activity - then we have to allow for the twofold level of the teacher's activity in each of the five areas specified above.

1   Teachers instruct, educate, evaluate, counsel, and professionally develop themselves and their pupils by appropriate direct activity, that is by means of deliberate classroom interventions, and also by official evaluation through testing, giving specific advice, and the processing and application of subject content and method-specific innovations into their teaching (surface level).

2   In addition, teachers act and thus affect their pupils in an indirect manner, while instructing, educating, evaluating, counselling, and developing them by the way in which they carry out and organize their deliberate interventions, for example in the manner in which teachers comport themselves while performing them, in the style of their own relationships with their pupils, and by how they encourage or discourage their attitudes to the teachers and towards each other. This also affects the pupils' attitudes to the subject which teachers orchestrate through their teaching (deep level).

This second, deep (or non-deliberate) level on which teachers carry out their professional tasks is possible because their pupils' personalities are determined to only a very limited extent by their genetic make-up. Indeed, because of the pupils' disposition, curiosity, and desire to learn and to model themselves on others, pupils are easily influenced in their self-concept, their social relations, and their world outlook by the teacher's every act in performing classroom duties. As a result of the pupils' human make-up, the specific forms assumed by the professional techniques of the teachers not only have a 'service' effect in terms of subject learning but also exert their influence in the formation of their pupils' personalities. From this interplay of the pupils' human make-up with the specific techniques used by teachers in the performance of their classroom role on the surface level, there emerge lines of force of their influence on their pupils in respect of each of the five professional tasks described above. This will now be explored more closely. It is not our intention to provide here an exhaustive catalogue of teachers' activities on the level of their indirect influence, nor is it possible to provide one in the space available. However, the examples to be given will demonstrate some quite significant ways of realizing on this deep level the five tasks of teachers so that the dimension of their impact on this level can be adequately demonstrated.

Instructing

Teachers instruct indirectly in the classroom by influencing their pupils' attitudes to the subject-specific contents they transmit and the ways through which teachers encourage certain social interpretations on this or on any subsequent encounter of a similar subject matter. Such cumulative experiences affect positively or negatively the attitude towards the subject. (14) Another important example is the facilitation, or closure, of the pupils' capacity for learning the subject matter which will depend upon how adequately teachers have prepared their material with respect to their pupils' personal and social readiness to learn. (15)

Educating

Teachers educate indirectly in their lessons as was demonstrated in our analysis of the mathematics episode

294

discussed in the first part of this chapter. This activity depends on the relationships which teachers establish between themselves and their pupils and which they encourage amongst the pupils themselves, or just allow to develop freely. This further affects both the learning outcomes and the personality development of their pupils, which they further or thwart with respect to their individual or social personalities. (16) Teachers also educate indirectly by being figures with whom the pupils identify in their pursuit of the process of learning. (17)

Evaluating

Teachers evaluate indirectly when they reveal the bias of their attitudes towards either individual pupils or towards a whole group of learners, (18) and in the reasons they give for accounting for their social behaviour or their intellectual performance. (19) Teachers' views and attitudes of this kind are usually expressed by means of non-verbal signals and are communicated to the pupils by gestures, assumed intonations, modulations of voice, physical proximity to, or distance from, the pupil singled out in the classroom. (20) Such signals can have a considerable impact on the formation of the pupils' self-images and confirm, or otherwise, their behaviour patterns suddenly confronted in this way by their position in their social and physical environment. Teaching is, after all, an act of communication; you cannot non-communicate as shown by Watzlawik, (21) and each communication is bound to entail judgements expressed in a non-verbal way about their partners by those taking part in the act. (22) Every teaching situation represents, therefore, an act of judgement of the pupil by the teacher.

Counselling

Teachers counsel indirectly particularly when they award marks, or otherwise assess their pupils' school-work as is contractually expected of them. Teachers do this also in various other less formal ways of praising or censuring the pupils, as well as in the attitudes they adopt in class as already explained above. All these direct and indirect acts of evaluation by the teacher contain at the same time an indirect counselling element, since any assessment is usually taken by the individuals concerned as a piece of advice, for example as approving, or rejecting, as the case might be, the ranking position they have reached in class or school. They may, or may not, wish to act on it.

Professional development

Teachers engage in indirect professional development of their pupils whenever they organize their teaching in such a way that it allows and encourages their independent activity in class, leaving room for individual contributions in the analytical process, and furthering and appreciating their efforts in tackling the subject tasks in hand. They perform the same function when they exhibit attitudes towards their pupils, which can again be seen in their basic classroom stance, as one of a trusting behaviour with positive expectations of their pupils for example. Ways of organizing teaching along these lines so as to adopt positive attitudes of pupil encouragement provide important stimuli to the latter's personality development which in later post-school social life may enable them to contribute in turn qualitatively similar positive achievements of their own which society needs successfully to meet the ever-new challenges facing it. As against that, teachers who rely upon worn-out, over-used techniques in their teaching marked by reproductive, non-adaptive approaches to their task, indirectly act as disinnovating, retarding agents. We may mention findings made about the innovating function of 'relaxed learning periods', (23) and the constricting effect of over-burdened, strained learning situations. (24) Impressive case studies of both the innovatory and disinnovatory approaches in everyday situations can be found in Thomae. (25)

THE TEACHERS' PROFESSIONAL TASKS IN THE CONTEXT OF THE CLASSROOM

We have already summarized the gist of the teacher's role in the pupil and classroom teaching centred approach advocated by us. We now wish to examine the five specific professional tasks of teachers more fully in order to emphasize their role both as perceived by themselves and as expected of them by others. These five tasks are inseparably linked with the act of teaching itself, and form an integrated whole. In carrying out their 'primary' function, that of instructing, (26) teachers are at the same time committed to their other tasks as is evident in the way they are expected to set about carrying out their duties in the explicit descriptions of them. (27)

Considering teaching activity on the direct surface level, however, might lead to the mistaken assumption that the five professional tasks are merely additive, that is the primary function of instructing is merely rounded off by the supplement of more or less important extras. 'You cannot omit evaluating your pupils' performance; however you may withdraw from educating or counselling them', or so the teacher may think. In fact, in the school reality nowadays we can find a number of well-intentioned and interesting innovations intended to lighten the teachers' burden mistakenly interpreted as releasing them from some of their tasks. Such, for example, is the role of the school counsellor or tutor, who functions in isolation from the other teachers advising pupils on their career, curriculum, or personal problems. The counsellor relieves the classroom teacher of these tasks as if there were no link whatsoever between the school curriculum, the teacher's lesson organization and teaching style, and problems like pupils' drug abuse. (28) The school psychologist to whom the problem pupil is referred for special treatment is a further example. Whereas the treatment of those affected is usually carried out within their normal social environment and their everyday context as a matter of policy in cases occurring in the school the classroom teacher is eliminated. The 'objective' test which is intended to liberate the teacher from an evaluation too subjectively justified is another case in point. (29)

The pupil and classroom teaching centred approach, on the other hand, by revealing the second, deep level of the teacher's function and role, makes clear that the complementary interrelation of the five teaching tasks is more radical and qualitatively more far reaching and rewarding than their surface realization in isolation. It has further shown that the five tasks in the teaching process form an indissoluble whole. There can be no teaching in which teachers, while instructing, do not at the same time educate, evaluate, counsel, and develop themselves and their pupils professionally through innovations. As teachers fulfil their task of instructing through the use of particular interpersonal and subject-related techniques, they also provide stimuli which develop their pupils' personalities. They thus act as educators. By their use of the necessary skills of communication between themselves and their pupils in accomplishing their teaching, teachers also give non-verbal signals expressing approval, or disapproval, of individual pupils, groups of pupils, and/or the teaching situation. In so doing they engage in their evaluating function. Teachers' assessments, in turn, indicate their advice about the usefulness, or otherwise, of various parts of the teaching process and their pupils' own contributions to it. This acts as an impulse or stimulus to the pupils' self-concept and thus has a counselling effect on them. The extent to which constricting, or expansive, approaches which characterize teachers' lessons are, or are not, compatible with the experience, maturity, thought, judgement, and, indeed, the performance of their pupils act in an innovating or disinnovating capacity on them as the teacher qua teacher widens, or narrows, their personal and subject specific horizons. The same indivisible quality attaches also to the direct, deliberate actions which teachers perform in the other expected task areas in the course of their lessons. Through them they also affect their pupils in areas not directly or deliberately intended.

Thus even the possibility of releasing teachers from their educational, evaluating, counselling, and professionally developing functions on the direct level of their professional activity so as to limit them to instructing alone would not destroy the unity of the five roles and their realization on the indirect, deep level. All it does do is to abandon it to accidental and unconscious factors. Indeed accident and chance may then allow all manner of inappropriate cuts, deformations, distortions, and naiveties to occur. Of course, we must be aware that the second indirect, deep level of teaching activity is only partially accessible to reflection and is, therefore, inevitably bound to be, in parts at least, subject to unconscious impulses and motivations. This fact confirms the importance of the teacher personality which reveals itself precisely in such impulses and motivations.

However we may note in this context that the quality of teachers' personalities is not an inborn phenomenon, but is confirmed in important aspects in the course of their socialization into the profession and in their own learning processes. The simple transmission of teaching techniques in the training of teachers is, of course, not sufficient to

Figure 8 The teacher's professional tasks and their accomplishment

		Levels on which the teacher accomplishes his professional tasks	
		Teacher's conscious activity	Outcomes arising
The teacher's professional tasks	Instructing		
	Educating		
	Evaluating/ assessing		
	Counselling		
	Professionally developing.		

(Complete the spaces in the matrix given above)

Figure 9 The fixed links between the five professional tasks of the teacher in the classroom

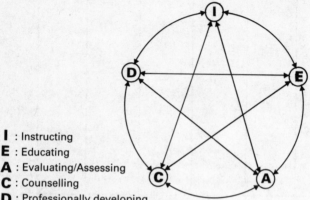

I : Instructing
E : Educating
A : Evaluating/Assessing
C : Counselling
D : Professionally developing

produce the necessary competencies as outlined in this section.

Figures 8 and 9 summarize this discussion by illustrating the contribution made by the pupil and classroom teaching centred approach to the realization of the link between the overt 'service' function of instructing and the inherent, covert role of teachers: the twofold manner in which they carry out their professional task.

The pupil and classroom teaching centred approach breaks the restrictive view of teachers as that of being mainly, or exclusively, purveyors of subject matter in their classrooms as indicated in the opening paragraphs of this chapter and contributes to an awareness of the more comprehensive function and role of the subject-specialist teacher as an orchestrator of lessons. No transmission of subject knowledge happens without at the same time an impact on the pupil's personality. This applies to all manner of teachers in all types of school, as already mentioned. Since this realization is a decisive yardstick for an understanding of teachers' roles it does have important consequences for a full appraisal of their work and, in particular, should lead to a more appropriate professional preparation for their roles.

IMPLICATIONS OF A PUPIL AND CLASSROOM TEACHING CENTRED APPROACH FOR TEACHER EDUCATION

A preparation for teaching that is to do adequate justice to new teachers in the successful pursuit of their professional task, including the level of their indirect activity, must clearly be based on an understanding of the approach suggested above and include a recognition of the important role subject teachers' lessons have in the classroom for their pupils' all-round development. Thus in addition to an appropriate grounding in subject methodology it must also include an adequate preparation for dealing with the pupil's developing personality. Moreover both domains must be integrated, not just added together. Therefore methods work in a particular subject is not to be equated solely with a knowledge of the corresponding academic discipline's method of inquiry. Academic scholarship in the humanities or sciences operates selectively; it largely excludes from its inquiry the affective, the social, the aesthetic, the moral, the realization in activity, and the teaching methodology implications of its subject matter. For example few classical scholars carry out archaeological digs. Yet these practical aspects of the discipline are those which pupils need to concern themselves with, as much as the cognitive ones, if they are to arrive at a balanced awareness of their environment and be ready to play an active part in it. (30)

A pupil-centred teacher preparation must include the following:

1　It must sensitize new teachers to enable them to 'experience' the pupils adequately as people, to be aware of them as reflective individuals with a life story of their own already behind them and at the same time actually present in front of the teacher in the very moment of learning.
2　It must make teachers conscious of their own impact on the pupil in the classroom.
3　It must provide teachers with an adequate knowledge of the pupils and the actual conditions of the pupils' existence and the forms it assumes (which is not to be understood as confined to school). It must also include the ability to understand the changes which occur in the pupils' situation. (31)
4　It must support teachers as they form appropriate attitudes towards their pupils.

301

5   It must equip the teacher to act in a way commensurate
     with a proper appraisal of the individual and social
     personalities of his pupils (pupil-diagnosis).

The aim of integrating the two levels described above is
to enable the beginning teacher to combine subject-specific
and pupil-personality specific objectives of teaching in such
a way as to satisfy the pupils as individuals in need of
learning, who find themselves in a primarily teaching-
oriented environment. Both their subject-specific
(professional and vocational) as well as personality-related
learning requirements must be linked in a way which is
acceptable to the pupils as individuals and as members of
society. The ability to act purposefully requires an
integration of intellectual, emotional-motivational,
attitudinal, social, moral, somatic, and other elements.
Since cognitive learning serves essentially only those
elements appropriate to the acquisition of content-
knowledge, future teachers must also be offered learning
facilities and training opportunities which satisfy precisely
these emotional, social, moral learning needs which they
must possess to discharge satisfactorily their professional
tasks in a way appropriate to the respective learning needs
confronting them.

All such learning opportunities new teachers find most
easily in contact with pupils in the schools and in classroom
situations. They can make use of the following:

1   Observation of pupils in lessons (in the presence of
     different teachers and in different subjects), during
     break, on the way to school, among their friends, at
     play, in leisure activities, and so forth. (32)
2   Help with preparation of homework and similar tasks,
     the supervision of sport, leisure, field-trip and holiday
     activities of pupils.
3   Extended school experience as visitor, assistant, or
     subject teacher, with an adequate preparation before,
     and debriefing after, these activities, and including
     meaningful supervision while so engaged.

Of course such learning opportunities also exist in the form
of various exercises for new teachers in which they
themselves experience events similar to those likely to
happen to a pupil in corresponding contexts, such as
workshops, role-play, simulation, as if they were happening

to or existing within themselves. The new teachers are thus able to derive important lessons from these personal experiences which they can subsequently apply to themselves as well as to others.

If it is not possible for the student-teacher to visit a school and take part in lessons either as an observer or by doing some small group teaching, there are a number of substitute solutions available. (33) For example, these might include the observation and analysis of actual lessons on video tape, of film documentaries through which the basic elements of a lesson, its planning and development, can be discovered in which the personal, situational, contextual, and methodological factors have been integrated into the totality of the target lesson. Further techniques could include case studies of pupils, observation of teachers in different classroom situations, workshops involving participation in replicated events alongside the original performers, role-play, the use of the participant beginning teachers' own past school experience, and subject method tutorial sessions in the teacher-education institution structured in such a way as to allow the student-teachers as participant members to carry out various tasks themselves in a responsible manner, taking account of the topic in hand and their fellow seminar members' specific requirements at the time. (34) This approach paves the way to a conscious pedagogical creativity, to learning not exclusively cognitive but subsuming all the other aspects mentioned. Insights and perceptions gradually gained can be 'tried out' by acting them out during subsequent methods sessions, in lessons, or parts of lessons, in simulations, when prepared lessons are taken by some students acting as teachers with the others playing the part of pupils, and which are at the end submitted to the whole group for a rigorous and thorough discussion. A teacher education which would meet the demands of a pupil and classroom teaching centred approach could assume the form illustrated in Figure 10.

The model shown in Figure 10 can be interpreted thus: the entire concurrent teacher preparation and university/college education course consists of four study areas extending over eight or nine semesters.

1 A study area involving regular experience and direct activity involving the student-teacher with actual school pupils, schools, and classroom teaching from the first semester onwards.

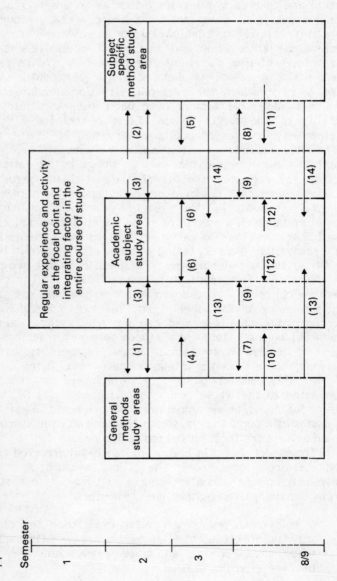

Figure 10 Model of a teacher-education course based upon a pupil and classroom centred approach

2   A general methods study area which is concerned with basic problems of a pedagogical, developmental, philosophical, psychological, and sociological nature.
3   An academic subject study area which caters for an acquisition of the knowledge and skills of the discipline which will be taught by the future teacher as a subject specialist.
4   A subject-specific methods study area which looks at the teaching and learning processes and their organization in respect of the school subject to be taught.

The regular experience and activity area provides a focal point giving meaning to and serving as an integrating feature for the entire course of study. It starts in the first semester and serves to introduce the student-teacher to experiencing pupils and their world in a concrete context through directed observation, supervision, and helping with school visits. To this, unstructured observation and the student-teacher's own teaching attempts are added in the following semesters so as to widen the experience and activity study. This actual school and classroom experience leads student-teachers to ask questions and to seek explanations. They also feel a growing wish satisfactorily to fulfil the requirements and skills demanded in the three other study areas, that is general methods, subject-specific content, and subject-specific methods (1) (2) (3) - which will then be addressed and dealt with in those parts of the course in turn. Their newly acquired insights and abilities the student-teachers refer back to the regular experience and activity area for further practical confrontation (4) (5) (6). These open up this area still further, but reveal, in addition, new and more differentiated questions and requirements demanded in turn by the other three areas (7) (8) (9), leading to the acquisition of still further insights and abilities, in turn opening up still further experiences and opportunities for activities in the regular experience and activity area (10) (11) (12). This area, then, as a result of student-teachers' own participation in it, focuses the questions raised in the other three study areas, highlighting their meaning and purpose. This enables student-teachers to use their newly found insights and abilities to enhance the effectiveness of their school and classroom experience and activity in a constant feed-back action. The subject method study area applies the findings of the general methods area and the academic study area to the specific dimensions of school subject teaching with its own subject and personality specific teaching and learning problems and adapts them accordingly (e.g. how general questioning techniques might be applied to the school subject 'Biology') (13) (14).

Editorial note

The model presented here seems to avoid the fundamental question of who is responsible for the teaching of the different areas in teacher-education institutions. The desired integrative effect will not be achieved unless some consideration is given to the allocation of responsibilities among tutors so that the teaching pattern itself as well as the organizational structure will encourage the desired integration. The author's own argument with respect to schools is logically equally applicable to teacher education.

Chapter Seventeen

CURRICULUM INTERPRETATION AND THE ROLES OF TEACHERS IN THE CURRICULUM ENTERPRISE

Miriam Ben-Peretz

INTRODUCTION

School curriculum can be perceived in different ways, using a variety of conceptual frameworks. From the starting-point of learners' needs one may claim that curriculum has to deal with problems which are relevant and important to pupils. (1) Viewing subject matter as the dominant component of the curriculum may lead to a search for structures of disciplines and their embodiment in curriculum materials. (2) Recent scholarship in political economy and sociology of knowledge has argued that the school curriculum in advanced industrial societies serves the reproduction of class structures. (3) This approach views society as the starting-point for curriculum inquiry.

In spite of these different approaches to curriculum there seems to be agreement about the crucial role that teachers play in curriculum development and implementation: the curriculum enterprise. (4) This crucial role of teachers may take different forms. Teachers may act as implementors of curricula which are determined and constructed by agents functioning outside schools, such as ministry of education officials or university scholars. Conversely teachers may be creators of the curriculum, when they are responsible for the development of their own curricula. Thus, curriculum development may be school based with only minimal input from external agencies. (5) The different roles of teachers are determined by the nature of the school system, whether it is largely centralized as in France, or decentralized, as in England. Other factors influencing teachers' role in the curriculum are related to school level, subject matter area, school climate, and teachers' personalities.

At the primary-school level one often finds a more flexible and less prescriptive curriculum than at the high-school level, giving teachers more space for autonomous involvement in curriculum construction. Humanities and social sciences disciplines may be more open to teacher-planning than mathematics or natural sciences. An extremely hierarchic and structured school climate may be less conducive to school-based curriculum development than a more open and informal one. Last, but not least, the personal inclinations, orientations, and abilities of teachers may determine the extent to which they are inclined to be implementors or creators of curricula.

This chapter focuses on teachers' interactions with curricula. The thesis of this chapter is that in both roles, either as curriculum implementors or as curriculum creators, teachers have to be able to engage in curriculum interpretation and have to be extremely sensitive to curricular potential.

CURRICULUM INTERPRETATION

Curriculum guidelines and curriculum materials, such as pupils' textbooks and teacher guides, can be interpreted in many ways. Any set of curriculum materials may be viewed as an embodiment of rich and complex educational potential beyond the predetermined intentions of their developers. (6) It is possible to reveal the educational potential of curriculum through the process of curriculum interpretation.

Curriculum interpretation may take diverse forms, from an intuitive, non-structured, and informal grasp of the meaning of a certain curricular unit, to the structured process of curriculum analysis. Curriculum interpretation may be a subjective, personal experience. Teachers may ask themselves 'How do I read this curriculum unit? What difficulties does it present for my pupils or for myself?' On the other hand, curriculum interpretation may be carried out through the systematic use of schemes of curriculum analysis. Different frames of reference may serve as sources for categories of curriculum analysis. Frames of reference may stem from the rationale of curriculum developers and lead to an 'internal' scheme of analysis. Thus one may use goals and objectives stated by the developers, as categories for the analysis of pupils' textbooks or other instructional materials.

Another approach is to use 'external' categories, stemming for instance from theories of teaching or from models of curriculum development. Thus, the models of teaching identified by Joyce and Weil may yield categories for uncovering the intended environments for learning envisioned by developers and incorporated in sets of curriculum materials. (7) Among the teaching models identified by Joyce and Weil one finds Taba's inductive thinking model and Gordon's synectics model for promoting creativity. (8) One of the strategies of the inductive thinking model includes the following elements: enumerating and listing of data that are relevant to a problem; grouping those items according to some basis of similarity; and, finally, developing categories and labels for the groups. These elements may serve as a framework for the curriculum analyst, searching for instances of instructional sequences calling for listing of data, grouping, and categorizing.

The other model, synectic strategies, uses metaphoric activities to develop imagination. Three types of metaphor form the basis of synectic strategies and are incorporated in this teaching model: personal analogy, requiring empathy; direct analogy, a comparison of two objects or concepts and, finally, compressed conflict, a description of an object or concept that incorporates two opposite frames of reference. These metaphorical forms may serve as an 'external' frame for analysing curriculum materials. An analyst using this frame will search for such metaphors in curriculum materials, providing insights into their potential use to promote creativity.

Whenever external frames of reference guide the process of curriculum analysis, it is assumed that the interpretative outcomes are objective and replicable, independent of the subjective views and preferences of the analysts.

MODES AND PROCEDURES OF CURRICULUM INTERPRETATION

Analytical schemes based on 'internal' frames of reference may aid teachers to identify and classify general characteristics that were deliberately introduced into curriculum materials by their developers. General characteristics may be identified as pertaining to each of the four commonplaces of curriculum: subject matter, learner, milieu, and teacher. (9) A scheme of analysis including questions relating to these commonplaces, as viewed by the developers, will disclose the general characteristics of the curriculum and their expression in the curriculum materials. General characteristics may relate to the specific content chosen by the developers, to special instructional strategies suggested by them, or to the diverse target population of students or teachers for whom the materials were developed. For instance, a biology curriculum may be characterized by emphasizing principles of homeostasis. This represents a subject matter, content orientation. The curriculum may adopt an inquiry approach to learning based on a certain perception of learners. Because of certain guiding perceptions of teachers and their role in society they may be expected to participate in environmental action in the community. The expressions of these general characteristics, which are part of the developers' rationale, may be disclosed by systematic analysis of curriculum materials.

A convenient procedure for curriculum analysis is the use of the 'matching wheel', which is a simple instrument for matching categories of curriculum characteristics with their concrete expressions in the materials. (10) Categories for analysis are noted in the inner part of the wheel. One may note, for instance, various substantive structures of biology or elements of instruction which are part of a teaching model expressing a certain approach to learning. The middle part of the wheel is used for noting the appropriate sections of curriculum materials which are considered to constitute an expression of these categories. Thus, for instance, a description of the physiology of a fish species may be matched with the substantive structure of homeostasis. The use of direct metaphors may be noted to indicate sections of curriculum materials which could be used to promote creativity. The matching wheel has an additional, external part, which may be used for noting teachers' ideas for complementing curriculum materials which are conceived as lacking certain characteristics. If, for instance, the materials are conceived as lacking opportunities for experiencing doubts and uncertainty, which constitute an important element in the structures of a discipline, teachers may devise learning experiences to complement the

Figure 11 The matching wheel

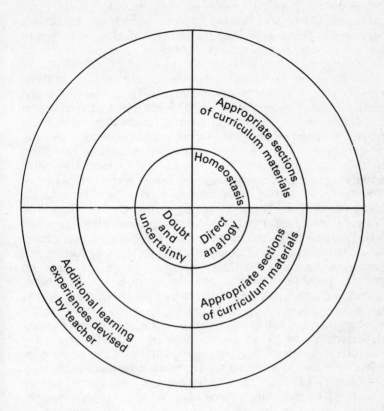

materials (see Figure 11).

Content analysis was a methodology used by Adar and Fox in order to disclose expressions of developers' intentions in a history curriculum. (11) The investigators used the main innovative features of the curriculum as categories for their analysis.

However, 'internal' frames of reference provide only a partial interpretation of curriculum. Teachers need a rich repertoire of criteria for interpreting curriculum materials, revealing the possible educational opportunities embodied in them, as well as their limitations and shortcomings.

As noted before categories for formal curriculum

analysis may come from diverse sources. The construction of 'internal' schemes of curriculum leads to an interpretation which provides answers to two main questions: What are the intended meanings of curriculum developers? How, where, and with what degree of intensity are these intended meanings expressed in the products of the development process?

Setting up 'external' schemes of curriculum analysis may provide answers to additional divergent questions and yield different interpretations. The nature of the question posed and the choice of frameworks for dealing with these questions determines the scope and character of the interpretation. For instance, questions related to the form of the curriculum and to its roots in certain curricular assumptions may be answered by using 'external' schemes such as those developed by Eash, Morrisset and Stevens, or Eraut et al. (12) These schemes are partly based on the Tyler rationale of curriculum development which supplied categories for curriculum analysis. (13) Categories include, for instance, the use of behavioural objectives or curriculum evaluation modes. The interpretation based on such an analysis provides insights into the process of curriculum development used by the developers. Teachers may find it useful to interpret a certain curriculum unit as the outcome of careful formative evaluation. Regarding curriculum objectives, teachers may discover limitations and shortcomings which may enable them to judge whether a curriculum unit fits their specific educational situation.

Models of curriculum development are not the only sources for curriculum analysis. In the subject matter domain Schwab's notions of substantive and syntactical structures of disciplines may provide categories for curriculum analysis. (14)

Substantive structures are conceived as the conceptual devices which are used by scientists for defining and analysing the subject matter under investigation. Some biologists, for instance, conceive the organism in terms of structures and functions. Other biologists may treat the organism as a collection of equilibrium points with a limited degree of variation: a homeostatic viewpoint. Each of these substantive structures leads to different methods of verification and justification of conclusions. These methods of experimentation, data collection, and interpretation constitute the logical structures of an academic discipline, its syntactical structures. Curriculum analysis guided by the notions of substantive and syntactical structures would reveal whether curriculum materials present the students with examples of differences of interpretations and with insights into issues of principles which characterize the disciplines. Such an analysis would disclose narratives of inquiry included in the materials and would reveal to what extent students are granted glimpses into the processes of determining which research questions to ask, what evidence to collect, and how to decide among alternative conclusions.

Curriculum interpretation related to the nature of the subject matter may guide teachers in their implementation efforts by providing insights into the particular pedagogical issues raised by certain perceptions of the discipline and by the nature of the concepts to be taught. Questions may be posed as to the social relevance and the social implications of the curriculum. Curriculum analysis guided by categories stemming from this domain yields an interpretative account which may lead teachers to complement the curriculum accordingly. (15)

An interesting set of questions related to curriculum concerns the image of teachers and teachers' roles embodied in curriculum materials. Thus, one may ask whether the materials offer teachers information about the deliberations leading to curricular choices made by the developers. Other questions pertain to the scope and amount of choices left to teachers in implementing the curriculum. Analysing curriculum materials, especially teachers' handbooks, using 'teacher autonomy' as a frame of reference, may yield an interpretation which may be most relevant to teachers implementing it. (16)

There are many other questions about curriculum that may guide systematic curriculum analysis and interpretation. A more refined and differentiated mode of teacher thinking about curriculum and its meanings could lead to a better and more comprehensive grasp of the richness and complexities of the educational opportunities offered by curriculum materials.

Let us turn now to the subjective, personal, mode of curriculum interpretation. How do teachers answer questions related to the curriculum without resorting to formal schemes of analysis. Kelly's theory of personal constructs provides one possible conceptual framework for exploring teachers' own criteria for interpreting curriculum materials. (17) Kelly claims that a central feature of human functioning is the forming of an ever-shifting picture of

313

reality. By developing a set of personal constructs, based on past experiences, we become capable of processing information contained in new experiences and, in turn, are able to formulate a reaction to these experiences. A construct system thus represents a person's knowledge and views of the world. A construct is unlike a logical concept in that its boundaries are personally defined on the basis of individual and personal experience. Fundamentally Kelly's theory is a theory of human action - of an experiential cycle in which people develop their personal construct systems in interaction with their environment. Constructs may be considered forerunners of action. Thus,

> the teacher who construes block building as an exercise for large muscle development will make different predictions about this activity and undoubtedly act in different ways from one who construes it as 'play' or from another who construes it as the child's concrete representation of his thoughts. (18)

Curriculum materials are part of the professional environment of teachers. Adopting Kelly's conceptual framework, teachers are conceived of as using personal constructs, based on past experience for examining, making sense of, and using available curriculum materials. This sense-making - teachers' personal interpretations forms the basis of teachers' lesson planning, and of curriculum implementation.

The Curriculum Item Repertory (CIR) instrument, developed as an extension of the Role Construct Repertory Test Form, serves as a tool for eliciting teachers' personal constructs in relation to curriculum items. (19)

Teachers responding to the CIR instrument are asked to sort ten triads of curriculum items. They do this by proposing a way in which two of the three items in each triad are similar and different from the third item. Curriculum items, the elements to be sorted, are sections of guidelines, paragraphs in student textbooks, worksheets, illustrations, and so on. The criterion which is used to differentiate two items of each triad from the third item is a personal construct elicited by the participating teacher. For example, in sorting triads of items taken from a set of English as a second language curriculum materials, teachers suggested constructs such as difficult versus easy, motivating versus non-motivating, and structured versus non-structured. As a research tool CIR can be used to explore consistency, complexity, and priorities of teachers' personal constructs used in interpreting curriculum materials. Teachers' own awareness of the personal constructs they use in making sense of curriculum materials is perceived as an enrichment of their interpretative abilities. These interpretative abilities are considered to be prerequisites for making professional decisions about the ways curriculum materials could be implemented in diverse educational situations.

The ability to interpret curriculum materials is perceived as crucial for teachers not only as implementors but also in their role as curriculum developers, creators of their own curriculum. Teachers' decisions about content and instructional strategies lead to the construction of curriculum units. Interpreting these with a varied set of criteria, using formal means, is important for the construction and formative evaluation of valid, relevant, useful, and rich curriculum units. With the aid of curriculum interpretation teachers may be able to judge the appropriateness of school-based curriculum for present and future educational situations.

Curriculum interpretation abilities cannot be taken for granted; they are not innate characteristics of teachers. Therefore it is deemed necessary to include curriculum interpretation in programmes of teacher pre- and in-service education.

CURRICULUM INTERPRETATION IN TEACHER EDUCATION

In order to participate in the curriculum enterprise, as implementors or developers, teachers have to acquire the necessary knowledge and skills. Appropriate curricular knowledge for teachers could encompass theories of curriculum development, implementation, and evaluation. Guided experiences in curriculum development would allow teachers to gain the necessary skills for involvement in the curricular enterprise.

It is argued that the learning of curriculum interpretation skills is an important component in teachers' curricular knowledge, whether they are involved in curriculum implementation or in curriculum development. Understanding the nature of divergent curriculum materials may give teachers the necessary overview of the range of curricular possibilities. Engaging in curriculum interpretation is considered to be an exercise in getting to know what curriculum is about. Familiarity with modes of transformation of scholarly knowledge into curricula may create a repertoire of possibilities that teachers may use in their everyday activities of implementing external curricula, or in the process of school-based curriculum development. Moreover, it is argued that curriculum interpretation for implementation is a prerequisite for autonomous curriculum development. Teacher education in the art of curriculum interpretation is seen as a strategy for engaging teachers and student-teachers reflectively in one of their major professional activities, namely making educational sense of curriculum materials.

Two points of intervention related to teacher education are conceived of as crucial for curriculum implementation. These intervention points are situated on a path which starts with the 'formal' curriculum, as presented to teachers, and ends with the 'operational' curriculum (see Figure 12). Formal and operational curricula are terms proposed by Klein and associates as components of a conceptual model for viewing the curriculum enterprise. (20) In this framework the 'formal' curriculum encompasses what it is expected that students will learn. The formal curriculum is brought to the attention of teachers in the form of written statements and a variety of materials prepared by external developers.

Teachers perceive the formal curriculum on the basis of their value screens, their professional competencies, assessed students' needs, and their own interests. This 'perceived' curriculum is what teachers believe they are offering to their students. Teachers' perceptions of curriculum are transformed into an 'operational' curriculum which is actually taught and implemented in the classroom. However, the operational curriculum may differ from the perceived curriculum as a result of concrete factors of unique and changing classroom interactions. Figure 12 shows this situation graphically.

The first point of intervention (A) aims at aiding teachers in perceiving curriculum materials. The second point of intervention (B) aims at aiding teachers in planning instructional activities based on their perceptions. (21)

This chapter relates to teacher education at the first intervention point (A), namely the process of curriculum

Figure 12 A model of teacher-intervention in education

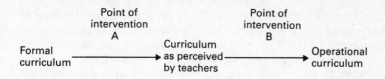

interpretation through which the formal curriculum is transformed into the perceived curriculum. It is contended that teachers' interpretative abilities can be developed by repeated experiences in curriculum analysis, using internal or external analytic schemes. Another important strategy for promoting teachers' power of interpretation is by raising their awareness of personal construct systems. Such awareness can be achieved through group discussions about varying constructs and their educational implications.

The examples of possible learning experiences are given herewith. Silberstein and Ben-Peretz propose the use of syllabus analysis in teacher education. (22) The analysis of a sample of syllabuses and guidelines in the humanities and natural sciences showed that all relate to a number of curriculum aspects, such as the nature of the discipline and appropriate modes of teaching. Engaging teachers and student-teachers in the analysis of syllabuses and guidelines aims at fostering their abilities to understand and evaluate the conceptual frameworks embodied in these documents. By discussing the dominant orientations and concerns that are expressed in the syllabuses teachers clarify their own positions and viewpoints regarding the conceptual frameworks revealed in the analysis.

Another approach is presented by Ben-Peretz and associates. (23) Using the Curriculum Item Repertory instrument, mentioned above, in teacher-education programmes, is believed to lead to self-awareness of the limitations of personal construct systems employed by teachers in the process of curriculum interpretations. Group discussions and confrontations with a variety of personal grids may serve to expand the scope of constructs used, thus providing teachers with richer and more complex

317

views of the educational potential of curriculum materials. Interesting questions that may be raised relate to perceived regularities in constructs or to the variance between grids supplied by teachers with different backgrounds who teach in different school contexts. The educational significance of variations in construct systems employed by teachers is an important issue to be treated in teacher education.

Group discussions may focus on individual personal constructs and emphasize the uniqueness of each construct system. On the other hand, one may use categories of constructs to highlight commonalities and variance between different teacher populations. By 'comparing notes' with each other, teachers may discover the hierarchies and limitations of their own constructs as well as those of peers. Thus their grasp of potentially useful criteria for curriculum interpretation may be expanded. Probing into differences between construct systems of certain teacher populations may raise awareness of the impact that educational situations and experiences have on teachers' scope of curriculum interpretations. The use of CIR in teacher-education programmes may be viewed as an attempt to remove 'blind spots' in teachers' perceptions of curriculum materials.

In-service teacher-education programmes focusing on curriculum interpretation are useful for teachers involved in the process of implementing innovative curricula, or in the development of a school-based curriculum. Particularly teachers confronted with educational situations which pose special difficulties, such as teaching multicultural groups of students, may benefit from expertise in curriculum interpretation. Matching existing curriculum materials to the needs of diverse student populations cannot be accomplished without in-depth understanding of the nature and educational potential of these materials.

Initial teacher-education programmes too could use curriculum interpretation to introduce students to curriculum inquiry. Curriculum interpretation would lead to the identification of curricular trends and their expression in teaching materials. Getting to know curriculum materials in various subject matter areas may be perceived as one of the prerequisites for teaching those areas.

The value of involving classroom teachers as partners in development (24) is clearly demonstrated in the Rand Change Agent Study which investigated factors leading to successful programme implementation. (25) Promotion of interpretative abilities is conceived as a prerequisite for teacher partnerships in curriculum development and implementation.

NOTES AND REFERENCES

1 UK EDUCATION IN THE LATE 1980s: PRESSURES AND CONTEXTS FOR CHANGE

1   DES, Education Act 1988, London, HMSO. 1988; W. Tulasiewicz, 'The development of the education system in England and Wales under the Conservative Administration of Mrs. Thatcher', in Zeitschrift für Internationale Erziehungs- und Wissenschaftliche Forschung. Vergleichende Bildungsforschung, Köln-Wien, Böhlau, Sonderheft, pp. 189-217, 1987.
2   R.H. Tawney (ed.) Secondary Education for All: A Policy for Labour, London, Allen & Unwin, nd.
3   DES, A Language for Life, Bullock Report, London, HMSO, 1975.
4   J. Callaghan, Speech at Ruskin College, Oxford, 13 October 1976. For details, especially on government control of the school curriculum, see The Times, London, 13 October 1976, p. 1, and Times Educational Supplement, London, 15 October 1976, p. 1.
5   DES, Primary Education in England: A Survey by HMI, London, HMSO, 1978; DES, Aspects of Secondary Education in England, London, HMSO, 1979.
6   ibid.
7   I.R. Findlay, Education in Scotland, Newton Abbot, Devon, David & Charles, 1973.
8   DES, Circular 10/65, The Organisation of Secondary Education, London, HMSO, 1965.
9   DES, Education Act 1976, London HMSO, 1976.
10 There was a positive spate of official publications on the curriculum in the late 1970s and the early 1980s.

These included the following: DES, Local Authority Arrangements for the School Curriculum (Circular 14/77), London, HMSO, 1977; DES, Education in Schools: A Consultative Document, Green Paper, London, HMSO, 1977; DES, The School Curriculum, London, HMSO, 1981; DES, Curriculum 11-16: Working Papers by HM Inspectorate: A Contribution to Current Debate, London, HMSO, 1977; DES, A View of the Curriculum, HMI series Matters for Discussion 11, London, HMSO, 1977; DES, Curriculum 11-16: Towards a Statement of Entitlement, London, HMSO, 1983; Schools Council for Curriculum and Examinations, The Whole Curriculum 13-16, Working Paper no 53, London, Evans/Methuen, 1975; Schools Council for Curriculum and Examinations, The Practical Curriculum, Working Paper no 70, London, Methuen, 1981.

What was interesting about these documents was the clear split that they revealed between DES policy and the view of HMI. For a commentary on some aspects of this see D. Lawton, The Politics of the School Curriculum, London, Routledge & Kegan Paul, ch. 3, 1980. See also HMI Series, Matters for Discussion (London, HMSO), a series of booklets presenting HM Inspectorate's view, among other matters, on curriculum content over a number of different subject areas, which came out at about this time.

11 For details of the Assessment of Performance Unit, set up by the DES as a direct outcome of the Bullock Report, op. cit., see Lawton, op. cit., ch. 4.

12 For information about the proposed reform of the A Level examination see Schools Council for Curriculum and Examinations, 16-19 Growth and Response: 1 Curricular Bases, Working Paper no 45, London, Evans/Methuen, 1972; Schools Council for Curriculum and Examinations, 16-19 Growth and Response: 2 Examination Structure, Working Paper no 46, London, Evans/Methuen, 1973; Schools Council for Curriculum and Examinations, Preparation for Degree Courses, Working Paper no 47, London, Evans/Methuen, 1973.

For reform of the examination system at 16-plus see DES, Examinations at 16+: A Statement of Policy, London, HMSO, 1982; DES, GCSE: General Certificate of Secondary Education, A General Introduction, London, HMSO, 1985. The national criteria for individual subjects were published in most cases in the same year in the same format.

13 The Youth Opportunities Programme (YOP) was introduced in 1978 as a temporary measure designed to alleviate what was seen as a short-term problem of school-leaver unemployment caused by the coincidence of a cyclical economic downturn and the coming of age of the 'baby-boom' generation born in the early 1960s. The aim was to smooth over the transition from school to work and make young people more attractive to potential employers by giving school-leavers six months of work experience backed by state allowances.

The YOP scheme grew progressively more unpopular and by 1981 there were many calls for an overhaul of the programme. In May of that year the Manpower Services Commission (MSC) published a consultative document entitled A New Training Initiative which was to form the basis of new government policy, beginning in autumn 1983, of the Youth Training Scheme (YTS) which sought to introduce a compulsory element so that all 16-year-olds would be either in continuing education or in some form of training; this included the Certificate of Pre-Vocational Education (CPVE), a qualification of pre-vocational studies introduced instead of a long-awaited examination of post-compulsory education at 17-plus (Certificate of Extended Education: CEE).

14 DES, A New Partnership for our Schools, Taylor Report, London, HMSO, 1977.

15 Circular 14/77, op. cit.

16 In the Education Bill, 1979, which sought to establish the partnership recommended in the Taylor Report, op. cit.

17 DES, Education Act 1980, London, HMSO, 1980.

18 Stuart Hall, 'The great moving right show', in Marxism Today, January 1979.

19 Education Act 1980, op. cit.

20 DES, Education (No 2) Act 1986, London, HMSO, 1986.

21 ibid.

22 See Education Act 1980, op. cit., Section 8 and DES, Admission to Schools, Appeals, Publication of Information and School Attendance Orders (Circular 1/81), London, HMSO, 1981.

23 This was made very clear in a Radio 4 phone-in programme conducted by Mr Kenneth Baker, Sir Keith

Joseph's successor as Secretary of State for Education
and Science, on 14 April 1987 when he stressed his view
of the importance of greater parental choice of schools.

24   Education Act 1980, op. cit.
25   See for example D. Lawton, The Tightening Grip:
Growth of Central Control of the School Curriculum,
Bedford Way Papers no 21, London, University of
London Institute of Education, 1984.
26   In March 1988 the chairman of the Mathematics
Curriculum Working Party set up to advise on the
mathematics element in the National Curriculum,
Professor Roger Blin-Stoyle, resigned after the
secretary of state's rejection of the working party's
interim report. His replacement, Duncan Graham,
immediately wrote to the members of the working
party stressing that they must steer clear of policy
issues and obey government priorities.
27   B. Salter and T. Tapper, Education, Politics and the
State, London, Grant McIntyre, 1981. See also
D. Lawton and P. Gordon, HMI, London and New York,
Routledge & Kegan Paul, 1987.
28   On 24 April the Prime Minister said in Parliament that
the Conservative Manifesto would include plans to stop
unemployment benefits to 16- to 18-year-olds who
refused offers of jobs or training and did not propose to
continue education (The Times, London, 24 April 1987,
p. 1). A White Paper, 18 February 1988, proposed to
tighten up procedure further to make the young school-
leavers take the first job or training place available, or
remain in 'education' despite their real wishes. These
proposals took effect on 12 September 1988 with
serious implications for young people wishing to
continue their studies on a part-time basis.
29   K. Webb, 'Classroom interaction and political
education', Teaching Politics, 8, 3, 1979.
30.   A. Adams, The Humanities Jungle, London, Ward Lock,
1976.
31   See J.S. Bruner, Towards a Theory of Instruction, New
York, W. W. Norton, ch. 4, 1968, and Adams, op. cit.
32   S. Marshall, An Experiment in Education, Cambridge,
Cambridge University Press, 1963.
33   For the proposed national curriculum see DES, The
National Curriculum 5-16: A Consultation Document,
London, HMSO, 1987 and also DES, The Curriculum
5-16, Curriculum Matters 2, HMI Series, London,

HMSO, 1985.

34 For profiling see P. Broadfoot (ed.) <u>Profiles and Records of Achievement</u>, London, Holt, Rinehart & Winston, 1986.

35 A.G. Watts, <u>Education, Unemployment and the Future of Work</u>, Milton Keynes, Open University Press, 1983.

36 For a discussion of the issues raised here see L. Stenhouse, <u>An Introduction to Curriculum Research and Development</u>, London, Heinemann Educational, 1975; Adams, op. cit.; A. Adams, <u>The Humanities Project: An Introduction</u>, London, Heinemann, 1970. Revised by J. Rudduck, Norwich, School of Education Publications, University of East Anglia, 1983.

37 For the changing approach to teaching contemporary society and the world of politics in schools see <u>DES, Curriculum 11-16</u>, op. cit.

38 Details given in DES, <u>Report of the Interim Awards Committee on School Teachers' Pay and Conditions 31 March 1988</u>, Chilver Report, London, HMSO, 1988.

39 <u>DES, Initial Teacher Training: Approval of Courses</u> (Circular 3/84), London, HMSO, 1984.

40 See P.H. Hirst, 'The PGCE course: its objectives and their nature', and B. Simon, 'Theoretical aspects of the PGCE course', in <u>British Journal of Teacher Education</u>, 2, London, Methuen, 1976.

41 A term coined by Arthur Clark of Rhodes University, Grahamstown, RSA, and used in an unpublished lecture.

42 W. Tulasiewicz, 'Inter-disciplinary tutor-led discussion groups in the new pattern of teacher education in England', <u>European Journal of Teacher Education</u>, 9, 2, 1986.

43 DES, <u>Teacher Education and Training</u>, James Report, London, HMSO, 1972.

44 Circular 3/84, op. cit.

45 These proposals were put forward in a Green Paper published towards the end of May 1988 to which interested parties were asked to respond by 14 October 1988.

46 DES, <u>Teaching Quality</u>, White Paper, London, HMSO, 1983.

47 Circular 3/84, op. cit.

48 DES, <u>Teachers' Pay and Conditions Act 1987</u>, London, HMSO, 1987, followed by the appropriate Order, Statutory Instrument no. 1433.

49 The Council for the Accreditation of Teacher Education

(CATE) was established under the provisions of Circular 3/84, op. cit.

50 DES, Achievement in Primary Schools, Third Report from the Education, Science and Arts Committee, London, HMSO, 1986.

51 The appraisal of teachers was first mentioned in the White Paper, Teaching Quality, op. cit. and followed up in DES, Better Schools, London, HMSO, 1985. The Inspectorate revealed its proposals in DES, Quality in Schools: Evaluation and Appraisal, London, HMSO, 1985. Several schemes were piloted in the following year. The Education (No 2) Act 1986, op. cit., gives the necessary reserve powers for teacher appraisal to proceed. This is also enshrined in the Teachers' Pay and Conditions Act 1987, op.cit.

52 Education (No 2) Act 1986, op. cit.

53 E. Holmes, What is and what might be, London, Constable, 1911.

54 A good example of how this may be achieved is provided in R. Hull, The Language Gap: How Classroom Dialogue Fails, London, Methuen, 1985.

55 DES, Special Educational Needs, Warnock Report, London, HMSO, 1978.

2 RECENT TRENDS IN EDUCATIONAL POLICIES IN THE FEDERAL REPUBLIC OF GERMANY

The following select bibliography is largely confined to titles in English or English/German.

O. Anweiler, and A. Hearnden, (eds) Sekundarschulbildung und Hochschule (From Secondary to Higher Education), Köln/Wien, Böhlau (Bildung und Erziehung, 1983, Beiheft 1), 1983.

J. Baumert and D. Goldschmidt, 'Centralization and decentralization as determinants of educational policy in the Federal Republic of Germany (FRG)', Social Science Information, 9, 6, 1980, London and Beverly Hills, Calif., Sage, pp. 1029-70.

Ch. Fuhr, Education and Teaching in the Federal Republic of Germany, München und Wien, Hanser Verlag, in co-operation with Inter Nationes, Bonn, Bad Godesberg, 1979.

C. Kuhlmann, Schulreform und Gesellschaft in der

Bundesrepublik Deutschland 1946-1966, with an introduction by S.B. Robinsohn, Stuttgart, Klett, 1970, vol. 1.1 of Robinsohn, S.B. Schulreform im Gesellschaftlichen Prozess, Ein Interkultureller Vergleich.

Max Planck Institute for Human Development and Education, Between Elite and Mass Education: Education in the Federal Republic of Germany, Foreword by J.S. Coleman, Albany, NY, State University of New York Press, 1983.

W. Mitter, 'Concept and realization of the comprehensive schools', in K. Dahmen, et al. (eds) Comprehensive Schools in Europe, Köln/Wien, Böhlau, 1984, pp. 133-50.

W. Mitter, The Organization and Content of Studies at the Post-Compulsory Level. Country Study: Germany, OECD Educational Monographs no. 7569, October 1987, Paris, Organization for Economic Co-operation and Development, 1987.

S.B. Robinsohn, et al., Bildungsreform als Revision des Curriculums, Neuwied, Berlin, Luchterhand, 1969.

Concerning recent educational reforms in the Federal Republic of Germany and, in particular, in the State (Land) of Hesse, the author has referred to the relevant bulletins published by the Standing Conference of Ministers of Education and Cultural Affairs and the Hesse Ministry of Education, as well as to public debate as mirrored in the press. The former are published as follows: Sekretariat der Ständigen Konferenz der Kultusminister der Länder in der Bundesrepublik Deutschland, Pressemitteilungen der Kultusministerkonferenz, Bonn: as appropriate. See also Land Hessen, Amtsblatt des Hessischen Kultusministeriums und des Hessischen Ministeriums für Wissenschaft und Kunst, Wiesbaden.

3 TEACHER PREPARATION AND THE REFORM OF COLLEGES IN FRANCE

1 A. Prost, Histoire générale de l'enseignement et de l'éducation en France, vol. 4, L'Ecole et la famille dans une société en mutation, Paris, Nouvelle Librairie de France, 1981.

2 Organisation de Cooperation et du Developpement Economiques (OCDE) Conference; Kungälu,

Proceedings, A.H. Halsey (ed.) Aptitude intellectuelle et éducation, Paris, Presses Universitaires de France, 1961.

3   B. Bernstein, Class, Codes and Control, London, Routledge & Kegan Paul, 2nd edn, 1974; B. Bernstein (ed.) Primary Socialisation and Education, London, University of London Institute of Education Sociological Research Unit, 1970.

4   F. Cros, 'Le développement intellectuel des élèves de sixième', Orientation scolaire et professionelle, 3, 1985.

5   J.S. Bruner, Savoir faire, savoir dire, Paris, Presses Universitaires de France, 1983.

6   C. Dinnat, Les Adolescents du béton, Paris, Casterman, 1980.

7   L. Schwartz, La France en mai 1981: l'enseignement et le développement scientifique, Paris, La Documentation Française (Etudes et Rapports de la Commission du Bilan), 1981.

8   L. Legrand, 'La formation des professeurs enseignant dans les collèges', European Journal of Teacher Education, 6, 3, pp. 249-58; 1983; L. Legrand, La Différenciation pédagogique, Paris, Scarabée, 1986.

9   A. Prost, 'La formation des professeurs de lycée ou peut-on bien faire un métier que personne ne prend au sérieux', European Journal of Teacher Education, 6, 13, pp. 259-70, 1983.

10 T. Tixeront and N. Leselbaum, 'La formation des enseignants du secondaire, quels enjeux?', Recherche et formation, 1, pp. 37-49, 1987.

11 Legrand, op. cit.

12 M. Navarro, La relation d'aide en éducation: l'aide aux enseignants du second degré, Paris, Institut National des Recherches Pédagogiques, 1981.

13 A. Leon, 'La profession enseignante: motivations, recyclage, promotion', in F. Lebigre, X. Amiel, J. Berbaum, M. Debesse, and G. de Landsheere (eds) Fonction et formation des enseignants, vol. 7, 1979, of M. Debesse and G. Mialaret, Traité des sciences pédagogiques, Paris, Presses Universitaires de France, pp. 27-49, 1969 foll. J.M. Chapoulie, Les professeurs de l'enseignement secondaire: un métier de classe moyenne, Paris, Editions de la Maison des Sciences de l'Homme, 1987.

14 A. de Peretti, L'Ecole plurielle, Paris, Larousse, 1987.

15 Navarro, op. cit.

327

16 A. Prost, Eloge des Pédagogues, Paris, Seuil, 1985.
17 Legrand, op. cit.
18 A. de Peretti, La formation des personnels de l'éducation nationale, Rapport au Ministre, Paris, La Documentation Française, 1982.
19 ibid.
20 Recteur, civil servant in control of académie (France is divided into educational regions, académies, each with a university, teacher-training establishments, an inspectorate, lycées, and other schools).
21 R. Bourdoncle and M. Lumbroso, La formation continue des enseignants du second degré, Paris, Institut National des Recherches Pédagogiques, 1986.
22 ibid.
23 Legrand, op. cit.
24 Ministère de l'Education Nationale, Bulletin officiel, 6, 7 February 1985, Paris, 1985.
25 H. Hamon and P. Rotman, Tant qu'il aura des profs, Paris, Seuil, 1984.

4 TEACHERS' EXPECTATIONS IN THE PRESENT EDUCATIONAL CONTEXT OF ISRAEL

1 This number does not include the nearly half a million (436,554) students in the occupied territories, Central Bureau of Statistics, The Statistical Yearbook, Jerusalem, Government Printer, 1985.
2 Tertiary education is carried out in teachers' colleges and universities that provide advanced training in the humanities, the social sciences, law, medicine, life sciences, physics and mathematics, agriculture, and engineering (Central Bureau of Statistics, op. cit.).
3 Y. Preisel, Laws of Education, Jerusalem, Government Printer (Hebrew), 1983.
4 A. Yogev and H. Roditi, 'The counsellor as a gatekeeper: guidance of "disadvantaged" and "privileged" pupils by school counsellors', Megamoth, 28, 4, (Hebrew), 1984.
5 Central Bureau of Statistics, The Statistical Yearbook. Jerusalem, Government Printer, Tables XXII/16, 17, 18, 1984.
6 The total number of teachers' colleges was forty-three in the school year of 1983; since then, there has been a concerted effort to reduce the number of colleges by

amalgamating institutions: cf. M. Halvetz Becoming a Teacher: Professional Socialization for Teaching in Teacher-Training Colleges in Israel, unpublished MA thesis, University of Haifa, (Hebrew), 1985; Ministry of Education and Culture, Data on Institutions of Teacher Training, Department of Teacher Training, Jerusalem, Government Printer, (Hebrew), December 1983.

7   E. Manneberg, The Evolution of Jewish Educational Practices in the Sancak (Eyalet) of Jerusalem under Ottoman Rule: An Historical and Philosophical Analysis of the Relationships Between the Social and Philosophical Changes of the Local Jewish Communities, the Western Consulates, the Evolution of Jewish Educational Practices, and their Effect on the Emergence of the Hebrew Educational System, Ph.D. dissertation, University of Connecticut, Ann Arbor, Mich., Xerox University Microfilms, 1976.

8   S.K. Mar'i, Arab Education in Israel, Syracuse, NY, University of Syracuse, 1978; N. Nardi, Education in Palestine, Washington, DC, Zionist Organization of America, 1945.

9   Mar'i, op. cit.

10   S. Reshef, 'The educators' movement', Studies in Education, 32, (Hebrew), 1981.

11   A. Kleinberger, Society, Schools and Progress in Israel, London, Pergamon, 1969.

12   ibid.

13   Preisel, op. cit.

14   H. Ormian, Education in Israel, Jerusalem, Ministry of Education and Culture, (Hebrew), 1973.

15   Kleinberger, op. cit.

16   Mar'i, op. cit.

17   Preisel, op. cit.

18   E. Peled (ed.) Education in Israel in the Eighties, Jerusalem, Ministry of Education and Culture (Hebrew), 1976.

19   M. Hen, A. Lewy, and H. Adler, The Procedure and the Result: An Evaluation Study of Intermediate Schools, Jerusalem, The Hebrew University, (Hebrew), 1978; E. Rimalt, Report on Proposed Changes in the Structure of Primary and Post-Primary Education in Israel, Jerusalem, Government Printer (Hebrew), 1970.

20   Central Bureau of Statistics, 1985, op. cit.

21   Ministry of Education and Culture, Guidelines for the Institution of the Reform in Education, Jerusalem,

Government Printer (Hebrew), 1970.

22 There are no legal restrictions. Arab parents may register their children for Jewish schools, and this is often the practice in cities with mixed Arab-Jewish populations.

23 In the academic programme courses for students of physics and mathematics are ranked highest, biology next, then the humanities, and last, the social sciences. This ranking does not reflect the demands of universities where departments in the faculty of the social sciences demand higher scores in entrance examinations than do the humanities, and the medical schools have more stringent requirements than do faculties of physics and mathematics. In vocational schools, students judged to be of the highest ability are permitted to study electronics, while those of the lowest are consigned to courses in automobile mechanics or technical drawing for the building trades. The secondary school created by the reform is a comprehensive school in which both academic and vocational classes study side by side. But the ranking of courses of study has not changed drastically (Yogev and Roditi, op. cit.).

24 Ministry of Education and Culture, 1970, op. cit.

25 Central Bureau of Statistics, 1985, op. cit.

26 A. Berlak and H. Berlak, Dilemmas of Schooling: Teaching and Social Change, London and New York, Methuen, 1981.

27 W. Klein and Y. Eshel, 'Towards a psycho-social model of integration', Megamoth, 23, pp. 17-40, (Hebrew), 1977; Y. Dar and N. Resh Homogeneity and Heterogeneity in Education, Jerusalem, Hebrew University School of Education (Hebrew), 1981.

28 Hen, Lewy and Adler, op. cit.

29 S. Eden, Curricula in Israel, Jerusalem, Ministry of Education and Culture (Hebrew), 1971.

30 Hen, Lewy and Adler, op. cit.

31 The Minister of Education and Culture at that time, Zevulon Hammer, was a member of the National Religious Party. The report of the Commission, headed by Supreme Court Judge Etzioni, has been a source of contention ever since it was published. Since it proposes to organize teaching in such a way that there are many more demands on the teachers' time, commitment, and responsibility, it might be expected that the teachers'

unions would be contesting it. What has in fact happened is that the employers (the central government and the local councils) have opposed the conclusions of the report because it also proposes to raise teachers' salaries. Cf. Ministry of Education, Special Newsletter of the Director-General, Report of the Etzioni Commission, Jerusalem, Government Printer, p. 14, 1979; see also S.F. 'Is the report of the Etzioni commission a promise of change?', Mah'beroth L'Mehkar Ul'Vikoreth, 6, pp. 45-61 (Hebrew), 1981.

32 The entire project included an exploratory stage for grounding in the theoretical basis, a written questionnaire and observations, as well as an investigation of sources in order to establish the development of teaching during the last century. Cf. D. Kalekin-Fishman, 'Burnout or alienation: a context-specific study of occupational fatigue among secondary school teachers', Journal for Research and Development in Education, 19, 3, pp. 24-34, Spring 1986, D. Kalekin-Fishman (forthcoming), 'From "my teacher, my Rabbi" to "workers in education", in M. Shalev, G. Shafir, and S. Swirski (eds) Political Economy in Israel, Tel Aviv, Sifriat Hapoalim (Hebrew); D. Kalekin-Fishman (in progress), Good Intentions Going Wrong: The Teacher in Israel Today.

33 Berlak and Berlak, op. cit.

34 W. Moore, 'Professional socialization', in D. Goslin (ed.) Handbook of Socialization Theory and Research, Chicago, Rand McNally, 1969.

35 S. Eden, S. Mozes, and R. Amiad, Interaction between 'Centre' and 'Periphery', Jerusalem, The Curriculum Centre (Hebrew), 1985; N. Sabar and N. Shafriri, 'The teacher as curriculum developer: a model for in-service training of teachers in Israel', Journal of Curriculum Studies, 12, 3, 1980.

36 C. Lacey, Socialization of Teachers, London, Methuen, 1977.

37 Halvetz, op. cit.; W. Tulasiewicz, 'Interdisciplinary tutor-led discussion groups in the new pattern of teacher education in England', European Journal of Teacher Education, 9, 2, pp. 133-51, 1986.

38 B. Bernstein, 'On the curriculum', in Class, Codes and Control: Towards a Theory of Educational Transmissions, London, Henley and Boston, Routledge & Kegan Paul, 1975.

5 TEACHERS' EXPECTATIONS, TEACHING REALITY, AND TEACHER PREPARATION IN EASTERN CANADA

1 J. Herndon, The Way it Spozed To Be, New York, Simon Schuster, 1968.
2 K. M. Zeichner, 'Reflective teaching and field-based experience in teacher education', Interchange, 12, 4, p. 4, 1982.
3 M. Polanyi, Personal Knowledge, London, Routledge & Kegan Paul, 1958.
4 V. Spolin, Improvisation for the Theatre, Evanston, Ill., Northwestern University Press, 1963.
5 J. Moffett, Teaching the Universe of Discourse, Boston, Mass., Houghton-Mifflin, 1968.
6 D. Barnes, From Communication to Curriculum, Harmondsworth, Penguin, 1976.

6 'AND GLADLY TEACH': THE ENGLISH MOTHER-TONGUE CURRICULUM

1 This helpful term was first used in P. Doughty, Language, 'English' and the Curriculum, London, Edward Arnold, 1974.
2 DES, A Language for Life, Bullock Report, London, HMSO, 1975.
3 J. Dixon, Growth Through English, Huddersfield, National Association for the Teaching of English, 1967.
4 A.M. Wilkinson, Spoken English, 'Educational Review', Occasional Publication no 2, Birmingham, University of Birmingham, 1965.
5 A. Adams in S. Tchudi (ed.) Language, Schooling and Society, Upper Montclair, Boynton Cook, 1985.
6 This is made clear in an extract from the Alan Palmer lecture given by Kenneth Baker on 7 November 1986 and published in The Times, London, of that date. Although some of the more dogmatic remarks in that article have since been retracted, the guidance offered to the National Curriculum: English Working Group (DES, 29 April 1988) state:

The programme of study should certainly be detailed enough to ensure a proper balance between learning about the grammatical structure of the English language and about its use and the study of English literature including poetry and drama. In particular they (the Working Group) should ensure that pupils have proper exposure to the great works of our literary heritage.

7   DES, Report of the Committee of Inquiry into the Teaching of the English Language, Kingman Report, London, HMSO, 1988.
8   A. Adams and E. Hopkins, Sixth Sense, Glasgow, Blackie, 1981.
9   P. Griffiths, Literary Theory and English Teaching, Milton Keynes, Open University Press, 1987.
10 A. Adams and E. Hadley, 'A study in method', in A. Adams (ed.) New Directions in English Teaching, Brighton, Falmer Press, 1982.
11 D. Fader, Hooked on Books, Oxford, Pergamon, 1966.
12 Of Oliver Goldsmith's 'Village Schoolmaster' it will be remembered

    In arguing too, the parson own'd his skill,
    For e'en though vanquish'd he could argue still;
    While words of learned length, and thund'ring sound
    Amazed the gazing rustics rang'd around,
    And still they gaz'd and still the wonder grew,
    That one small head could carry all he knew

13 In the Cambridge University Department of Education all PGCE students now undergo a basic course of training in both educational technology and information technology irrespective of the subject in which they specialize.
14 A.G. Watts, Education, Unemployment and the Future of Work, Milton Keynes, Open University Press, 1983.
15 DES, Initial Teacher Training: Approval of Courses, Circular 3/84, London, HMSO, 1984.
16 D. Barnes, From Communication to Curriculum, Harmondsworth, Penguin, 1976.
17 See for example D. Barnes, J.N. Britton and H. Rosen, Language, the Learner and the School, Harmondsworth, Penguin, 1970; J.N. Britton, Language and Learning, Harmondsworth, Penguin, 1970.
18 B. Simon, 'Theoretical aspects of the PGCE course', British Journal of Teacher Education, 2, 1976.
19 J. Dixon, Growth through English: Set in the Perspectives of the Seventies, Oxford, Oxford

University Press, 1975.

20 A record of this seminar is presented in Tchudi, op. cit.

7 TEACHING THE MOTHER-TONGUE CURRICULUM IN GERMANY

1 Sitta (p. 22) quotes the complaint of a German minister of education and concludes that the situation has meanwhile quietened down. See H. Sitta, 'Syntax - Die Lehre vom Bau des Satzes', Praxis Deutsch, 68, 1984.

2 Cf. for example, F. Hundsnurscher (ed.) T.S.G. Transformationelle Schulgrammatik Erster Versuch, Formale Grammatikmodelle, Göppingen, Kümmerle, 3rd edn, 1970; W. Hartmann, 'Unterrichtsbeispiele zur Arbeit mit der generativen Grammatik im Deutschunterricht', Wirkendes Wort, 19, pp. 289-310, 1969.

3 Cf. the critical discussion of such views by W. Menzel, Die deutsche Schulgrammatik, Paderborn, Schöningh, pp. 72-6, 1972.

4 H. Weydt, Noam Chomskys Werk: Kritik - Kommentar - Bibliographie, Tübingen, Narr, 1976, has some criticism to make of the grammatical bases of this.

5 There are still no compendia available for teaching at university level. There is no book such as that of A. Radford, Transformational Syntax: A Student's Guide to Chomsky's Extended Standard Theory, Cambridge, Cambridge University Press, 1981, in German.

6 Here the main concern is about the impact and further development of L. Tesnière, Elements de Syntaxe Structurale, Paris, Klincksieck, 1959. Cf. especially G. Helbig and W. Schenkel, Wörterbuch zur Valenz und Distribution deutscher Verben, Leipzig, VEB Bibliographisches Institut, 1969; and J. Erben, Deutsche Grammatik: Ein Abriss, München, Hueber, 1972; and H.J. Heringer, Formale Logik und Grammatik, Tübingen, Niemeyer, 11th edn, 1972, with further literature.

7 Cf. for example the very popular book over many years by the Klett publishing firm, K. Beilhardt et al. (eds) Sprachbuch - (A/B Ausgabe für Gymnasien, Realschulen und entsprechende Kurse an Gesamtschulen, C - Ausgabe für Hauptschulen und entsprechende Kurse an Gesamtschulen) Stuttgart, Klett, 1970 foll.

8 Cf. B. Bernstein, 'Elaborated and restricted codes:

their origins and some consequences', in J.J. Gumperz and D. Hymes (eds) The Ethnography of Communication, and in American Anthropologist, 66, 6, pt. 2, pp. 55-69, 1964; also B. Bernstein, Soziale Struktur, Sozialisation und Sprachverhalten Aufsätze 1958-1970, vol. 1, Amsterdam, de Munter, 1970; B. Bernstein, Class, Codes and Control, St Albans, Paladin, vol. 1, 1971.

9 Cf. especially U. Oevermann, Sprache und soziale Herkunft, Frankfurt/Main, Suhrkamp, 1972.

10 Cf. for example U. Ammon, Dialekt, soziale Ungleichheit und Schule, Weinheim/Basel, Beltz, 1972; U. Ammon, U. Knoop and I. Radtke (eds) Grundlagen einer dialektorientierten Sprachdidaktik Weinheim/ Basel, Beltz, 1978; Altenhofer et al., Die hessischen Rahmenrichtlinien für das Fach Deutsch (Sekundarstufe I) in der wissenschaftlichen Diskussion, Kronberg, Scriptor, 1974.

11 Cf. for example, A. Gutt and R. Salffner, Sozialisation und Sprache. Didaktische Hinweise zu emanzipatorischer Sprachschulung, Frankfurt/Main, Europäische VerlagsAnstalt, 1972; and critically S. Jäger, '"Sprachbarrieren" und Kompensatorische Erziehung: Ein bürgerliches Trauerspiel', Linguistische Berichte, 19, pp. 80-99, 1972.

12 W. Hartung and H. Schoenfeld (eds) Kommunikation und Sprachvariation, Berlin, Akademie Verlag, 1981.

13 Bernstein, 1970, op. cit.

14 Oevermann, op. cit.

15 The study areas of linguistic pragmatics are accessibly presented in H. Pelz, Linguistik für Anfänger, Hamburg, Hoffmann und Campe, 5th edn, pp. 221-53, 1975. Cf. also H.J. Tymister, 'Curricula', in M. Gorschenek and A. Rucktäschel, Kritische Stichwörter zur Sprachdidaktik, München, Fink, 1983, who discuss the pragmatic turn in the role of the learner.

16 Cf. for example J. Streeck, 'Sprechakttheorie, soziologische Sprachtheorie und Sprachunterricht. Einige Anmerkungen und Vorschläge', Linguistik und Didaktik, 6, pp. 260-9, 1975; and the article by E. Dobnig-Jülch, 'Text und Sprechakttheorie', in O. Beisbart, E. Dobnig-Jülch, H.-W. Eroms, and G. Koss, Textlinguistik und ihre Didaktik, Donauwörth, Auer, 1976.

17 Cf. the progress report by A. Betten, 'Erforschung

gesprochener deutscher Standardsprache', in Deutsche Sprache, pt I, vol. 5, pp. 335-61 and pt II, vol. 6, pp. 21-44, 1978.

18   A more detailed contribution can be found in W. Seifert, 'Sprachdidaktische Analyse der Erörterung', in A. Weber and H. Melzer (eds) Sprachdidaktische Analysen, Modelle zur Unterrichtsvorbereitung, Freiburg/Basel/Wien, Herder, 1981.

19   Beisbart et al., 1976, op. cit.

20   Cf. the critical remarks in E. Dobnig-Jülch, O. Raith and K. Matzel, 'Zur Sprachbuch-Diskussion. Drei Werke kritisch betrachtet', Linguistik und Didaktik, 15, pp. 204-17, 1973.

21   G. Haas, 'Texttheorie als Fundierungskategorie des Deutschunterrichts auf der Primarstufe', in H. Halbfas, F. Maurer and W. Popp, Sprache, Umgang und Erziehung, Stuttgart, Klett, pp. 117-41, 1975.

22. Cf. for example P. Pauly, Integrativer Sprachunterricht, Grundzüge einer didaktischen Grammatik, Heidelberg, Quelle und Meyer, 1975.

23   Cf. Tymister, op. cit., p. 14.

24   Cf. W. Ulrich, 'Fachdidaktik, eigensprachlich', in Gorschenek and Rucktäschel, op. cit. pp. 63ff.

25   W. Boettcher and H. Sitta, Der andere Grammatikunterricht, München/Wien/Baltimore, Urban und Schwarzenberg, 1978.

26   Cf. Boettcher and Sitta, op. cit., pp. 23ff, and following notes.

27   ibid., p. 33.

28   ibid., p. 36.

29   ibid., pp. 42ff.

30   ibid., pp. 125ff.

31   ibid., p. 127.

32   ibid., p. 130.

33   ibid., p. 131.

34   ibid., p. 249.

35   ibid., p. 243.

36   ibid., pp. 245ff.

37   H. Kreye, H.J. Schmidt, E. Schoenke, and W. Ulrich, Sprachbuch Deutsch 6, Gymnasium. Braunschweig, Westermann, p. 5, 1984; H.Kreye, H.J. Schmidt, E. Schoenke, and W. Ulrich, Sprachbuch Deutsch 6, Gymnasium, Lehrerband, Braunschweig, Westermann, 1984.

38   ibid.

39 ibid.
40 Kreye et al., op. cit., p. 7., and the following notes.
41 ibid.
42 ibid., p. 8.
43 E. Dingeldey, 'Projektunterricht', in E. Dingeldey and J. Vogt (eds) Kritische Stichwörter zum Deutschunterricht, Ein Handbuch, München, Fink, 2nd edn, pp. 284-95, 1974.
44 Kreye et al., op. cit., p. 8.
45 O. Beisbart and M. Krejci, 'Sprechanlässe. Ein Beitrag zum mündlichen Sprachgebrauch im Deutschunterricht', Pädagogische Welt, 31, pp. 605-15, 1977.
46 Kreye et al., op. cit., p. 12.
47 ibid., pp. 64-7.
48 ibid., p. 76.
49 Pelz, op. cit.
50 This is also emphasized by U. Steinmüller, 'Grammatik im Deutschunterricht. Zum Verhältnis von wissenschaftlicher und didaktischer Grammatik', Diskussion Deutsch, 10, pp. 183-93, 1979.

9 KNOWLEDGE OR COMMUNICATION: TOWARDS A NEW ROLE FOR MODERN FOREIGN LANGUAGES IN THE SCHOOL CURRICULUM

1 There are probably more books in English about individual schools than in any other language. Those by Thomas and Matthew Arnold, A.S. Neill, and researchers of the 'public' schools like Royston Lambert could be singled out. There have of course been books about the educationally more innovative comprehensive schools, like Risinghill and Countesthorpe; see also W. Tulasiewicz, 'Teaching modern languages and European studies to the less and not so less able'..., in M.-L. van Herreweghe (ed.) Personality - Education - Society, Proceedings of the VIIIth World Congress of the World Association for Educational Research, Gent, WAER/AMSE, 1984.
2 Board of Education, Modern Studies, Report to the Prime Minister of Committee on the Position of Modern Languages in the Educational System of Great Britain, Leathes Report, London, HMSO, 1918.
3 Post-war non-selective 'secondary modern' schools acquired a new respectability when they could offer a

modern foreign language and compete with the grammar schools. The figures which follow were culled from DES booklets of statistics.

The 1963 Newsom Report (Half our Future) advocated modern foreign languages for the less able students. The National Curriculum legislated for in the 1988 Education Reform Act, though not yet available everywhere, has for the first time made the subject compulsory for all students.

4 Ministry of Education, Report on the Teaching of Russian, Annan Report, London, HMSO, 1962; Schools Council for Curriculum and Examinations, French in the Primary School, Working Paper no 8, London, HMSO, 1966; C. Burstall, French in the Primary School: Attitudes and Achievement, Slough, National Foundation for Educational Research, 1970; see also Burstall et al., 1974.

5 Scottish Education Department, Modern Languages in Secondary Schools, London, HMSO, 1950; Scottish Education Department, The Place and Aims of Modern Language Teaching in Secondary Schools, 4th Report of the Scottish Central Committee for Modern Languages, London, HMSO, 1972.

6 DES, Modern Languages in Comprehensive Schools, HMI Series Matters for Discussion 3, London, HMSO, 1977. The continuing dissatisfaction with modern foreign languages was noted in a Consultative Paper prepared in connection with the proposed National Curriculum; DES, Foreign Languages in the School Curriculum, A Consultative Paper, mimeo, 1983.

7 See DES, Curriculum 11-16, Working Papers by HM Inspectorate, A Contribution to the Current Debate, London, HMSO, 1977; also the Working Paper by the Modern Languages Committee on Modern Languages, 1978; cf. also the extensive literature on taxonomies of educational objectives.

8 See U. Aselmeier, An Analysis and Critique of School Syllabuses in Secondary Schools (German Federal Republic) prepared by the Arbeitsgruppe Anthropologie und Schule, Institute of Education, Johannes Gutenberg Universität Mainz, Mainz, 1980, and a similar analysis by W. Tulasiewicz, (Great Britain), mimeo, 1981. Some positive, but also conflicting views of modern foreign languages (French) held by 13-year-old students can be found in DES, Assessment of Performance Unit, Foreign

Language Performance in Schools (1985 Survey), London, HMSO, 1987.

9   Information about the concept and practice in schools of 'European Studies' (or 'French etc. Studies') can be found in a book of this title by H. Williams. These 'Studies' are unique to schools in the United Kingdom and consist of simple factual information about individual countries. Administered to the weaker and reluctant linguists, they did little to foster European understanding (see Tulasiewicz in Personality - Education - Society, op. cit.). 'European Studies' must be distinguished from the challenging concept of 'European Awareness' which should permeate all school subjects across the curriculum and make a contribution to international understanding resulting in fruitful co-operation in the cultural, political, and economic spheres, and which emerged ten years later. Suggestions emanate at intervals from the European Community offices and are picked up by the United Kingdom Centre for European Education (UKCEE), the Central Bureau for Educational Visits and Exchanges and other organizations. The DES has shown a somewhat belated interest recently; see also selected papers by the Centre for Information on Language Teaching and Research in London.

10 J. Searle, Speech Acts, Cambridge, Cambridge University Press, 1969; see also Hawkins in note 19.

11 M. Buckby, P. Bull, R. Fletcher, P. Green, B. Page and P. Roger, Graded Objectives and Tests for Modern Languages, an Evaluation, Schools Council - University of York, York, 1981; A. Harding, B. Page and S. Rowell, Graded Objectives in Modern Languages, London, Centre for Information on Language Teaching and Research, 1980, provides full details of the tests themselves.

12 Figures communicated by the Cambridgeshire LEA in 1987, also statistics collected by the author. Positive changes, students staying on in modern language classes, have also been noted in samplings taken by HM Inspectorate, published in 1987 (mimeo).

13 For details of the GCSE and the National Criteria see DES, GCSE: General Certificate of Secondary Education, The National Criteria: French, London, HMSO, 1985; also DES, GCSE: General Certificate of Secondary Education, General Criteria, London, HMSO,

1985; see also note 27.

14 The United Kingdom Centre for European Education has been responsible for facilitating teenagers' work placings abroad.

15 Our adaptation of Stenhouse's seminal procedural style of teaching to work with language. See L. Stenhouse, An Introduction to Curriculum Research and Development, London, Heinemann, 1975.

16 M. Edgerton, 'The study of languages: A point of view', Liberal Education, 51, 4, 1965.

17 In theory this could result in Punjabi speakers in Britain acquiring French through the medium of Punjabi; while certainly possible in the case of older speakers of the language, this would not necessarily apply to young Punjabis attending English schools since they would have been educated bilingually. It is an intriguing thought.

18 The Kingman Report on the Teaching of English has recommended a co-ordinated language teaching policy in schools, which includes modern foreign languages. This has been interpreted as giving some attention to 'language awareness', an idea rather less warmly received in some modern foreign language circles. Hawkins (see note 19) has given his full support. See DES, Report of the Committee of Inquiry into the Teaching of English Language, Kingman Report, London, HMSO, 1988.

19 E.W. Hawkins, Modern Languages in the Curriculum, Cambridge, Cambridge University Press, 1981; E.W. Hawkins, Awareness of Language: An Introduction, Cambridge, Cambridge University Press, 1984.

20 See P. Guberina, Zvuk i Pokret u Jeziku, Zagreb, Matica Hrvatska, 1952; P. Guberina, 'La methode audio-visuelle structuro-globale', Revue de Phonétique Appliquée, 1, 1965; also W. Tulasiewicz, 'Some experiences with the verbo-tonal method in teaching the deaf', Revue de Phonetique Appliquée, 3, 1966; R. Renard, Introduction à la méthode verbo-tonale de correction phonétique, Paris, Didier, 1971.

21 N. Beattie, 'Use or ornament? Values in the teaching and learning of modern languages', in P. Tomlinson and M. Quinton, (eds) Values across the Curriculum, Lewes, Falmer Press, 1986.

22 A. Convey has prepared for UKCEE a Survey with Recommendations on the European Dimension in Initial

Teacher Training Courses in the United Kingdom, London, UKCEE, mimeo, 1988; see also note 9.

23 In the days when modern foreign languages were more of an elitist subject, the singing of foreign songs was regarded as a pleasant pastime activity reserved for the end of term.

24 While learning the international language of iconography students might also develop a more sympathetic understanding for the pecularities of foreign reality.

25 So far modern foreign languages has largely excluded the ethnic languages spoken in Britain for this purpose. They have been used occasionally for language awareness.

26 S. Krashen, Second Language Acquisition and Second Language Learning, Hemel Hempstead, Prentice-Hall, 1981.

27 DES, Modern Foreign Languages to 16, Curriculum Matters 8, An HMI Series, London, HMSO, 1987; DES, The Curriculum from 5 to 16, Curriculum Matters 2, An HMI Series, London, HMSO, 1985; see also note 13 for the GCSE National and General Criteria.

28 At the time of writing the findings have not been published.

29 Secondary Examinations Council, GCSE - A Guide for Teachers: French, Milton Keynes, Open University Press, 1986.

30 E. Bird and M. Dennison, Teaching GCSE, Modern Languages, London/Sydney/Auckland/Toronto, Hodder & Stoughton, 1987.

31 H.B. Altman, 'Foreign language teaching: Focus on the learner', AILA Conference Proceedings, in H.B. Altman and C.V. James (eds), Foreign Language Teaching: Meeting Individual Needs, Oxford, Pergamon Press, 1980.

10 INDUCTING THE HUMANISTIC TEACHER

1 I have for the past twenty years been developing a 'Method group' in integrated humanities at the University of Leicester School of Education. This started as a 'Combined arts' group and metamorphized through 'Combined studies' to 'Combined humanities' to 'Humanities' and, most recently, to 'Integrated

humanities'. The metamorphosis has interacted closely with the developing practice in this area of Leicestershire schools.

2 D. Holly (ed.) Humanism in Adversity: Teachers' Experience of Integrated Humanities in the 1980s, Brighton, Sussex: Falmer Press, 1986.

3 Such as HM Inspectorate's Matters for Discussion series, London, HMSO.

4 The rather gnomic phrase used in Circular 3/84 (DES, London, HMSO, 1984) to describe the criteria by which the Council for the Accreditation of Teacher Education (CATE) will approve courses for initial teacher training. There is no indication of what criteria were employed by the secretaries of state to decide on the competence of the persons to be members of CATE and, therefore, judges of the professional suitability of teacher-education courses.

5 See especially P. Freire, Education for a Critical Consciousness, London, Sheed & Ward, 1974.

6 For an extremely illuminating edition of Tolstoy's writings about his work with peasant children at Yasnaya Polyana, see A. Pinch and M. Armstrong (eds) Tolstoy in Education: Tolstoy's Educational Writings 1961-62, London, Athlone Press, 1982.

7 Anton Semeonovitch Makarenko wrote in 1935 one of the most 'creative' works ever to be attempted by an educationalist: The Road to Life: An Epic of Education, Foreign Languages Publishing House, Moscow 1951. In it he describes his despairs and triumphs - and running battle with progressive education - as he tried to turn the street-hardened delinquent orphans of revolution and civil war, the bezpriziorni, into socially conscious beings. His stories certainly carry the shock of recognition for anyone who has had dealings with the rougher end of education.

8 This has been recognized by Sunderland LEA, for instance, which has made integrated humanities a main strand of the LEA's Training and Vocational Education Initiative (see Technical and Vocational Educational Initiative - Sunderland LEA Submission).

9 H.M. Warnock (chairman) Special Educational Needs: A Report of the Committee of Inquiry into the Education of Handicapped Children and Young People, London, HMSO, 1978.

10 For details of the IHA the interested reader should

contact the membership secretary, currently Nina Wroe, of 3 South Brook Cottages, South Brook Lane, Bovey Tracey, Devon.

11 RESEARCH-ORIENTED TEACHER-TRAINING: THE CASE OF MATHEMATICS

1   In an article 'Handlungsforschung im Schulfeld', Zeitschrift für pädagogik, 19, 4, 1973, W. Klafki started a discussion on action research in German pedagogics. He ascribed to this mode of school-based research the following properties. First, from the very beginning this kind of research is concerned with problems of educational practice: it aims at solving problems of everyday schooling. Second, it is carried out in the closest collaboration with educational practice: it immediately intervenes in the actual process of teaching and learning. Third, it reduces the gap between researchers, on the one hand, and classroom practitioners, on the other, thus encouraging co-operation between them.
        See also W. Klafki, Aspekte Kritisch-Konstruktiver Erziehungswissenschaft, Weinheim, Beltz, 1977; Ch. Cremer and R. Wolf, Aktionsforschung, Weinheim, Beltz, 1978; and T. Heinze, Handlungsforschung im Pädagogischen Feld, München, Reinhardt, 1975.

2   In particular a translation of the hand-outs, dialogues, and notes from German into English seems unnecessary while to give detailed information about the results would be premature, since the work done in the course was only seen as a trial run for a following definitive study; see also H. Maier, 'Thesen zu einer Schüler- und Unterrichtsorientierten Fachdidaktik aus der Sicht des Mathematikdidaktikers' in U. Aselmeier, K.-W. Eigenbrodt, F.W. Kron, and G. Vogel (eds) Fachdidaktik am Scheideweg, Zum Zusammenhang von Fachunterricht und Persönlichkeitsentwicklung, München/Basel, Reinhardt, 1985.

3   The works recommended were A.R. Luria, Language and Cognition, Chichester, Wiley, 1982; J.R. Searle, Speech Acts: An Essay in the Philosophy of Language, Cambridge, Cambridge University Press, 1969; H. Maier, and L. Bauer, Zum Problem der Sprache im Mathematikunterricht, Bielefeld, Cornelsen-Velhagen

& Klasing, 1987.

12 HUMAN HANDICAP AS A PROFESSIONAL EXPERIENCE FOR TEACHERS OF NATURAL SCIENCES

1   E. Klee, Behinderten-report, revised edn, Frankfurt/Main, Fischer, 1981.
2   R. Bilz, Palaoanthropologie, vol. 1, Frankfurt/Main, Suhrkamp, p. 127, 1971.
3   G. Vogel, 'Fachdidaktische Dimensionen des Humanbiologieunterrichts - dargestellt am Beispiel menschlier Behinderung', in U. Aselmeier, K.W. Eigenbrodt, F.W. Kron, and U. Vogel (eds) Fachdidaktik am Scheideweg zum Zusammenhang von Fachunterricht und Persönlichkeitsentwicklung, München/Basel, Reinhardt, pp. 115-20, 1985.
4   Processes such as the rising and falling of the plane or space capsule, the various noises during the flight, weightlessness and others, are 'simulated' in such a perfect manner that the impression of real flight is conveyed, complete with all senses of seeing, hearing, and feeling. This perfect illusion is achieved by means of computer-operated equipment. It is possible to proceess approximately 50 calculations and their resulting reactions per second. It comes as no surprise that such 'simple' practice equipment costs Lufthansa 14 million DM a year.
5   C. Abt, Serious Games, New York, Viking Press, 1970; S. Boocock, and E.O. Schild, Simulation Games in Learning, Beverly Hills, Calif., Sage, 1968; J. Lehmann, Grundlagen und Anwendungen des pädagogischen Simulationsspiels, Weinheim, Beltz, 1975; J. Lehmann and G. Portele (eds) Simulationsspiele der Erziehung, Weinheim, Beltz, 1976.
6   Lehmann and Portele, op. cit., p. 121.
7   G. Clauss (ed.) Wörterbuch der Psychologie, Leipzig, VEB Bibliographisches Institut, 1979.
8   J.R. Raser, 'Theorien, Modelle und Simulationen', in Lehmann and Portele, op. cit., p. 11.
9   J.L. Taylor and R. Walford, Simulation in the Classroom, Harmondsworth, Penguin, 1972.
10   G. Vogel, 'Begegnungen mit einem Rollstuhlfahrer', Unterricht Biologie, 54, February, 1981.

11 G. Vogel, 'Menschliche Behinderung als Erfahrungsfeld für Lehrer und Schüler', in E.E. Kobi, et al., <u>Zum Verhältnis von Pädagogik und Sonderpädagogik</u>, Luzern, <u>Verlag der Schweizerischen Zentralstelle für Heilpädagogik</u>, pp. 219-24, 1984.

12 E. Preuss and H. Rasper, 'Behindertsein - Möglichkeiten und Grenzen der Simulation in der Sonder - und Regelschullehrerausbildung', in Kobi <u>et al.</u>, op. cit., pp. 162-7.

13 E. Klee, <u>Behindert</u>, Frankfurt/Main, Fischer, 1980.

14 ibid.

15 M. Ben-Peretz, 'Das Curriculum als Potential für erzieherische Möglichkeiten in Schule und Unterricht', in Aselmeier <u>et al.</u>, op. cit.

16 ibid., p. 71.

17 Deutscher Bildungsrat, <u>Empfehlungen der Bildungs-</u> <u>kommission</u>, Bonn, 1973.

18 F.W. Kron, 'Sinn und Grenzen des sogenannten "pädagogischen Freiraums" des Lehrers', <u>Der</u> <u>Evangelische Erzieher</u>, 35, 5, pp. 433-42, 1983.

19 H. Forster, 'Lehrplanentwicklung in Rheinland-Pfalz', <u>Recht der Jugend und des Bildungswesen</u>, 28, pp. 327-38, 1980.

20 Rheinland Pfalz: Kultusministerium, G. Golter, 'Elternbrief '82', Mainz, Ministry of Education, 1982.

13 COMPUTER-ASSISTED LEARNERS: AUTOMATONS OR THINKING INDIVIDUALS?

1   S. Papert, <u>Mindstorms: Children, Computers and</u> <u>Powerful Ideas</u>, Brighton, Sussex, Harvester Press, p. viii, 1980.

2   M. MacLuhan, <u>Understanding Media</u>, London, Ark, 1987.

3   R.T. Green and V.J. Laxon, <u>Entering the World of</u> <u>Number</u>, London, Thames & Hudson, 1978.

4   A. Adams, 'Talking and listening with microcomputers', in D. Chandler, and S. Marcus, <u>Computers and Literacy</u>, Milton Keynes, Open University Press, 1985.

5   J. Hebenstreit, 'The 10,000 microcomputers plan', in J. Megarry <u>et al.</u> (eds) <u>Computers and Education</u>, London, Kogan Page, p. 128, 1983.

6   A. Toffler, <u>Future Shock</u>, London, Bodley Head, ch. 18, 1970.

7   R. Sperry in <u>Science</u>, 24 September 1982, p. 1,263,

quoted in A. Bork, Personal Computers in Education, New York, Harper & Row, p.88, 1985.

8   J. Anglin, Jerome Bruner, Beyond the Information Given, New York, Norton, p. 397, 1973.

14   THE POLITICS OF TEACHER EDUCATION

1   G. Psacharopoulos, and M. Woodhall, Education for Development, World Bank, Oxford, Oxford University Press, 1985.

2   C. Jencks et al., Inequality and Reassessment of the Effect of Family and Schooling in America, Harmondsworth, Penguin, 1973.

3   S.C. Purkey and M.S. Smith, 'Effective schools: a review', Elementary School Journal, 83, University of Chicago, 1983.

4   P.H. Coombs, The World Crisis in Education, Oxford, Oxford University Press, 1985.

5   DES, Teaching Quality, White Paper, London, HMSO, 1983.

6   J.D. Wilson et al., Judgments of Quality: Assessing Candidates for Entry into Initial Teacher Training in Scotland, Moray House, Edinburgh, mimeo, 1985.

7   DES, Teacher Education and Training, James Report, London, HMSO, 1972.

8   G. Rhoades, The Costs of Academic Excellence in Teacher Education, Graduate School of Education, University of California, Berkeley, 1985.

9   P.H. Hirst, 'Educational Studies and the PGCE', British Journal of Educational Studies, 33, 3, Oxford, 1985.

10   D. Lortie, Schoolteacher, Chicago, University of Chicago Press, 1975.

11   S.J. Catling, 'The B.Ed. degree: a degree for teachers, not for teaching', Education for Teaching, 84, pp. 21-7, 1971.

12   A.M. van der Dussen, 'New teacher training experiments in Leyden', ATEE Journal, Elsevier, Amsterdam, 4, 3, 1981.

13   DES, Children and Their Primary Schools, Report of the Central Advisory Council for Education (England), Plowden Report, London, HMSO, 1967.

14   R. Bolam and K. Baker (eds) The Teacher Induction Pilot Schemes Project, Bristol School of Education, University of Bristol, 1975.

15 DES, Statistics of Education: Special Series No 2, London, HMSO, 1970.
16 Lortie, op. cit.
17 V. Vance and P. Schlechty, 'Do academically able teachers leave education?', Phi Delta Kappa 63, 2, pp. 106-12, 1981.
18 L. Darling-Hammond, A.E. Wise and S.R. Pease, 'Teacher evaluation in the organizational context: a review of the literature', Review of Educational Research, 53, 3, pp. 285-328, 1983.
19 ibid.
20 N. Gage, The Scientific Basis of the Art of Teaching, New York, Teachers College Press, p. 15, 1978.
21 ibid.
22 W. Eisner Elliott, The Educational Imagination: on the Design and Evaluation of School Programs, New York, Macmillan, 1979.
23 DES, Better Schools, London, HMSO, 1985; DES, Teaching Quality, op. cit.
24 These proposals were published as a matter for consultation in May 1988, to which interested parties were asked to give a response by 14 October 1988. For the details of the proposals and a commentary see Times Educational Supplement, London, 27 May 1988, p. 14.

15 THE NATURE AND LIMITATIONS OF TEACHERS' PROFESSIONAL AUTONOMY

1 Both are recognized, especially in secondary schools, and allocated weekly or daily periods on the timetable which teachers with responsibility for pastoral and year groups and ordinary classroom teachers use for informal tutorial contact. See J. Baldwin, and H. Wells, Active Tutorial Work, Books 1-5, Oxford, Basil Blackwell, 1979-81, which gives a useful list of activities.
2 F.W. Kron, 'Sinn und Grenzen des sogenannten "pädagogischen Freiraums" des Lehrers', Der Evangelische Erzieher, 35, 5, pp. 433-42, 1983; F.W. Kron, (ed.) Antiautoritäre Erziehung, Bad Heilbrunn/Obb, Klinkhardt, 1973.
3 Rheinland-Pfalz, Kultusministerium, Lehrpläne, Soziologie, Hauptschule, Mainz, 1978 and 1984.
4 Rheinland-Pfalz, Kultusministerium, Elternbrief, 1985

edn, Kultusminister, Mainz, January 1985.

5 U. Aselmeier, et al., 'Zum erzieherischen Auftrag der Schule', in U. Aselmeier, K.-W. Eigenbrodt, and F.W. Kron, (eds) Schule und Persönlichkeitsbildung des Schülers, 2, Publications of the 'Authropologie und Schule', Institute of Education, der Johannes Gutenberg Universität, Mainz, Arbeitsgruppe, pp. 3 and 24, mimeo, 1983.

6 A. Schnitzer, (ed.) Der Pädagogische Bezug-Grundprobleme Schulischer Erziehung (Pädagogische Grund- und Zeitfragen), München, Oldenbourg, 1983. As against that see P.H. Hirst and R.S. Peters, The Logic of Education, London, Routledge & Kegan Paul, 1970, and D. Lawton, Class, Culture and the Curriculum, London, Routledge & Kegan Paul, 1975.

7 Deutscher Bildungsrat Strukturplan für das Bildungswesen, Stuttgart, Klett, 3rd edn, p. 217, 1971; U. Aselmeier, K.-W. Eigenbrodt, F.W. Kron, and G. Vogel (eds) Fachdidaktik am Scheideweg, Der Zusammenhang von Fachunterricht und Persönlichkeits-entwicklung, München/Basel, Reinhardt, 1985.

8 Aselmeier, 1983, op. cit.

9 S. Hilsum, The Teacher's Day, Windsor, NFER, 1971; S. Hilsum and C. Story, The Secondary Teacher's Day, Windsor, NFER, 1978.

10 H. Nohl, Die Pädagogische Bewegung in Deutschland und ihre Theorie, Frankfurt/Main, Schulte-Bulmke, 6th edn, 1963.

11 F.W. Kron, 'Der Zusammenhang von sozialem Lernen und Persönlichkeitsentwicklung', in F.W. Kron (ed.) Persönlichkeitsbildung und soziales Lernen, Bad Heilbrunn/Obb, Klinkhardt, pp. 13-24, 1980.

12 P. Bourdieu, 'Systems of education and systems of thought', in M.F.D. Young, Knowledge and Control, London, Collier Macmillan, pp. 189-207, 1971.

13 H.-H. Groothoff, Funktion und Rolle des Erziehers, München, Juventa, 1972.

14 F.W. Kron, 'What is critical phenomenology?' in Pedagogiek-Joernaal, 1, pp. 56-70, 1981.

15 W. Flitner, Allgemeine Pädagogik, Stuttgart, Klett, 10th edn, 1965; M.J. Langeveld, Die Schule als der Weg des Kindes, Braunschweig, Westermann, 3rd edn, 1966.

16 L. Kremer-Hayon, 'Pedagogical autonomy as perceived by teachers - a cross-cultural comparison', Lecture given on 11 February 1985 at the University of Mainz

for the Arbeitsgruppe 'Anthropologie und Schule', unpublished.

17 F.W. Kron, 'Das erzieherische Verhältnis oder Chancen für gemeinsam gestaltete schulische Wirklichkeit', in Schnitzer, op. cit.

18 J.J. Schwab, 'The practical 3: translations into curriculum', School Review, 81, 4, pp. 501-22, 1975.

19 J.S. Bruner, The Process of Education, Cambridge, Mass., Harvard University Press, 1960.

20 W. Sacher, 'Kodifizierte Bestimmungsfaktoren curricularer Lernereignisse, Lehrpläne', in U. Hameyer, K. Frey, and H. Haft (eds) Handbuch der Curriculumforschung, Weinheim/Basel, Beltz, pp. 325-35, 1983.

21 M. Ben-Peretz, 'Das Curriculum als Potential für erzieherische Möglichkeiten in Schule und Unterricht', in Aselmeier, 1985, op. cit.

22 ibid.

23 Kron, 1980, op. cit.; A. Adams, 'Lernen und Lehren in und durch Englisch: Das muttersprachliche Curriculum in England', in Aselmeier, et al. 1985, op. cit.

24 H.-U. Stephan, 'Lernsituation für Lehrer? Fallbeschreibung des Umgangs eines Lehrers mit einer Unterrichtseinheit aus dem Curriculum Mensch und Technik', Neue Sammlung, 22, 1, pp. 55-63, 1982.

25 Kron, 1983, op. cit.

26 A. Gehlen, Der Mensch, Frankfurt/Main, Athenaeum, 8th edn, 1966; P.L. Berger, and T. Luckmann, The Social Construction of Reality, Harmondsworth, Allen Lane, The Penguin Press, 1967.

27 Club of Rome, Das Menschliche Dilemma, Molden/Wien, 3rd edn, 1979.

28 F.D.E. Schleiermacher, Pädagogische Schriften, vol. 1, Düsseldorf, Kuepper, 1957.

29 F. Klatt, Die Schöpferische Pause, Jena, Diederichs, 1923.

30 W. Meyer, 'Freiräume im Rhythmus der geselligen Schule', Lecture given to the European Educational Symposium in Oberinntal, mimeo, pp. 44-56, 1976.

31 ibid.

32 M. Brown and N. Precious, The Integrated Day in the Primary School, London, Ward Lock Educational, 1968.

33 Meyer, op. cit.

34 Gehlen, op. cit.

35 G. Velthaus, 'Didaktische Leitvorstellungen des sozialen

Lernens in der Grundschule', in W. Loch (ed.) Modelle Pädagogischen Verstehens, Essen, Neue Deutsche Verlagsgesellschaft, pp. 103-40, 1978.

36 Schwab, op. cit.; M. Ben-Peretz, 'The concept of curriculum potential', Curriculum Theory Network, 5, 2, pp. 151-9, 1975.

37 J. Connelly and M. Ben-Peretz, 'Teachers' role in using and doing of research and curriculum development', Journal of Curriculum Studies, 12, 2, pp. 95-107, 1980.

38 G. Grace, Teachers, Ideology and Control, London, Routledge & Kegan Paul, 1978.

39 G. Vogel 'Fachdidaktische Dimension des Humanbiologie unterrichts dargestellt am Beispiel menschlicher Behinderung', in Aselmeier et al. 1985, op. cit.

40 Schwab, op. cit.

16 RECONCILING THE TEACHER'S PROFESSIONAL TASK AND SOCIAL INFLUENCE

1 K.U. Neulinger, Muss die Schule krank machen? Möglichkeiten der Konfliktbegegnung in Unterricht und Unterrichtsplanung, Freiburg (Br.), Herder, p. 69, 1978.

2 See U. Aselmeier, 'Gegen einen fachdidaktischen Reduktionismus oder für eine Schüler - und unterrichtsorientierte Fachdidaktik', in U. Aselmeier, K.-W. Eigenbrodt, F.W. Kron, and G. Vogel (eds) Fachdidaktik am Schweideweg - Der Zusammenhang von Fachunterricht und Persönlichkeitsentwicklung, München/Basel, Reinhardt, pp. 12-41, 1985, for the theoretical background and literature. J. Henry, 'Spontaneity, initiative and creativity in suburban classrooms', American Journal of Orthopsychiatry, 29, pp. 266-79, 1959, provides the relevant school and lesson observations; J. Henry, Culture against Man, New York, Vintage Books, 1965; P.W. Jackson, Life in Classrooms, New York, Holt, Rinehart & Winston, 1968; P.W. Jackson, 'The student's world', Elementary School Journal, 66, pp. 345-57, 1966.

3 W.Klafki, 'Zum Verhältnis von Didaktik und Methodik', Zeitschrift für Pädagogik, 22, pp. 77-94, 1976.

4 Klafki, op. cit., p. 90.

5 Cf. Freudenthal's reference to pupils' mathematical trauma in H. Freudenthal, 'Die Stufen im Lernprozess und die heterogene Lerngruppe im Hinblick auf die

Middleschool', Neue Sammlung, 14, pp. 161-72, 1974, see p. 163. For further implications see E.E. Geissler, Erziehungsmittel, Bad Heilbrunn/Obb, Klinkhardt, 4th revised edn, pp. 41-4, 1973; E.E. Geissler, Analyse des Unterrichts, Bochum, Kemp, 5th edn, p. 47, 1982; R. Lercher, 'Die Wechselbeziehung zwischen der Haltung zur Lehrperson und der Haltung zur Mathematik', PhD dissertation, Innsbruck University, 1974.

6 A. Bandura, 'Analysis of modeling process', in A. Bandura (ed.) Psychological Modeling: Conflicting Theories, Chicago, Aldine Atherton, 1971; H. Bauersfeld, Research Related to the Mathematical Learning Process: Report for the 3rd International Congress on Mathematical Education in Karlsruhe 1976, Bielefeld, University Publication, 1976; V. Reiss, 'Zur theoretischen Einordnung von Sozialisationsphänomenen im Mathematikunterricht', Zeitschrift für Pädagogik, 25, pp. 275-89, 1979; D. Ulich, Pädagogische Interaktion, Weinheim, Beltz, 1976.

7 For the influence of classroom experiences on the rise and change of pupils' attitudes see Aselmeier, op. cit., pp. 12-27; Geissler, op. cit., ch. 1; L. Schenk-Danzinger, Handbuch der Legasthenie im Kindesalter, Weinheim, Beltz, pp. 367-73, 1968; C.F. Graumann, 'Soziale Interaktion', in F.E. Weinert, C.F. Graumann, H. Heckhausen, M. Hofer, et al., Funkkolleg Pädagogische Psychologie, vol. 1, Frankfurt/Main, Fischer, pp. 333-53, 1974; E. Höhn, Der schlechte Schüler, Sozialpsychologische Untersuchungen über das Bild des Schulversagers, München, Piper, pp. 7, 15-22, 1980.

8 See the literature on self-concept formation, as for change of attitudes, in note 7.

9 W. Belschner, and P. Kaiser, 'Darstellung eines Mehrebenenmodells primarer Prävention', in S.-H. Filipp (ed.) Kritische Lebensereignisse, München/Wien/Baltimore, Urban und Schwarzenberg, see esp. pp. 180-2, 1981. For stress situations see W. McQuade and A. Aikman, Stress, New York, 1974; H. Selye (ed.) Guide to Stress Research, New York, Van Nostrand, Reinhold, 1980.

10 Klafki, ibid.

11 H. Thomae, 'Das Problem der Persönlichkeitsveränderung', in H.v. Bracken and H.P. David (eds) Perspektiven

der Persönlichkeit, Bern/Stuttgart, Huber, pp. 196-205, 1959.

12 We would like here to draw attention to the changes in socialization theory from the viewpoint of the individual as a passive recipient to one in which he or she is an active participant in the shaping of his or her personality, and which has been accompanied by changes in the theories of cognitive psychology. See G.A. Kelly, The Psychology of Personal Constructs, New York, Norton, 2 vols, 1955; H. Thomae, Das Individuum in seiner Welt, Göttingen, Hohgrefe, 1968; H. Thomae, 'Theory of ageing and cognitive theory of personality', Human Development, 13, pp. 1-16, 1970; A.L. Baldwin, 'A cognitive theory of socialization', in D.A. Goslin (ed.) Handbook of Socialization: Theory and Research, Chicago, Rand McNally, 1969.

13 Deutscher Bildungsrat, Strukturplan für das Bildungswesen, Stuttgart, Klett, pp. 217-20, 1973.

14 Bandura, op. cit.; R. Fuchs, 'Mathematische und naturwissenschaftliche Schulbildung als Sozialisation und Enkulturation', in Th. Scharmann (ed.) Schule und Beruf als Sozialisationsfaktoren, Stuttgart, Enke, pp. 156-88, 1974; Bauersfeld, op. cit.; Ulich, op. cit., pp. 155-91; Reiss, op. cit., Geissler, op. cit. The boundary between the two personality affecting outcomes is of course fluid. The sheer quantity of learning outcomes in all areas necessitates the schematic presentation used here.

15 Geissler, op. cit., ch. II.; F. Vester, Denken, Lernen, Vergessen, München, dtv, 1978.

16 Aselmeier, 1985, op. cit., plus literature; E.E. Geissler, 'Unterricht (und Erziehung)', in L. Roth (ed.) Handlexikon zur Erziehungswissenschaft, Reinbek, Rowohlt, pp. 438-42, 1980; Geissler, 1982, op. cit.

17 A. Bandura, Social Learning Theory, Englewood Cliffs, NJ, Prentice-Hall, 1977; D.R. Sears, 'Identification as a form of behavior development', in D.B. Harries, (ed.) The Concept of Development, Minneapolis, Minn., University of Minnesota Press, pp. 149-61, 1957.

18 Geissler, 1982, op. cit., ch. I; Höhn, op. cit.

19 For causal attribution see H. Heckhausen, 'Lehrer-Schüler-Interaktion', in Funkkolleg Pädagogische Psychologie, vol. 1, op. cit., pp. 547-73.; M.D. Vernon, Perception through Experience, London, Methuen, ch. IX. 4, 1970; B. Weiner, J. Frieze, A. Kukla, L. Reed,

S. Rest and R.M. Rosenbaum, Perceiving the Causes of Success and Failure, New York, General Learning Press, 1971.

20   M. Argyle, Social Interaction, London, Methuen, 1969; M. Argyle, Bodily Communication, London, Methuen, 1975; K.R. Scherer and H.G. Walbott (eds) Nonverbale Kommunikation, Forschungsberichte zum Interaktions-verhalten, Weinheim/Basel, Beltz, 1979.

21   P. Watzlawik, J.H. Beavin, and D.D. Jackson, Pragmatics of Human Communication, New York, Nortona Company, 1967.

22   A. Mehrabian, Nonverbal Communication, Chicago and New York, Aldine-Atherton, 1972; K.R. Scherer, 'Kommunikation', in Scherer and Walbott, op. cit., pp. 14-24.

23   B. Hassenstein, Verhaltensbiologie des Kindes, München, Piper, pp. 51-6, 131, 231-5, 343, 1973. B. Hassenstein, 'Das spezifisch Menschliche nach den Resultaten der Verhaltensforschung', in H.-G. Gadamer and P. Vogler (eds) Neue Anthropologie, vol. 2, Biologische Anthropologie, pt 2, Stuttgart, Thieme/dtv, pp. 60-97, 1972; Geissler, 1982, op. cit., pp. 106ff; Vernon, op. cit., ch. II. 2.

24   H.-W. Krohne, 'Der Einfluss von Angstvermeidung auf das Niveau der Informationsverarbeitung', Zeitschrift für Experimentelle und Angewandte Psychologie, 20, pp. 408-43, 1973; K. Singer, Verhindert die Schule das Lernen?, Psychoanlytische Erkenntnisse als Hilfe für Erziehung und Unterricht, München, Ehrenwirth, 2nd edn, 1976.

25   H. Thomae, 'Persönlichkeitsmerkmale und soziale Merkmale von guten und schlechten Schülern', in H. Thomae, Vita humana. Beiträge zu einer genetischen Anthropologie, Frankfurt/Main, Athenäum, 1969, see esp. pp. 186 ff.

26   Deutscher Bildungsrat, op. cit., p. 217.

27   Cf. the example of the statements of the Deutsche Bildungsrat, op. cit., pp. 217-20.

28   U. Aselmeier, K.-W. Eigenbrodt, and F.W. Kron, 'Sozialanthropologische und anthropologische Erwägung-en zur Situation des Schülers unter besonderer Berücksichtigung des Drogenmissbrauchs durch den Schüler', in Aselmeier, Eigenbrodt and Kron (eds) Schule und Persönlichkeitsentwicklung des Schülers, 2, Publication of the Institute of Education, Drei Studien

der Arbeitsgruppe 'Anthropologie und Schule' des Pädagogischen Instituts der Universität Mainz, vol. 2, Schriftenreihe des Pädagogischen Instituts der Johannes Gutenberg Universität Mainz, Mainz, Universität, pp. 25-47, mimeo, 1983.

29 E. Heimenhdal, Dialog des Abendlandes: Physik und Philosophie, München, List, 1966, gives a telling example from physics.

30 Aselmeier. 1985, op. cit., pp. 28-34.

31 We refer to the bitter indictments seen in article titles like K. Nitsch, 'Was wissen Lehrer schon von Kindern?' Die Zeit, 7, 1975; or H.-K. Beckmann, 'Die Verleugnung des Kindes in der Pädagogik', Westermanns Pädagogische Beiträge, 30, pp. 150-5, 1978.

32 Approaches pointing in this direction were made years ago, cf. W. Hinrichs, 'Kooperation von Schule und Hochschule im Schulpraktikum', Die Deutsche Schule, 63, pp. 502-6, 1971; and U. Aselmeier, 'Hochschul Curriculum - Anmerkungen zu einem Studienelement', Die Pädagogische Hochschule, 12, pp. 43-6, 1972.

33 This procedure is based on a course model devised by the author of this chapter which has been successfully tried out by him in practice.

34 W. Tulasiewicz, 'Interdisciplinary tutor-led discussion groups in the new pattern of teacher education in England', European Journal of Teacher Education, 9, 2, 1986.

17 CURRICULUM INTERPRETATION AND THE ROLES OF TEACHERS IN THE CURRICULUM ENTERPRISE

1 N. Postman and C. Weingartner, Teaching as a Subversive Activity, Harmondsworth, Penguin Education Specials, 1969.

2 J. Bruner, The Process of Education, Boston, Mass., Harvard University Press, 1960; J.J. Schwab, 'The structure of the disciplines: meanings and significances', in G.W. Ford and L. Pugno (eds) The Structure of Knowledge and the Curriculum, Chicago, Rand McNally, 1964.

3 J. Anyon, 'Social class and school knowledge', Curriculum Theory Network, 5, 2, pp. 3-42, 1975; M.W. Apple, Ideology and Curriculum, London, Routledge & Kegan Paul, 1979.

4 L. Adar and S. Fox. An Analysis of the Content and Use of a History Curriculum, Jerusalem, Hebrew University School of Education Publication, 1978; F.M. Connelly, 'The functions of curriculum development', Interchange, 2, 3, pp. 161-77, 1972; F.M. Connelly, and M. Ben-Peretz, 'Teachers' role in using and doing of research and curriculum development', Journal of Curriculum Studies, 12. 2, pp. 95-107, 1980; J. Goodlad, A Place called School" New York, McGraw Hill, 1984; M.W. McLaughlin and D.D. Marsh, 'Staff development and school change', Teachers' College Record, 80, 1, pp. 69-94, 1978.

5 M. Skilbeck (ed.) Readings in School Based Curriculum Development, London, Harper & Row, 1984.

6 M. Ben-Peretz, 'The concept of curriculum potential', Curriculum Theory Network, 5, 2, pp. 151-9, 1975.

7 B. Joyce and M. Weil, Models of Teaching, Englewood Cliffs, NJ, and London, Prentice-Hall, 2nd edn, 1980.

8 W.J.J. Gordon, Synectics: The Development of Creative Capacity, New York, Harper & Row, 1961; H. Taba, 'Teachers' Handbook for elementary social studies', in Social Science in the Schools: A Search for Rationale, Reading, Mass., Addison-Wesley, 1967.

9 J.J. Schwab, 'The practical 3: translations into curriculum', School Review, 81, 4, pp. 501-22, 1975.

10 M. Ben-Peretz and M. Lifman, Teacher Education for Curriculum Implementation: Procedures Instruments and Assignments, Jerusalem, Ministry of Education and Culture, Government Printer, 1978.

11 Adar and Fox, op. cit.

12 M.J. Eraut, L. Goad, and G. Smith, The Analysis of Curriculum Materials, Brighton, Sussex, University of Sussex Occasional Paper no 2. 1975; I. Morrisset, and W.W. Stevens jr (eds) Curriculum Materials Analysis System, New York, Holt, Rinehart & Winston, Social Science Education Consortium Publication, 1974; M.J. Eash, 'An instrument for the assessment of instructional materials', Curriculum Theory Network, 9, 3, pp. 192-220, 1981-2.

13 R.W. Tyler, Basic Principles of Curriculum and Instruction, Chicago, University of Chicago Press, 1949.

14 Schwab, 1964, op. cit.

15 M. Ben-Peretz and B. Bar-Yoav, 'Social issues and science teacher education', in P. Tamir, A. Hofstein, and M. Ben-Peretz (eds) Preservice and Inservice

Training of Science Teachers, Rehovot, Balaban International Science Services, Philadelphia, 1983.

16 M. Silberstein and M. Ben-Peretz, 'The use of syllabus analysis in teacher education programs', in Tamir, Hofstein, and Ben-Peretz (eds), op. cit.

17 G.A. Kelly, The Psychology of Personal Constructs, New York, Norton, 2 vols, 1955.

18 A.M. Bussis, E.A. Chittenden, and M. Amarel, Beyond Surface Curriculum, Boulder, Col., Westview Press, 1976.

19 M. Ben-Peretz, S. Katz and M. Silberstein, 'Curriculum interpretation and its place in teacher education programs', Interchange, 13, 4, pp. 47-55, 1982.

20 M.F. Klein, K.A. Tye and J.Goodlad, 'A conceptual model for the analysis of discrepancies between curriculum intent and curriculum practice', unpublished paper presented at the annual meeting of AERA, Washington, DC, 1975.

21 Schwab, 1964, op. cit.

22 Silberstein and Ben-Peretz, op. cit.; Ben-Peretz, Katz, and Silberstein, op. cit.

23 ibid.

24 Connelly, op. cit.

25 McLaughlin and Marsh, op. cit.